Eating Lite

& Loving It

"Eating Lite

&

Loving It"

Published in Springville, Utah
By Art City Publishing

First Printing: September 1992
Second Printing: March 1993
Revision and Third Printing July 1994
Forth Printing: July 1995
Revision and Fifth Printing: October 1996

Printed in the United States of America

ISBN NUNBER   0-9649325-0-4

CONTENTS

INTRODUCTION

Healthier eating is a major objective of more and more people today. This cookbook was designed to meet this growing concern. Through a variety of creative and taste-tempting recipes, it demonstrates how you can prepare and enjoy foods with less sugar, fat and salt, while enjoying the benefits of more fiber.

You and your family will discover a variety of taste sensations through the use of new seasonings and flavorings.

Cutting back doesn't mean your have to cut out your favorites.

Healthy eating doesn't have to be boring!

APPRECIATION

This book is dedicated to all my special friends, who have enjoyed my recipes, suggested I compile them into a book, and encouraged me to do so.

My appreciation also, to my wonderful family who's encouragement and help has been so valuable to me, and for their unselfishness in giving it.

Rebecca R. Young

THE EQUIVALENT GIVEN FOLLOW THE GUIDELINES SET FORTH BY THE U.S.D.A. FOOD PYRAMID, AMERICAN HEART ASSOCIATION, NATIONAL CANCER SOCIETY, AND THE AMERICAN DIABETIC ASSOCIATION.

A healthy diet of less fats should also incorporate good sources of fiber. Whole grains, breads and cereals, fresh fruits, fresh vegetables and legumes are good sources of fiber. Fruits with seeds such as strawberries are especially high in fiber as well as our favorite apple.

Anyone who is following a specific restricted diet plan administered by a Physician or Health Professional, may wish to evaluate these recipes and adjust to their physicians recommendations.

KEY

(M)   MAINTENANCE RECIPES

ALL OTHERS NOT SPECIFIED ARE REDUCING RECIPES

HELPFUL HINTS

1. *Try experimenting with other seasonings to compensate for less salt. Be sure to read your labels, some seasonings contain sugar and salt. Fresh lemon is a great way to give food a salty taste.*

2. *Food & Drug Administration proposed guidelines for product labeling are established on a per serving basis.*

"Sodium Free"	*5 mg. or less*
"Low Sodium"	*less than 35 mg*
"Moderate Sodium"	*less than 140 mg*
"Reduced Sodium"	*a 75% reduction in sodium from comparable food*

3. *Instead of heavy desserts, use the natural sweetness of fruits to satisfy sweet cravings, or one of the light desserts in this book.*

4. *Many baked goods need to be kept refrigerated.*

5. *In cake and muffin recipes that call for several eggs, you may use egg substitutes.*

6. *Tofu is a very versatile food which is very high in protein, calcium, and low in calories, sodium, fats and carbohydrates.*

There is also no cholesterol in it! Try the new "Lite" versions available and save even more fat. I found that Mori-Nu Tofu has the best consistency and taste of all tofu products I tested.

7. *"Eating Light & Loving It" uses the microwave in some of it's recipes. It is an excellent way of preparing foods for many reasons. Many foods do very well in the microwave so don't be afraid to try it for more than just warming foods.*
Recipe Timing:
Microwaves vary widely so don't count on cooking time only to determine if food is done. Check often and adjust times just as you would in other cooking methods. Colder foods from the refrigerator will take longer cooking times than those that are at room temperature.

8. *Seasonings make all the difference in how wonderful or bland our food tastes. I am usually liberal with seasonings, and you may prefer to cut back at bit on suggested amounts.*

   I suggest Teton Valley and Parsley Patch seasonings. Parsley Patch is a Shilling McCormick product and available in most large grocery stores. They are both sugar free and Parsley Patch is salt free. If unavailable see substitution list on following page.

9. *Pam and Vegalene are excellent options to using oils and fats in cooking and in helping foods to brown.*

10. *When chicken broth is specified in a recipe, homemade stock is preferable, if not available, there are low-sodium choices in the grocery store.*

11. *If a recipe calls for bran, be sure to allow 10 minutes before baking for the liquid to be absorbed and thus making for a better overall texture.*

12. *Packets of dressing called for in recipes are 1 ounce servings, each containing 1 tsp oil, 40 calories each, with 4 g of fat. Reduced calorie and Fat-Free choices may be used as well, but the calorie and ingredient analysis may vary because of your choice and the ingredients.*

13. *Many recipes call for cornstarch as a thickener. Always add cool liquids to cornstarch and mix well to a thin paste, then add to recipe.*

14. *If you wish to cook dry beans, be sure to soak first. The fastest method is to add 8 cups of hot water for every 1 pound of dry beans. Bring to a rapid boil for 2 minutes. Cover and let beans stand for 1 hour. Drain, rinse, add fresh water and simmer until tender.*

PRODUCTS

Diet Center Teton Valley Seasonings, Shapelite Protein Powder, Diet Center Dressings; *are all Trademarks of Diet Center, Inc.*

Mori-Nu: *is a registered Trademark of Morinaga Milk Co. LTD.*

Pam: *is a registered Trademark of American Home Food Products, Inc.*

Ryvita: *is a registered Trademark of Shaffer, Clark & Co., Inc.*

Wasa: *is a registered Trademark of Wasa GmbH.*

NutraSweet: *is a registered Trademark of the NutraSweet Co.*

Diet 7-Up: *is a registered Trademark of the Seven-Up Co.*

Crystal Light & Jell-O: *are registered Trademarks of Kraft General Foods, Inc.*

Equal: *is a registered Trademark of the NutraSweet Co.*

Season All: *is a registered Trademark of McCormick & Co.,Inc.*

Pace Picante Sauce: *is a registered Trademark of Pace Food,Ltd*

Tabasco: *is a registered Trademark of the McIlhenny Company*

Appetizers

CLAM DIP

Ingredients:

4 oz fat-free cream cheese
1 cup non-fat cottage cheese
2 T mayonnaise
2 T fat-free mayonnaise
1/2 cup plain non-fat yogurt
1 can (6 1/2 oz) chopped clams, drained
2 T chopped green onion
2 tsp lemon juice
1/2 tsp Teton Valley Nice n Spicy or Season-All
1/4 tsp lemon pepper
1/8 tsp salt, or to taste

Instructions:

In a blender or food processor, add softened cream cheese, cottage cheese, mayonnaise, yogurt, and seasonings. Stir in other ingredients.
Chill at least 1 hour before serving. Serve with fresh vegetables or crackers.

Equivalent to:

4 Servings
Each =
3/4 oz protein
1 dairy
1 oil
1 additional food

157 calories
5 g total fat
1 g saturated
21 mg cholesterol
616 mg sodium

CRABMEAT TIDBITS

Appetizers

Ingredients:

1 T mayonnaise
1 T fat-free mayonnaise
1 T plain non-fat yogurt
1 can crabmeat, drained
1 shallot, minced
2 oz fat-free cheddar cheese, grated
1 tsp curry powder
Salt and pepper, to taste
1/8 tsp lemon pepper
1 tsp lemon juice
Crackers, rice cakes, english muffins, bagels,
  etc.

Equivalent to

2 Servings
Each =
1 1/2 oz
protein
1 oil
1 starch
1 dairy

230 Calories
5.9 g total fat
1.1 g saturated
61 mg
cholesterol
789 mg sodium

Instructions:

Combine the mayonnaise, yogurt, crabmeat, shallots, lemon juice, 1/2 cheese and seasonings. Mix well. Mound mixture on crackers, top with remaining cheese, brown lightly under broiler until cheese is melted.

CRAB & WATER CHESTNUT APPETIZER

Ingredients:

*8 oz fresh crab meat, chopped or equal amount
  canned
1/2 cup minced water chestnuts
1 T low-sodium soy sauce
2 1/2 T mayonnaise
1/4 cup plain non-fat yogurt
2 T green onion, minced
English muffins, crackers, Ryvita, bagel, etc.*

Instructions:

Combine all ingredients. Serve with crackers or
other starch choice.

Equivalent to:

4 Servings
Each =
1 oz protein
Scant dairy
1 starch
2 oil

204 calories
7 g total fat
1.4 g saturated
53 mg
cholesterol
268 mg sodium

Appetizers

CRAB STUFFED EGGS

Ingredients:

4 hard-boiled eggs
2 oz crab meat
2 T fat-free mayonnaise
2 T finely chopped celery
1 finely chopped green onion
1 T chopped pimento
2 tsp Dijon-style mustard
1/8 tsp salt
1/4 tsp Teton Valley Nice n Spicy or Season All
1/4 tsp lemon pepper

Equivalent to

2 Servings
Each =
2 1/2 oz
protein
2 oil
1 additional
food

201 calories
11 g total fat
3 g saturated
451 mg
cholesterol
537 sodium

Instructions:

Slice eggs lengthwise, remove yolks and smash in a small bowl. Add mayonnaise and mustard, cream together. Add crab, celery, onion, pimento and seasonings; mix together. Fill egg white halves with mixture, garnish with parsley if desired and sprinkle a dash of Nice n Spicy on top of eggs for color.

CARROT DIP

Ingredients:

4 oz fat-free cream cheese
1 cup fat-free cottage cheese
1/2 cup finely shredded carrot
1/4 tsp fresh dill, chopped
1/8 tsp salt
1 tsp Teton Valley Nice n Spicy or Season All
1/2 tsp lemon pepper
1 T chopped chives

Instructions:

In a food processor, or blender, mix cottage cheese and cream cheese until smooth.
Add vegetables and seasonings and mix until well blended. Chill and serve with vegetable dippers.

Equivalent to:

4 Servings
Each =
1/2 dairy
1 additional
food

72 calories
< 1 g total fat
< 1 g saturated
7 mg
cholesterol
237 mg sodium

FRUIT WITH DIP

Ingredients:

3 cups fresh fruit, cut up (may use melons,
berries, kiwi, oranges, apples, peaches, etc).

Dip:
2 T light mayonnaise
1/2 cup vanilla non-fat, sugar-free yogurt
3 T sugar-free raspberry preserves
1/2 tsp grated orange rind

Instructions:

Combine all ingredients for dip; mix well.
Chill.
Cut fruit into serving size pieces. Arrange
attractively on serving plate alongside dip.

Equivalent to:

3 Servings
Each =
2 oil
Scant dairy
1 fruit
1 additional
food

334 calories
7.6 g total fat
1.5 g saturated
8 mg
cholesterol
222 mg sodium

CREAM CHEESE

Ingredients:

1/2 cup non-fat cottage cheese
9 oz Lite Mori-Nu Tofu
3/4 tsp Crystal Lite Lemon Drink Mix, dry
2 tsp butter extract
1/4 tsp salt, or to taste
2 tsp sweetener

Instructions:

Wrap tofu in several layers of paper toweling and press for 5 minutes. Place tofu and other ingredients in a food processor or blender and blend until smooth and creamy.
Excellent as a fruit dip or as icing for a favorite recipe.

Variation: These both make excellent fruit dips.

Coconut: Add 1 tsp coconut extract to basic cream cheese recipe.
Orange: Add 2 T orange concentrate to basic recipe.

Equivalent to:

2 Servings
Each=
2 1/2 oz protein
1/2 dairy

Woman Style:
2 Servings
Each=
1 1/2 legume
1/2 dairy

87 calories
1.3 g total fat
0 saturated
2 mg cholesterol
381 mg sodium

MEXICAN SHRIMP COCKTAIL

Ingredients:

7 oz shrimp (may use canned)
2 ribs celery, chopped
1 tomato, chopped
4 T Pace Picante Sauce

Instructions:

If using fresh shrimp, cook, cool and shell. If using canned shrimp, drain. In a cocktail dish place celery, tomato, and shrimp on top. Top with picante sauce.

Equivalent to:

2 Servings
Each =
31/2 oz protein
1 cup raw
vegetable

109 calories
2.9 g total fat
< 1 g saturated
151 mg
cholesterol
298 mg sodium

MEXICAN SALSA

Ingredients:

3 tomatoes, chopped
2 ribs celery, chopped
1/2 medium onion, chopped
1 medium green pepper, chopped
1 red pepper, chopped
1 small can green chilies, chopped
1/2 tsp mexican blend seasoning
1/2 tsp garlic powder
1/2 tsp Teton Valley Nice n Spicy or Season All
1 T cilantro, chopped
2 tsp oil
1 T apple cider vinegar
3 T red wine vinegar

Instructions:

Chop all vegetables well and mix with seasonings, vinegar and oil. Chill at least 3 hours. This is great on any mexican dish, eggs, crackers, or salads.

Equivalent to:

8 Servings
Each =
3/4 cup raw
vegetable
1/4 oil

31 calories
1 g total fat
< 1g saturated
0 cholesterol
20 mg sodium

BLACK BEAN AND CORN SALSA

Ingredients:

2 cups canned black beans, drained and rinsed
1 (16 oz) can whole kernel corn, drained
1/3 cup chopped fresh cilantro
6 T fresh lime juice
3 tsp vegetable oil
1/4 cup minced red onion
1/4 cup minced green onion
1 1/2 tsp ground cumin
1/2 cup chopped tomatoes

Instructions:

Mix first 8 ingredients in large bowl. Season to taste with salt and pepper. Cover and refrigerate until cold, (Can be prepared 1 day ahead; keep refrigerated.) Mix tomatoes into salsa and serve. Recipe makes 3 1/2 cups.

This salsa makes an excellent topping for grilled beef, chicken or fish.

Equivalent to:

6 Servings
Each =
1 1/2 starch
1/2 oil
scant vegetable

Woman Style:
6 Servings
Each =
2/3 legume
2/3 starch
1/2 oil
scant vegetable

174 calories
3 g total fat
< 1 g saturated
0 cholesterol
457 mg sodium

MEXICAN LAYERED DIP

Appetizer

Ingredients:

1/2 cup fat-free cream cheese
4 oz fat-free cheddar cheese, shredded
1 cup fat-free sour cream
3 drops of tabasco, optional
1/4 tsp onion powder
1/8 tsp garlic powder
1/2 tsp Mexican blend seasoning
1 can (15 oz) refried beans
1/2 cup green onion, sliced
2 medium tomatoes, diced
1 (4 oz) can green chiles

Instructions:

Combine cream cheese, sour cream and seasonings. To assemble dip, on a large round platter or serving dish, spread beans in an even layer on plate. Top with sour cream mixture next. Sprinkle with green onion, part of the tomatoes, and chiles. Top with cheese and another layer of tomatoes.
Serve with your favorite crackers or low-fat chips.

Equivalent to:

8 Servings
Each =
1/4 cup raw vegetable
1/4 dairy
1 1/2 starch
2 additional foods

Woman Style:
8 Servings
Each =
1/2 legume
1/4 cup raw vegetable
2 additional foods

105 calories
< 1 g total fat
< 1 g saturated
5 mg cholesterol
540 mg sodium

MARINATED FRESH MUSHROOMS

Ingredients:

4 T reduced calorie Italian dressing
1 pound fresh mushrooms
2 tsp lemon juice

Instructions:

In a saucepan, heat Italian dressing and cook mushrooms over medium heat stirring occasionally, about 3-4 minutes. Add lemon juice.

Remove mushrooms with dressing into a shallow dish.

Cover and marinate in refrigerator, 4 hours or overnight, stirring occasionally.

Serve cold in salads or as garnish.

Equivalent to:

2 Servings
Each =
1 cup cooked
vegetable
1 oil

73 calories
4 g total fat
< 1 g saturated
0 cholesterol
174 mg sodium

STUFFED MUSHROOMS

Appetizers

Ingredients:

1 pound large mushrooms, stems removed and chopped
1 small onion, chopped
1/2 cup dry bread crumbs
4 oz fat-free mozzarella cheese, shredded
1/4 tsp Season All
1/4 tsp lemon pepper
1/8 tsp garlic blend seasoning
1/8 tsp dill
2 T skim milk
2 tsp diet margarine

Instructions:

Rinse mushrooms, snap out and finely chop stems.
In a skillet heat 2 tsp diet margarine, saute onion and chopped mushrooms until tender. Remove from heat, add other ingredients and mix well.
Spray mushroom caps with Pam, mound stuffing mixture into mushroom caps.
Bake in a 400 degree oven 8-10 minutes.

Equivalent to:

4 Servings
Each =
1/2 dairy
1/4 fat/oil
1/4 starch
1/4 cup cooked vegetable

91 calories
1.2 g total fat
< 1 g saturated
5.1 mg cholesterol
461 mg sodium

EASY SPINACH DIP

Ingredients:

1 pkg (8oz) fat-free cream cheese
2 cups plain non-fat yogurt
10 oz package frozen chopped spinach, thawed
    and drained
1/3 cup fresh minced onion
1 tsp lemon juice
1 envelope Knorr or Lipton Vegetable Soup
    Mix, (dry)
1 round whole grain bread, center cut out to
    make a bowl
Assorted vegetables for dipping

Equivalent to:

3 cups
Entire recipe =
2 oz protein
1 cup cooked
vegetables
1 additional
food
(Count veggies
and bread used
used to dip)

119 calories
.5 g total fat
< 1 g saturated
10 mg
cholesterol
)7 mg sodium

Instructions:

In a medium bowl, combine cream cheese, yogurt, onion, lemon juice and dry soup mix; mix well. Place spinach in several layers of paper toweling or a clean kitchen towel and twist to wring out any water. Add to other ingredients and mix. Chill before serving.

Cut the center out of the round bread to make a bowl. Fill with chilled spinach dip. Break or cut removed bread into bite size pieces to use with assorted vegetables to dip.

TROUT MOUSSE

Ingredients:

7 oz canned trout
1 package unflavored gelatin
1/4 cup cold water
1 package Lite Mori-Nu Tofu, pressed
1 T mayonnaise
2 T fat-free mayonnaise
2 T chopped green onion
2 T chopped parsley
3 T lemon juice
1/4 tsp garlic seasoning & 1/4 tsp dill
1/2 tsp Teton Valley Nice n Spicy or Season-All
1/4 tsp lemon pepper

Instructions:

Spray a loaf pan or mold with Pam and set aside. Place drained trout in a small bowl; separate trout with a fork. In a small saucepan, combine gelatin and water. Stir over low heat until gelatin is dissolved. In a bowl, beat tofu and mayonnaise until smooth. Add trout, lemon juice, seasonings, and cooled gelatin. Spoon mixture into a mold and smooth top. Cover and refrigerate until set. Invert mousse onto a serving plate and garnish as desired. Serve with crackers and raw vegetables.

Equivalent to:

3 Servings
Each =
31/3 oz protein
1 fat/oil
1 add. food

Woman Style:

3 Servings
Each =
1 legume
1 fat/oil
21/3 oz protein

180 calories
8.4 g total fat
< 1 g saturated
1.6 mg
cholesterol
233 mg sodium

SHRIMP DIP

Ingredients:

4 oz non-fat cream cheese
1 cup non-fat cottage cheese
1/2 cup plain non-fat yogurt
2 T lemon juice
1 can shrimp, drained
1 to 2 finely chopped green onions
1/4 tsp prepared horseradish, optional
1 tsp Worcestershire sauce
1/4 tsp pepper
1/8 tsp garlic powder
1/2 tsp Season All
Salt, to taste

Equivalent to:

4 Servings
Each =
1 1/2 oz
protein
1/2 dairy
1 additional
food

115 calories
< 1 g total fat
< 1 g saturated
50 mg
cholesterol
380 mg sodium

Instructions:

In a food processor, or blender, mix cottage cheese until smooth and creamy. Add yogurt, lemon juice, seasonings and horseradish. Fold in remaining ingredients and chill to blend flavors. Serve with vegetables or low-fat crackers or chips.

SMOKEY SALMON SPREAD

Ingredients:

1 can (7 3/4 oz) salmon
4 oz Lite Mori-Nu Tofu
1/4 cup plain non-fat yogurt
1 to 2 drops liquid smoke
3 T sliced green onions
Crackers, bagels, english muffins, rice cakes, etc.

Instructions:

Drain and flake salmon. Combine tofu, yogurt, liquid smoke and blend thoroughly. Stir in green onions, then fold in salmon.
Refrigerate for at least 2 hours, or overnight to blend flavors.
Serve on crackers or bagels.

Equivalent to:

4 Servings
Each=
2 1/4 oz protein

Woman Style:

4 Servings
Each=
1/3 legume
1 3/4 oz protein

99 calories
3.9 g total fat
< 1 g saturated
18 mg cholesterol
435 mg sodium

NOTES

Beverages

FROZEN FRUIT SHAKE

Ingredients:

1 1/2 cup ice cubes
1/2 ripe banana, sliced
1/2 cup blueberries
1/2 orange, peeled
1/4 cup orange juice concentrate

Instructions:

Mix all ingredients in a blender until thick and smooth. Serve immediately.

Equivalent to:

1 Serving
Each=
2 fruit
1 additional
food

123 calories
< 1 g total fat
< 1 g saturated
0 cholesterol
1 mg sodium

FRUIT SHAKE

Ingredients:

1 1/2 tsp powdered skim milk
4 T plain non-fat yogurt
1 can diet black cherry soda
1/2 cup frozen strawberries, cherries, or any berries

Instructions:

Equivalent to:

1 Serving
Each=
1/2 fruit
1 diet drink
scant dairy
1 additional
food

66 calories
<1 g total fat
<1 g saturated
<1 mg
cholesterol
91 mg sodium

Place all ingredients into a blender or food processor, and blend until thick and creamy. Serve.

YOGURT SHAKE

Ingredients:

8 oz plain non-fat yogurt or 8 oz Vanilla non-
   fat, sugar free yogurt
1/2 cup skim milk
1 tsp vanilla

Instructions:

Place in a blender or food processor, blend
until frothy.

Variations:
Fruit: add 1/2 cup fruit or berries
        1/2 tsp sweetener
Banana: Add 1 small banana, sliced.

Equivalent to:

1 Serving
Each=
1 1/2 dairy
(Count fruit
accordingly if
used)

153 calories
< 1 g total fat
< 1 g saturated
2 mg
cholesterol
192 mg sodium

PEACH AND YOGURT SMOOTHIE

Beverages

Ingredients:

2 peaches, peeled and quartered
1/2 cup non-fat, sugar-free vanilla yogurt
1/4 cup skim milk
1 packet sweetener
Dash nutmeg
Ice cubes
1/8 tsp almond extract

Instructions:

Equivalent to:

1 Serving
Each =
3/4 dairy
2 fruit

153 calories
< 1 g total fat
< 1 g saturated
1 mg
cholesterol
92 mg sodium

In a blender combine all ingredients except ice cubes and blend. While blending add ice cubes through the lid until thick and smooth.

RISE 'N SHINE SHAKE

Ingredients:

1 cup strawberries
1/2 medium banana, cut into pieces
1 cup skim milk
1/2 cup plain non-fat yogurt
1 tsp sweetener
nutmeg

Instructions:

Reserve 2 strawberries. In a blender, combine remaining strawberries, banana, milk, yogurt, and sweetener. Cover and blend at medium-low speed until thick and smooth. Pour into chilled glasses; sprinkle with nutmeg. Garnish each glass with a whole strawberry.

Equivalent to:

2 Servings
Each =
1 fruit
3/4 dairy

245 calories
1.54 g total fat
< 1 g saturated
4 mg
cholesterol
209 sodium

STRAWBERRY PROTEIN SHAKE

Ingredients:

1 cup strawberries (frozen) or 1/2 cup
  strawberries and 1/2 peach
1 scoop Diet Center Vanilla Protein Powder
1 1/2 tsp powdered milk
1/2 can strawberry diet soda
6 ice cubes

Instructions:

Put all ingredients in a blender or food processor, and mix until smooth. Serve immediately.

Equivalent to:

1 Serving
Each =
1 fruit
2 additional
foods

128 calories
1 g total fat
< 1 g saturated
< 1 mg
cholesterol
190 mg sodium

FRUIT & TOFU SHAKE

Beverages

Ingredients:

1 (10 1/2 oz) Lite Mori-Nu Silken Firm Tofu
1/2 banana
1/2 cup frozen strawberries or 1/2 cup fresh
1/2 tsp Crystal Light Berry Drink Mix, dry
1/4 cup skim milk

Instructions:

In a blender or food processor, mix ingredients together until smooth and creamy.

VARIATION:
1 (10 1/2 oz) Lite Mori-Nu Tofu
1 cup cantaloupe
1/2 tsp Crystal Lite Pink Grapefruit drink mix, dry
1 tsp coconut extract
1/4 cup skim milk

Equivalent to:

1 Serving
Each =
3 1/2 oz
protein
1/4 dairy
1 fruit

Woman Style:
1 Serving
Each =
3 legume
1 fruit
1/4 dairy

165 calories
2.5 g total fat
<1 g saturated
1 mg
cholesterol
161 mg sodium

ORANGE YOGURT SHAKE

Ingredients:

1/3 cup orange juice concentrate
1 orange
1/2 banana
8 oz cup sugar-free, non-fat lemon yogurt
2 ice cubes

Instructions:

Add all ingredients, except ice cubes, in a blender and blend well. Add ice cubes gradually, and process until smooth and creamy.

Equivalent to:

1 Serving
Each=
2 fruit
1 dairy
1 additional
food

251 calories
<1 g total fat
<1 g saturated
0 cholesterol
121 mg sodium

STRAWBERRY PARTY DRINK

Ingredients:

*2 cups frozen, unsweetened strawberries, or any
  frozen fruit
2 cups mineral water, diet 7-up or Fresca,
  chilled
1/3 cup fresh lime juice, chilled
1 tsp or more sweetener
Sprig of fresh mint, optional*

Instructions:

Place chilled mineral water, lime juice, and
sweetener in a blender or food processor. Add
frozen fruit and blend at high speed until
smooth and creamy. Garnish with fresh mint.

Equivalent to:

4 Servings
Each =
1/2 fruit

30 calories
< 1 g total fat
< 1 g saturated
0 cholesterol
2 mg sodium

ORANGE JULIUS

Ingredients:

1 whole orange
1/2 cup Diet 7-up
1 egg white
1/4 tsp Crystal Lite Citrus Drink Mix, dry
2 ice cubes
2 tsp Diet Center Vanilla Protein Powder,
  optional

Instructions:

Equivalent to:

1 Serving
Each =
1 Fruit
1 additional
food

164 calories
1.2 g total fat
0 saturated
0 cholesterol
265 mg sodium

Place all ingredients in a blender or food processor and blend to desired consistency. Will be frothy.

WAKE-UP SHAKE

Ingredients:

3/4 cup skim milk
1/2 cup sugar-free, non-fat vanilla yogurt
1/3 cup orange juice
1 cup pineapple
2 ice cubes

Instructions:

Combine milk, yogurt, pineapple, orange and
ice in blender. Cover and blend until smooth.

Equivalent to:

1 Serving
Each =
1 1/4 dairy
1 1/2 fruit

301 calories
< 1 g fat
< 1 g saturated
3 mg
cholesterol
159 mg sodium

ROOT BEER FLOAT

Ingredients:

1 can diet root beer
1 (5 oz) container fat-free, sugar-free frozen
  yogurt

Instructions:

Place frozen yogurt in a large glass, slowly pour root beer over yogurt. Serve immediately.

Equivalent to:

1 Serving
Each =
1/2 dairy
1 diet drink
1/2 fruit

86 calories
0 fat
0 saturated
0 cholesterol
149 mg sodium

HOT HOLIDAY WASSAIL

Ingredients:

2 quarts water
1 (2 qt) package Crystal Lite Citrus drink mix
4 packets sugar-free apple cider drink mix
Cinnamon, to taste
Whole cloves
Orange and lemon slices
Juice of 1 orange

Instructions:

Mix all ingredients together and heat thoroughly. Add orange and lemon slices to hot wassail. Serve hot.

Equivalent to:

6 Servings
Each=
1 diet drink

21 calories
<1 g total fat
<1 g saturated
0 cholesterol
15 mg sodium

HOT FRUITED TEA

Ingredients:

5 cups boiling water
4 tea bags or 4 tsp tea
10 whole cloves
1/4 tsp cinnamon
1 tsp Crystal Light Lemon Drink Mix
1 tsp Crystal Light Citrus Drink Mix
1 T lemon juice
Orange slices

Instructions:

In a large teapot or pan, pour water over tea, cloves, cinnamon, and drink mixes. Cover; let steep 5 minutes.
Serve hot with orange slices.

Equivalent to:

5 Servings
Each=
1 tea serving
1 diet drink

12 calories
0 fat
0 saturated
0 cholesterol
2 mg sodium

APPLE PANCAKES

Ingredients:

1 apple, cored
4 egg whites, beaten
1 T Diet Center Vanilla Protein Powder
2 T oat bran
1/2 tsp sweetener
1/2 tsp vanilla extract
1/4 tsp cinnamon and nutmeg
2 tsp sugar-free fruit preserves or unsweetened
*   applesauce*

Instructions:

Mix all ingredients, except apple, in a blender or food processor. Add apple and grind. In a skillet sprayed with Pam, pour mixture on preheated skillet, (makes 4 pancakes). Cook as regular pancakes.
Top with fruit spread or unsweetened applesauce.

Equivalent to:

1 Serving
Each =
3 1/2 oz
protein
1 fruit
1 additional
food

264 calories
1.9 g total fat
<1 g saturated
0 cholesterol
372 mg sodium

CHEESECAKE CRUST

Ingredients:

9 whole graham crackers, crushed
2 T reduced calorie margarine, melted
1 tsp cinnamon, optional
1-2 packets sweetener
Pam

Instructions:

Spray a glass pie plate with Pam, add together ingredients and mix well. Press into a pie plate and up the sides. Compact with a spoon.
Spray with Pam again and continue pressing into plate.
* Bake at 350 degrees for 4-5 minutes, cool and fill with your favorite filling.

* Crust may also be used uncooked.

Equivalent to:

6 Servings
Each =
1 starch
1/2 oil

90 calories
3.7 g total fat
< 1 g saturated
0 cholesterol
162 mg sodium

CREPE TORTILLA

Ingredients:

1 egg, beaten
1 T Diet Center Vanilla Protein Powder,
  optional
2 T skim milk
2 T whole wheat flour or bran
Dash of salt

Instructions:

Combine ingredients and beat with a wire whisk. Prepare a pan by spraying with Pam spray coating and heat over medium-high heat. When pan is hot, pour and quickly swirl 1/2 of mixture to coat bottom of pan. Cover with a lid for about 30 seconds. Run a spatula around the edge of the crepe, it should start to pull away from the sides of the pan. Turn crepe and continue to cook 30 seconds longer.

Equivalent to:

1 Serving
Each =
1 1/2 oz
protein
2 additional
foods

176 calories
5.8 g total fat
1.6 g saturated
213 mg
cholesterol
184 mg sodium

CHICKEN SALAD SANDWICHES

Ingredients:

1 1/2 cans, or 7 oz cooked chicken, turkey,
*   tuna or trout*
1 1/2 T light mayonnaise
4 T plain non-fat yogurt
2 green onions, chopped
1 rib celery, chopped
1/3 cucumber, chopped
1/4 green pepper, chopped
2-3 mushrooms, chopped
1 oz fat-free cheddar cheese, shredded
Salt, to taste
1/2 tsp Teton Valley Nice n Spicy or Season All
1/4 tsp lemon pepper
2 starch selections, (crackers, whole grain roll,
*   pita, whole wheat bread, etc.)*
Alfalfa sprouts

Equivalent to:

2 Servings
Each =
3 1/2 oz
protein
1 starch
1 1/2 oil
Scant dairy

285 calories
9.3 g total fat
1.5 g saturated
41 mg
cholesterol
673 mg sodium

Instructions:

Mix all ingredients together except the alfalfa sprouts. Put filling between bread selection. Wrap in plastic wrap and chill. Top with alfalfa sprouts or lettuce just before serving.
May refrigerate overnight.

CLASSIC EGG SALAD SANDWICH

Ingredients:

2 hard boiled eggs, chopped
1/3 cup chopped celery
1/4 cup chopped green bell pepper
1 T light mayonnaise
1 T plain non-fat yogurt
1/2 tsp dry mustard
1/8 tsp lemon pepper
Salt, to taste
whole grain bread or roll, rice cakes, crackers,
english muffins, etc.

Instructions:

Mix eggs, celery, bell pepper, dressings and
seasonings. Spread on bread, crackers, etc.

Equivalent to:

1 Serving
Each =
2 oz protein
1 starch
2 oil

332 calories
20 g total fat
5 g saturated
431 mg
cholesterol
812 mg sodium

NECTARINE-CHICKEN FILLING

Ingredients:

7 oz chicken breast, cooked and diced
1 cup finely chopped nectarine
1/4 cup minced celery
1/4 cup plain yogurt
2 T chopped green onion
1 T fresh lemon juice
1/4 tsp salt
1/4 tsp dried tarragon, crumbled
1/4 tsp lemon pepper
Pita bread, rice cakes, Ryvita Crackers, etc.

Equivalent to:

2 Servings
Each =
31/2 oz protein
1/2 fruit
Scant dairy
1 starch

179 calories
1.6 g total fat
< 1 g saturated
57 mg
cholesterol
377 mg sodium

Instructions:

Combine all ingredients and chill to blend flavors.
Use filling for breads, crackers, rice cakes, etc.

HOT CRAB AND CHEESE SANDWICHES

Ingredients:

6 1/2 oz can crab meat, drained and flaked
1/2 cup green celery, chopped
1/2 cup green pepper, chopped
1 green onion, sliced
4 T water chestnuts, chopped
2 T reduced calorie ranch dressing
1 1/2 T light mayonnaise
1/4 cup plain non-fat yogurt
1/8 tsp red wine vinegar
1/2 tsp Season All
1 oz fat-free cheddar cheese
2 starch servings, (whole grain roll, english
    muffins, bagels, bread, rice cakes, etc.

Instructions:

Mix all ingredients together and place filling on a whole wheat roll, Ryvita crackers or rice cakes. Place under broiler for 2-3 minutes until hot and cheese is melted.

Equivalent to:

2 Servings
Each =
1 starch
1 1/2 oz
protein
2 oil
1 additional
food
1/4 dairy

245 calories
10 g total fat
2 g saturated
88 mg
cholesterol
690 mg sodium

CURRIED SHRIMP ROUNDS

Ingredients:

1 (4 1/2 oz) can shrimp, drained and rinsed
1 T light mayonnaise
1 T fat-free mayonnaise
1 T Diet Center Ranch Dressing or other
   reduced calorie Ranch dressing
2 T plain non-fat yogurt
2 T chopped green onion
1 tsp lemon juice
1/8 tsp curry powder
4 T sliced water chestnuts
1/2 tsp chopped fresh parsley
2 oz fat-free swiss cheese, grated
Crackers, rice cakes, bagels, english muffins
   etc.

Instructions:

In a small bowl, combine all ingredients together and mix well. Adjust seasonings.
Spoon mixture onto rolls, crackers or rice cakes.
Broil until warmed and cheese starts to melt, about 3 to 4 minutes.

Equivalent to:

2 Servings
Each =
1 1/4 oz
protein
1 1/2 oil
1 starch

264 calories
10 g total fat
2 g saturated
93 mg
cholesterol
806 mg sodium

LEMON FANTASY MUFFINS

Ingredients:

8 egg whites or equivalent of egg substitute
2 tsp vanilla
2 tsp butter flavor
1 cup unsweetened applesauce
1 banana, mashed
1/2 cup non-fat plain yogurt
1/2 cup Diet Center Vanilla Protein Powder
1/4 cup non-fat dry milk
1 1/2 tsp sweetener
1/3 cup flour
1/3 cup unprocessed oat bran
1/3 cup unprocessed wheat bran
1/3 cup oatmeal
1 tsp baking soda
1/2 tsp baking powder
1/2 tsp lemon peel, grated
1/2 package Crystal Lite Lemon Drink Mix

Instructions:

Beat egg with flavorings until light and fluffy using a electric mixer. Add dry ingredients to egg mixture, mix well. Add applesauce, yogurt and banana, fold in until well incorporated.
In a muffin tin sprayed with Pam, and dusted with flour, fill and bake at 350 for 20 minutes.

Equivalent to:

8 Servings
Each =
1/2 oz protein
1/2 fruit
2 additional
foods

172 calories
1 g total fat
< 1 g saturated
1 mg
cholesterol
360 mg sodium

BANANA-PINEAPPLE MUFFINS

Ingredients:

1 cup quick rolled oats
1/2 cup skim milk
3/4 cup crushed pineapple
1/2 cup unprocessed bran
1 banana, mashed
1/4 cup corn oil
2 eggs whites
1 cup whole wheat flour
2 tsp baking powder
1/4 tsp salt
1/4 tsp soda
1-2 T honey

Equivalent to:

12 Servings
Each =
1 starch
1 oil
1/4 fruit
1 additional
food

178 calories
5 g total fat
< 1 g saturated
1 mg
cholesterol
258 mg sodium

Instructions:

Mix all ingredients together and bake for 15-20 minutes at 400 degrees.
Yield: 12 muffins

GYRO SANDWICH

Ingredients:

*1/2 lb 95% lean ground round beef or turkey
   breast
1/2 tsp salt, or to taste
1/8 tsp allspice
1/4 tsp garlic seasoning
1/8 tsp dill
2 pocket breads, cut in half or 4 (1 oz) pitas
4 slices onion
1 medium tomato, cut in 4 slices
Shredded lettuce
Dressing:
1/2 cup plain non-fat yogurt
1/8 tsp salt
1/8 tsp garlic seasoning
1 1/2 tsp fresh lemon juice*

Instructions:

In a bowl combine beef and seasonings, mix
well. Shape into 4 patties. In a skillet sprayed
with Pam, fry patties over medium heat until
done (may also grill meat).
In a small bowl, combine dressing ingredients,
mix well. Warm pocket breads. Place shredded
lettuce, meat, onion and tomato in pocket and
top with dressing.

Equivalent to:

4 Servings
Each =
1 3/4 oz
protein
1 starch
1/2 cup raw
vegetable
Scant dairy

186 calories
3 g total fat
<1 g saturated
35 mg
cholesterol
416 mg sodium

TACO POCKETS

Ingredients:

8 oz lean ground round beef
1 large tomato, chopped
1/4 cup Pace Picante sauce
1/4 cup sliced green onions
1 tsp Mexican seasoning
1/4 tsp garlic herb seasoning
Dash cayenne pepper, optional
1 whole wheat pocket bread
1 cup shredded lettuce
1 oz fat-free cheddar cheese, shredded

Equivalent to:

2 Servings
Each =
31/2 oz protein
1 cup cooked
vegetable
1 starch
1/4 dairy

272 calories
7 g total fat
1.9 g saturated
72 mg
cholesterol
551 mg sodium

Instructions:

In a large skillet sprayed with Pam, brown beef; drain any fat. Add tomatoes, onions, water and seasonings. Simmer 10 to 12 minutes, may need to add a bit of water if mixture gets too thick. Cut pocket bread in half. Fill each pocket with meat filling; top with lettuce and cheese.

CRAB SALAD IN PITA POCKETS

Ingredients:

6 oz fresh crabmeat, excess liquid squeezed out,
   or 1 (6 oz) can crab, drained
1 8-inch whole wheat pita bread, cut in half
2 T minced red onion
1/2 medium tomato, chopped
2 T green pepper, chopped
2 T chopped cilantro
1/8 tsp lemon pepper
2 T fat-free mayonnaise
2 T plain non-fat yogurt
1 oz feta cheese, crumbled
4 large lettuce leaves, rinsed and dried

Instructions:

In a medium bowl, combine all ingredients
except the pita bread (or lettuce); mix well.
Chill. Cut pitas in half, line pita halves with
lettuce and fill with crabmeat mixture.

Equivalent to:

2 Servings
Each =
1 1/2 oz
protein
1/3 dairy
1/2 oil
1 starch

229 calories
4.2 g total fat
2.4 g saturated
88 mg
cholesterol
698 mg sodium

MUSHROOM BURGERS IN A POCKET

Ingredients:

8 oz extra lean ground round beef
1/3 cup onion, chopped
1/4 cup bread crumbs
1/3 cup beef broth
1/4 tsp lemon pepper
1/2 tsp Season All
Salt, to taste
1/2 cup sliced fresh mushrooms
1/4 green pepper, cut into stirps
2 (1 oz) whole wheat pocket bread

Equivalent to:

2 Servings
Each =
31/2 oz protein
1 starch
1/2 cup cooked
vegetable
1 additional
food

265 calories
6 g total fat
1.9 g saturated
70 mg
cholesterol
362 mg sodium

Instructions:

In a large bowl, combine beef, onion, bread crumbs, bran, broth and seasonings; mix well. Shape into 2 patties. In a skillet sprayed with Pam, cook patties as desired; remove from skillet and drain on paper towel.
In a skillet, cook mushrooms and green peppers 3-4 minutes or until crisp-tender.
Cut pocket bread in half, place 1 burger, half of mushrooms and green peppers in each. Serve immediately.

SHRIMP ON ENGLISH MUFFINS

Ingredients:

1 English muffin, sliced
3/4 cup mushrooms, sliced
2 T chopped green onion
1/2 cup skim milk
4 oz shrimp
Dash nutmeg
1 T cornstarch
2 oz fat-free cheddar cheese, grated
Salt, to taste
1/8 tsp lemon pepper

Instructions:

Place mushrooms and shallot in a microwave bowl sprayed with Pam. Microwave on high 1 minute. Mix cornstarch in milk and add to mushroom mixture, season to taste. Add shrimp, microwave again about 1-2 minutes, uncovered until starts to thicken. Using a knife, pare away some of bread in middle of english muffin. Place on cookie sheet and fill holes with shrimp mixture. Top with grated cheese and broil in conventional oven until melted.

Equivalent to:

2 Servings
Each =
1 starch
1 oz protein
1/2 dairy
1/3 cup cooked vegetable
1 oil

212 calories
1 g total fat
< 1 g saturated
93 mg cholesterol
736 mg sodium

LITE CORNBREAD

Ingredients:

1 1/2 cups cornmeal
1/2 cup flour
4 tsp baking powder
1/4 tsp baking soda
1/2 tsp salt
2 T canola oil
1 tsp sweetener
1 1/2 cups skim buttermilk
2 egg whites

Equivalent to:

8 Servings
Each =
1/3 dairy
1 starch
3/4 oil
1 additional
food

107 calories
4 g total fat
< 1 g saturated
2 mg
cholesterol
459 mg sodium

Instructions:

Preheat oven to 425 degrees. Sift together dry ingredients, pour in oil, buttermilk and egg, mixing well. Spray a 8-inch square baking pan with non-stick spray and pour in batter. Bake for 30 minutes or until bread tests done.

Breads

CHICKEN VEGETABLE PITA

Ingredients:

1 (5 oz) can chicken or 5 oz cooked chicken breast, cubed
1 packet Diet Center Italian Dressing or other reduced calorie Italian dressing
1/4 cup finely chopped celery
1/4 cup thinly sliced cucumber
1 small tomato, sliced
Lettuce leaves
Sliced red onion, optional
1 (2 oz) pita bread, sliced in half

Instruction:

In a medium bowl combine chicken, dressing and celery, cover and chill. To serve, line breads with lettuce, tomato, cucumber, and onion. Spoon in chicken filling.

Equivalent to:

2 Servings
Each =
1 Starch
2 1/2 oz protein
1/2 oil
1/2 cup raw vegetable

171 calories
3 g total fat
< 1 g saturated
25 mg cholesterol
306 mg sodium

APPLESAUCE OATMEAL MUFFINS

Ingredients:

1/2 cups oats, uncooked
1 1/4 cups flour
3/4 tsp cinnamon
1 tsp baking powder
1 cup unsweetened applesauce
1/2 cup skim milk
1/3 cup brown sugar substitute, well packed
2 T sweetener
2 T corn oil
1 egg white
Topping (recipe given)

Equivalent to:

10 Servings
Each =
1 starch
1/4 fruit
3/4 oil
2 additional
foods

174 calories
3.7 g total fat
< 1 g saturated
0 cholesterol
116 mg sodium

Instructions:

Heat oven to 400 degrees. Spray muffin tin with Pam spray coating. Combine oats, flour, cinnamon, baking powder and baking soda. Add applesauce, milk, brown sugar, oil and egg white. Mix just until ingredients are moistened. Fill muffin cups almost full. Combine topping ingredients and sprinkle evenly over batter.
Bake at 400 degrees 20 to 22 minutes or until golden brown.

Ingredients Continued:

TOPPING:
1/2 cup oats, uncooked
1 T brown sugar, well packed
1 tsp cinnamon
2 tsp diet soft tub margarine, melted
1 tsp vanilla

Instructions Continued:

Combine oats, brown sugar, cinnamon and margarine; sprinkle evenly over muffin batter after filling in muffin tins.

FRUIT MUFFINS

Ingredients:

2 cups oat bran
1/2 cup whole wheat pastry flour
1 T baking soda
1/2 tsp cinnamon
3/4 cup orange juice
2 T cup vegetable oil
2 egg whites or egg substitute
1 T sweetener or honey (not Equal)
3/4 cup fruit, chopped fine or unsweetened
  applesauce

Instructions:

Combine all ingredients, mixing gently until well blended. Spay a muffin tin with Pam, spoon batter into muffin tins 2/3 full. Bake at 350 degrees for approximately 20 minutes.

Equivalent to:

10 Servings
Each=
1 starch
1/3 fruit
1/2 oil

90 calories
3 g total fat
<1 g saturated
0 cholesterol
257 mg sodium

APRICOT MUFFINS (M)

Ingredients:

1 1/2 cups oat bran
1/2 cup rolled oats
3/4 cup whole wheat flour
2 1/2 tsp baking powder
1 tsp cinnamon
3/4 cup dried apricots
4 egg whites
3/4 cup skim milk
1 T vegetable oil
1/2 cup honey

Topping:
1/2 cup all-purpose flour
3 T diet soft tub margarine
1/2 cup rolled oats
1 tsp cinnamon
1/4 cup sugar

Instructions:

Combine all ingredients except those for the
topping. In a muffin tin sprayed with Pam, fill
to 3/4 full. Combine topping ingredients and
sprinkle over muffin batter. Bake at 350 for 15-
20 minutes.

Equivalent to:

12 Servings
Each =

167 calories
3.8 g total fat
< 1 g saturated
< 1 g
cholesterol
190 mg sodium

BANANA-OAT BRAN MUFFINS

Ingredients:

1 cup whole wheat flour
1 cup all-purpose flour
2/3 cup oat bran
2 tsp baking powder
1 tsp baking soda
1 tsp cinnamon
1/8 tsp nutmeg
4 egg whites or egg substitute
2 T brown sugar
1/4 cup corn oil
1/2 cup orange juice concentrate
1/2 cup skim milk or low-fat buttermilk
2 bananas, mashed

Instructions:

Combine all ingredients, mixing only until blended. Pour into a muffin tin sprayed with Pam.
Bake at 350 degrees for about 20 minutes.

Equivalent to:

14 Servings
Each =
1 starch
3/4 oil
1/3 fruit
Scant protein
and dairy

173 calories
4.7 g total fat
< 1 g saturated
< 1 mg
cholesterol
142 mg sodium

PANCAKES

Ingredients:

3 T oat bran
1 1/2 cups rolled oats
1 T baking powder
2 T whole wheat flour
1 1/2 cup skim milk
1 egg and 2 egg whites
2 tsp vegetable oil

Instructions:

In a food processor mix oats, bran, baking powder and flour together until blended well. Mix in the liquid ingredients and allow mixture to stand 5 minutes.
Cook in a hot skillet sprayed with Pam, turning when cakes edges are set and firm.

Equivalent to:

4 Servings
Each=
1 starch
1/3 dairy
1/2 oz protein
1/2 oil

200 calories
5 g total fat
<1 g saturated
55 mg cholesterol
206 mg sodium

APPLE-OATMEAL CEREAL

Ingredients:

1/3 cup rolled oats
3 T oat bran
1 cup skim milk
1/2 cup unsweetened applesauce
1/2 tsp sweetener
1/2 tsp cinnamon
Dash nutmeg
1/2 tsp vanilla

Equivalent to:

2 Servings
Each =
1/2 dairy
1/3 starch
1/4 fruit
1 additional
food

137 calories
1 g total fat
0 saturated
2 mg
cholesterol
77 mg sodium

Instructions:

Heat the skim milk until hot but not boiling, over medium heat. Add rolled oats and oat bran. Stir until well blended. Add other ingredients and stir well. Serve hot.

MUESLI   (M)

Ingredients:

1 cup rolled oats
1 cup oat bran
1 1/4 cup skim milk
1/2 cup dried fruits of choice
1 T grated orange rind
1/3 cup orange juice
1/3 cup wheat germ
1/3 cup honey
Nuts, optional

Instructions:

Combine all ingredients together in a bowl and blend well. Cover and refrigerate overnight or for at least 8 hours. Before serving, stir thoroughly.
This can be prepared and stored for as long as 24 hours.

Yield:

6 Servings
Each =

236 caloreis
3 g total fat
< 1 g saturated
0 cholesterol
89 mg sodium

NOTES

Breakfast
& Brunch

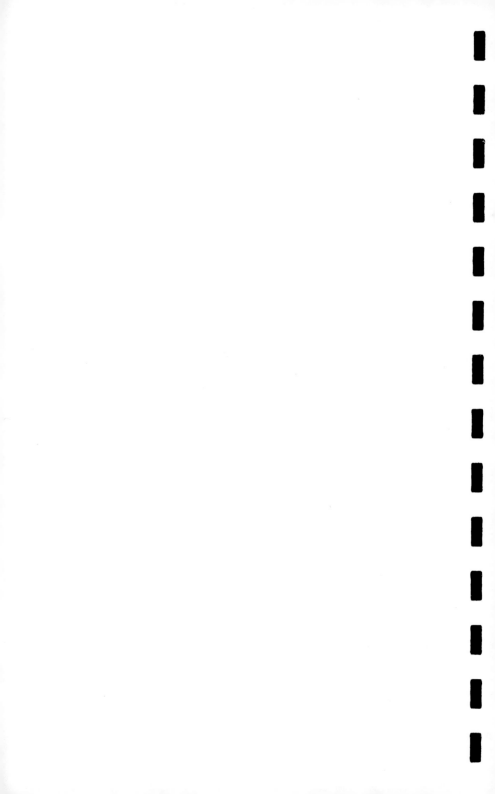

BAKED BROCCOLI FRITTATA

Ingredients:

1/2 cup sliced onion
1/3 cup sliced red or green bell pepper
1/4 tsp garlic powder
1/4 tsp dill
1/4 tsp each, basil and thyme leaves
1/2 tsp Season All
1/4 tsp lemon pepper
1 cup fresh or frozen broccoli cuts, cooked
  crisp-tender and drained
6 egg whites or 3/4 cup egg substitute
3 T skim milk
2 oz fat-free mozzarella cheese

Instructions:

Preheat oven to 425 degrees. In a skillet sprayed with Pam over medium-low heat, saute onions and peppers until tender; cool slightly. In large bowl, beat eggs, milk and seasonings until well mixed. Stir in onion-pepper mixture and broccoli. Pour into casserole dish sprayed with Pam, sprinkle with cheese. Bake at 425 for 10-15 minutes or until mixture is set (top will remain moist). Let stand 5 minutes before serving.

Equivalent to:

2 Servings
Each =
1 1/2 oz protein
3/4 cup cooked vegetable
1/2 dairy

135 calories
<1 g total fat
0 saturated
5 mg cholesterol
623 mg sodium

Breakfast & Brunch

CHILI RELLENO

Ingredients:

1 can (7 oz) green chilies
4 egg whites or 1/2 cup egg substitute
1/2 cup skim milk
1/2 cup non-fat cottage cheese
4 oz fat-free jack cheese, cubed and shredded
1/2 tsp salt, or to taste
1/2 tsp Teton Valley Nice n Spicy or Season All
Pepper, to taste
Mexican Salsa (recipe in Condiments) or Pace
   Picante sauce

Instructions:

Equivalent to:

4 Servings
Each =
1/2 oz protein
1 dairy

150 calories
3 g total fat
< 1 g saturated
116 mg
cholesterol
821 mg sodium

Split chilies open and remove seeds and pith. Stuff chilies with cottage cheese and a small amount of sliced jack cheese. Roll up each chili, place seam side down in a pan sprayed with Pam. Beat egg, milk, salt, and pepper add seasonings. Top with remaining cheese, Bake at 325 degrees for 40 minutes or until eggs are set. Top with Mexican Salsa or Picante sauce.

MEXICAN OMELET

Breakfast
& Brunch

Ingredients:

4 egg whites or egg substitute
1/4 cup green pepper, chopped
1/4 cup green onion, chopped
Hot green chilies, chopped, amount according
*   to taste, optional*
1/4 cup mushrooms, sliced
1 oz fat-free cheddar cheese, shredded
1/4 tsp salt
1/2 tsp Teton Valley Nice n Spicy or Season All
Dash lemon pepper
Mexican Salsa (recipe given in Condiments) or
*   Picante sauce*
Mock Sour Cream (recipe given in Condiments)
*   or 1 T fat-free sour cream*

Instructions:

Saute vegetables in a skillet sprayed with Pam. Add 1 T water to eggs and whip with a wire whisk. In a medium fry pan, add eggs and cook over medium-high heat until eggs start to set. Add vegetables and seasonings to one side of egg. Fold over other side and continue cooking until almost done. Add small amount of cheese and put on top of omelet. Finish cooking until done. Top with Salsa and Mock Sour Cream.

Equivalent to:

1 Serving
Each =
2 oz protein
1/2 cup cooked
vegetable
1 dairy

154 calories
2 g total fat
< 1 g saturated
10 mg
cholesterol
771 mg sodium

Breakfast
& Brunch

BASIC OMELET

Ingredients:

6 egg whites or 3/4 cup egg substitute
1 T water
Salt, to taste
Dash of garlic herb seasoning
Dash of Season All
Dash of lemon pepper

Instructions:

Gently beat eggs, water and seasonings. Pour into a pan sprayed with Pam. Cover and cook until puffy. Fold and serve.

Equivalent to:

1 Serving
Each =
3 oz protein

103 calories
0 total fat
0 saturated
0 cholesterol
560 mg sodium

ORIENTAL OMELET

Ingredients:

6 egg whites or 3/4 cup egg substitute
1 cup mushrooms, sliced
2/3 cup bean sprouts
1/2 cup sliced green onion
3-4 drops of low-sodium soy sauce
Salt, to taste
1/4 tsp garlic herb seasoning
1/4 tsp Oriental seasoning, optional

Instructions:

Beat eggs and mix in all seasonings. Pour eggs into a skillet sprayed with Pam, over medium high heat. Sprinkle bean sprouts, onions and mushrooms on top. Cover and cook until puffy, fold and serve.

Equivalent to:

1 Serving
Each =
3 oz protein
1 1/2 cup
cooked
vegetable

146 calories
<1 g total fat
0 saturated
0 cholesterol
345 mg sodium

CRUSTLESS CHILI QUICHE

Ingredients:

2 eggs
4 egg whites
3 T all-purpose flour
2 tsp diet soft tub margarine, melted
1 T Dijon mustard
1/8 tsp salt
3-4 drops red pepper sauce
3 oz shredded non-fat jack cheese
1 cup non-fat cottage cheese
1/4 cup chopped canned green chilies, drained
1/4 cup chopped roasted red pepper
1 T grated parmesan cheese

Equivalent to:

4 Serving
Each =
1 oz protein
1 dairy
1 additional
food
3/4 oil

131 calories
4 g total fat
1 g saturated
110 mg
cholesterol
253 mg sodium

Instructions:

Preheat oven to 350 degrees. Spray a 9" pie plate with Pam. In a medium bowl, lightly beat eggs. Whisk in flour, margarine, mustard, salt and pepper sauce. Stir in cottage cheese, jack cheese, chilies, and red pepper. Spoon mixture into prepared pie plate; sprinkle with parmesan cheese.
Bake 20-30 minutes, until filling is set and top is golden. Let stand 10 minutes before cutting into quarters.

EGG FOO YONG

Breakfast & Brunch

Ingredients:

3/4 cup egg substitute or 6 egg whites
1/4 cup finely chopped onion
1 T chopped green pepper
1/4 tsp salt, optional
1/8 tsp Oriental seasoning
Dash pepper
1 cup bean sprouts, rinsed and drained

Instructions:

In a medium bowl, beat eggs well. Add onion, green pepper, seasonings and bean sprouts; mix well. In a skillet sprayed with Pam, drop egg mixture by tablespoons into skillet; fry until golden. Turn and brown both sides.

Equivalent to:

1 Serving
Each =
3 oz protein
1/2 cup cooked vegetable

Serving =
199 calories
<1 g total fat
0 saturated
0 cholesterol
632 mg sodium

EASY ZUCCHINI QUICHE

Breakfast & Brunch

Ingredients:

1/2 cup sliced zucchini
1/2 cup sliced yellow crookneck
1/2 cup sliced mushrooms
1/2 onion, sliced
1/4 tsp garlic herb seasoning
1/4 tsp dill
1/4 tsp lemon pepper
1/2 tsp Teton Valley Nice n Spicy or Season All
Salt, to taste
4 egg whites or 1/2 cup egg substitute
2 oz fat-free cheddar cheese
1 tomato, diced

Equivalent to:

2 Servings
Each =
1 oz protein
1 cup cooked
vegetable
1/2 dairy

142 calories
2 g total fat
< 1 g saturated
5 mg
cholesterol
551 mg sodium

Instructions:

In a large skillet sprayed with Pam, saute vegetables until tender. Whip egg until foamy. Pour over vegetables and swirl pan to distribute egg evenly throughout pan. Cover and continue cooking until eggs are almost set. Add tomato and cheese on top and continue to cook until cheese melts.

HUEVOS RANCHEROS

Ingredients:

1/2 small onion, chopped
1/2 green pepper, chopped
1/2 tomato, peeled and chopped
2 T tomato paste
1/2 cup water
1 clove garlic, minced
1/2 tsp dried oregano leaves
1/4 tsp salt, or to taste
1/4 tsp Tabasco pepper sauce
8 egg whites or 1 cup egg substitute
Tortillas or English Muffins

Instructions:

In a skillet sprayed with Pam, cook onion and green pepper about 5 minutes or until tender. Add tomato, tomato paste, water, garlic, and seasonings. Cover; simmer 20 minutes. Break eggs, 1 at a time, into cup and slip into sauce. Cover; simmer over low heat 5 minutes or until eggs are set.
Serve over tortillas or English muffins.

Equivalent to:

2 Servings
Each =
2 oz protein
1 starch

168 calories
1 g total fat
< 1 g saturated
0 cholesterol
400 mg sodium

Breakfast
& Brunch

LITE EGG McMUFFIN

Ingredients:

4 English Muffins, toasted
2 slices fat-free cheddar cheese
2 eggs or egg substitute
Salt and pepper to taste
Dash of Season All
2 slices canadian bacon, lean ham or turkey
  breast

Instructions:

Equivalent to:

2 Servings
Each =
1 oz protein
2 starch
1/2 dairy

382 calories
2.3 g total fat
< 1 g saturated
14 mg
cholesterol
741 mg sodium

In a skillet sprayed with Pam, cook egg in manner preferred, (scrambled, fried, or poached). Toast muffins, top with eggs, cheese, meat, and muffin top.

BREAKFAST BURRITO

Ingredients:

4 egg whites or 1/2 cup egg substitute
1/4 cup green or red pepper, chopped
1/4 cup green onion, chopped
1 T non-fat sour cream
Pace Picante sauce
1/4 tsp Teton Valley Nice n Spicy or Season All
Pepper
2 tortillas

Instructions:

In a skillet sprayed with Pam, saute vegetables until crisp-tender. Add eggs and continue cooking until set. Fill tortilla with egg mixture and top with non-fat sour cream and picante sauce.

Equivalent to:

2 Serving
Each =
2 oz protein
1/4 cup cooked
vegetable
1 starch

149 calories
3 g total fat
< 1 g saturated
0 cholesterol
620 mg sodium

NOTES

Condiments

BEEF MARINADE

Condiment

Ingredients:

4 tsp oil
1/4 cup red wine vinegar
1 T low-sodium soy sauce
1/2 tsp Teton Valley Nice n Spicy or Season All
1/4 tsp thyme leaves, crushed
1/4 tsp lemon pepper

Instructions:

Score sirloin steak on both sides diagonally in a criss-cross pattern. Place in a shallow glass dish. In a small bowl, combine marinade ingredients; pour over meat, cover and refrigerate 8 to 24 hours.

Equivalent to:

2 Servings
Each =
2 oil

91 calories
9 g total fat
< 1 g saturated
0 cholesterol
38 mg sodium

SOY-GINGER MARINADE

Condiment

Ingredients:

2 T low-sodium soy sauce
4 tsp oil
1 tsp dry mustard
1/4 tsp ginger or 3/4 tsp grated fresh ginger
1 cloves garlic, finely chopped
2 green onions, sliced
1 small jalapeno pepper, seeded and chopped
3 T water

Instructions:

Whisk together all ingredients. Cover and let stand at room temperature for 1 hour to combine the flavors before using.

Equivalent to:

2 Serving
Each =
2 oil

109 calories
9 g total fat
< 1 g saturated
0 cholesterol
116 mg sodium

SOY MARINADE

Condiment

Ingredients:

1/2 tsp ginger
1 green onion, chopped
1 clove garlic, minced
1 T oil
2 T low-sodium soy sauce
1 tsp sweetener
2 T lemon or rice vinegar

Instructions:

In a small bowl, combine all ingredients and mix well. Makes 1/2 cup marinade.

Equivalent to:

2 Servings
Each =
1 1/2 oil

162 calories
13 g total fat
1.7 g saturated
0 cholesterol
158 mg sodium

TURKEY-CHICKEN MARINADE

Condiment

Ingredients:

1/2 diet lemon-lime soda
1-2 T low-sodium soy sauce
1 T oil

Instructions:

Mix ingredients together and place turkey or chicken in marinade. Cover and place in the refrigerator for 2-3 hours. Grill poultry on barbecue or under a broiler.

Equivalent to:

2 Servings
Each =
1 1/2 oil

70 calories
6 g total fat
< 1 g saturated
0 cholesterol
56 mg sodium

CAJUN MARINADE & BASTE

Condiment

Ingredients:

4 tsp oil
1/4 cup vinegar
1 clove garlic, crushed
1 tsp leaf oregano
1 tsp leaf thyme
1/4 tsp salt
1/2 tsp ground hot red pepper
1/2 tsp paprika
1/2 tsp black pepper

Instructions:

Combine all ingredients in a jar with a tight fitting lid. Shake vigorously until blended.
This marinade is great on chicken or beef. If your taste runs to milder food, use a little less hot pepper.

Equivalent to:

2 Serving
Each=
2 oil

94 calories
9 g total fat
1 g saturated
0 cholesterol
292 mg sodium

LEMONY LOW-CAL DRESSING

Condiment

Ingredients:

1/4 cup lemon juice
2/3 cup water
*1 (1.3 oz) packet low calorie Italian salad
   dressing mix*

Instructions:

In a pint jar with a tight-fitting lid or cruet, combine ingredients; shake well. Chill to blend flavors. Makes 1 cup.

Equivalent to:

4 Serving
Each=
2 additional
foods

67 calories
3 g total fat
< 1 g saturated
0 cholesterol
893 mg sodium

BASIL MARINADE FOR VEGETABLES

Condiment

Ingredients:

1 T oil
3 T lemon juice
2 T finely chopped fresh basil
1/8 tsp salt
1/8 tsp lemon pepper

Instructions:

Beat together oil, lemon juice, basil, and seasonings in a small bowl. Lightly brush on vegetables before grilling. Brush vegetables with marinade while grilling

Equivalent to:

3 Servings
Each =
1 oil

49 calories
4 g total fat
< 1 g saturated
0 cholesterol
100 mg sodium

CILANTRO-JALAPENO DRESSING

Ingredients:

1/2 bunch cilantro
1/3 cup oil
1/4 cup white wine vinegar
1 T fresh lime juice
1/2 jalapeno chili, stemmed, coarsely chopped.
1/4 shallot, halved
1/4 tsp salt
Dash Mexican seasoning

Instructions:

Combine all ingredients in a blender and puree. Refrigerate.

Equivalent to:

8 Servings
Each =
2 oil

85 calories
9 g total fat
< 1 g saturated
0 cholesterol
75 mg sodium

CURRIED APRICOT MAYONNAISE

Condiment

Ingredients:

1 egg
1/8 tsp dry mustard
1/8 tsp white pepper
dash paprika
1/2 tsp Teton Valley Nice n Spicy or Season All
1/4 tsp salt
1/4 tsp onion powder
1/8 tsp garlic powder
2 T apple cider vinegar, or lemon juice
3/4 cup corn oil
1/2 tsp curry powder
1/4 cup apricots
1/2 tsp sweetener

Instructions:

Place all ingredients, except oil, in a blender. Blend on high for 5 seconds. Add oil gradually to ingredients as mixing, add slowly because this thickens dressing. Adjust spices to taste, cover with a lid and refrigerate.
Serving = 4 teaspoons

Equivalent to:

16 Servings
Each =
2 oil

109 calories
11 g total fat
1.4 g saturated
14 mg cholesterol
4 mg sodium

DIJON MUSTARD DRESSING

Ingredients:

1 egg
2 T olive oil
2 T red wine vinegar
Salt, to taste
Dash of lemon pepper
Pinch sweetener
1 T Dijon-style mustard

Instructions:

Coddle the egg by placing in a bowl of very hot tap water. Let stand 15 minutes.
Place all ingredients in a food blender, and mix until well blended.

Equivalent to:

3 Servings
Each=
2 oil

112 calories
11 g total fat
1.8 g saturated
71 mg
cholesterol
180 mg sodium

CREAMY CUCUMBER DRESSING

Condiment

Ingredients:

1/4 cup fat-free mayonnaise
1/4 cup light mayonnaise
1/2 cup plain non-fat yogurt
1/2 cup chopped cucumber
1 T chopped chives
1 tsp finely chopped fresh parsley
1/4 tsp salt
1/4 tsp lemon pepper
1/4 tsp dill weed

Instructions:

In a small bowl, combine mayonnaise and yogurt, mix well. Stir in remaining ingredients. Cover; refrigerate to blend flavors.

Equivalent to:

1 1/2 cup
4 Servings
4 T= Serving
Each=
2 tsp oil
Scant dairy

119 calories
10 g total fat
2 g saturated
5 mg cholesterol
314 mg sodium

Condiment

COTTAGE CHEESE & DILL DRESSING

Ingredients:

1/2 cup low-fat cottage cheese
1/2 cup plain non-fat yogurt
1/2 cup skim milk
1 tsp olive oil
2 T wine vinegar or lemon juice
1 packet sweetener
Salt, to taste
1/2 tsp lemon pepper
1/4 tsp garlic herb seasoning
1/2 tsp dill weed

Instructions:

Blend together all ingredients.
Refrigerate for at least 24 hours before serving.

Equivalent to:

1 Serving
Each =
1 dairy
1 oil

55 calories
1 g total fat
< 1 g saturated
2 mg
cholesterol
108 mg sodium

VINAIGRETTE OIL-FREE DRESSING

Condiment

Ingredients:

1 tsp Knox Unflavored Gelatine
1/2 cup cold water
1 cup boiling water
1/4 cup red wine vinegar
1 T Dijon-style mustard
1 tsp fresh dill or 1 T dried dill weed
1/2 tsp garlic herb seasoning
1/4 tsp salt
1/8 tsp lemon pepper

Instructions:

In a blender, sprinkle unflavored gelatine over cold water; let stand 2 minutes. Add boiling water and process at low speed until gelatine is completely dissolved, about 2 minutes. Add remaining ingredients and process at low speed until blended. Pour into bowl; chill until slightly thickened, about 2 hours. Before serving, stir until smooth. Dressing can be stored covered in refrigerator up to 5 days. Makes about 3 cups dressing. May have as much as desired.

Equivalent to:

1 Serving
Each =
1 additional
food

10 calories
0 fat
0 saturated
0 cholesterol
193 mg sodium

Condiment

YOGURT DRESSING

Ingredients:

8 oz non-fat plain yogurt
1/2 tsp sweetener
1/4 tsp onion powder
1 1/2 tsp prepared mustard
1 tsp lemon juice·

Instructions:

In a small bowl, combine all ingredients; blend well and refrigerate.

Variations:
Curry Dressing: Add 1 tsp curry powder.
Horseradish Dressing: 1/2 tsp sweetener, 1/2 tsp prepared horseradish, 1/2 tsp worcestershire sauce.

Equivalent to:

1 Serving
Each=
1 dairy

31 calories
0 fat
0 cholesterol
64 mg sodium

ORANGE-ALMOND DRESSING

Condiment

Ingredients:

1/2 cup sunflower oil
1/3 cup red wine vinegar
1/3 cup orange juice
1 T orange peel
1/4 tsp salt
Orange peel (orange part only) cut into strips
1/4 tsp almond extract

Instructions:

Whisk all ingredients in a small bowl. Pour dressing over salad and toss gently. Garnish with orange peel strips and serve.
Serving = 1 1/2 Tablespoon

Equivalent to:

16 Servings
Equals =
2 oil

101 calories
11 g total fat
1 g saturated
0 cholesterol
58 mg sodium

Condiment

LIME POPPY SEED DRESSING

Ingredients:

Juice of 1 lime
2 T white wine vinegar
1 tsp sweetener
1 tsp Dijon mustard
Salt, to taste
1/4 tsp lemon pepper
2/3 cup corn oil
3 T poppy seeds

Instructions:

Combine lime juice, vinegar, sweetener, mustard, salt and pepper in a blender. Slowly add oil, blend until creamy. Stir in poppy seeds.

Equivalent to:

16 Servings
Each =
2 oil

91 calories
10 g total fat
1 g saturated
0 cholesterol
40 mg sodium

HERB BUTTERMILK DRESSING

Condiment

Ingredients:

1 cup low-fat buttermilk
2 T light mayonnaise
3/4 cup plain non-fat yogurt
1 tsp basil leaves
1/2 tsp garlic herb seasoning
1/4 tsp lemon pepper
1/4 tsp onion powder
1/2 tsp thyme
1/4 tsp salt

Instructions:

In a small bowl, combine ingredients; mix well.
Chill to blend flavors.
Serve with salads or as a vegetable dip.
Recipe makes 2 cups. Serving= 1/3 cup

Equivalent to:

6 Servings
Each=
2 oil
1/4 dairy

63 calories
3 g total fat
< 1 g saturated
3 mg
cholesterol
174 mg sodium

CHICKEN COATING MIX

Condiment

Ingredients:

2 T parsley flakes
1 T oregano
1 T marjoram
1 T thyme
2 tsp rosemary
1 tsp garlic powder
1 T paprika
1 tsp onion powder
1 T celery salt
1 T ginger
1 tsp pepper
1 tsp sage

Equivalent to:

May use as
much as you
desire

22 calories
< 1 g total fat
0 saturated
0 cholesterol
5 mg sodium

Instructions:

Mix all ingredients together and use as a coating for chicken or turkey. Store in an air tight container.

MEXICAN SPICE BLEND

Condiment

Ingredients:

6 T chili powder
3/4 tsp oregano
1/2 tsp cumin
1 tsp onion powder
1 tsp garlic powder

Instructions:

Mix together to use as a fast alternative to everyday seasonings.
Put in a shaker bottle for convenient use.

Equivalent to:

Use as much as desired

28 calories
1 g total fat
0 saturated
0 cholesterol
80 mg sodium

Condiment

CURRY CREAM SAUCE

Ingredients:

1 cup non-fat plain yogurt
1 tsp curry powder
1/4 tsp salt
dash hot pepper sauce

Instructions:

In a small bowl, combine yogurt and seasonings. Mix well. Cover and refrigerate to chill.

Great on fish or poultry.

Equivalent to:

1 Serving
Each =
1 dairy

29 calories
< 1 g total fat
0 saturated
0 cholesterol
186 mg sodium

CAJUN SPICE MIX

Condiment

94

Ingredients:

1 T sweet paprika
2 tsp salt
1 tsp onion powder
1/2 tsp garlic powder
1 tsp cayenne pepper
3/4 tsp black pepper
1/2 tsp dried thyme
1/2 tsp dried oregano

Instructions:

Mix all seasonings together and store in an air-tight container.

Equivalent to:

May use as
much as
desired

7 calories
0 fat
0 saturated
0 cholesterol
768 mg sodium

LITE HOLLANDAISE SAUCE

Condiment

Ingredients:

1 cup plain non-fat yogurt
4 egg yolks
1 T fresh lemon juice
Pinch paprika
Pinch cayenne pepper
1 T fresh minced herbs such as
    tarragon, basil, or parsley

Instructions:

Equivalent to

6 Servings
Each =
1/2 oz protein
scant dairy

59 calories
3 g total fat
1 g saturated
142 mg
cholesterol
32 mg sodium

Beat yogurt, egg yolks, lemon juice, pepper and paprika in a double boiler over simmering water until foamy and slightly thickened; sauce should register 170 degrees on a candy thermometer. Remove from over water. Season with salt and stir in herbs.

SEAFOOD COCKTAIL SAUCE

Condiment

Ingredients:

*2 T tomato paste, thinned with water to a thick
    tomato sauce consistency
1/4 cup Pace Picante Sauce
1/2 tsp celery seed
1 T lemon juice
1 tsp prepared horseradish
1/2 tsp Worcestershire sauce*

Instructions:

In a small bowl, combine all ingredients; mix
well. Cover and chill. Makes 3/4 cup.

Equivalent to:

1 Serving
Each =
1/4 cup
vegetable

41 calories
2 g total fat
<1 g saturated
0 cholesterol
265 mg sodium

Condiment

PINEAPPLE SALSA

Ingredients:

1 can (8 oz) crushed pineapple, drained
1/4 cup chopped red bell pepper
1 sliced green onion
1 T fresh lime juice
1 T low-sodium soy sauce
1/8 tsp red pepper
1/8 tsp black pepper

Instructions:

Combine all ingredients.
Serve over grilled or baked chicken breasts for a real taste treat.

Equivalent to:

4 Serving
Each =
1/3 fruit

46 calories
< 1 g total fat
0 saturated
0 cholesterol
22 mg sodium

EASY CHEESE SAUCE

Ingredients:

1/4 cup non-fat buttermilk
1 oz fat-free cheddar cheese, grated
Dash Teton Valley Nice n Spicy or Season All
Dash pepper

Instructions:

In a microwave safe bowl, combine buttermilk, cheese and seasonings. Microwave on medium setting, until cheese melts, stir often to mix sauce.

Equivalent to:

1 Serving
Each =
1 oz protein
1/4 dairy
1 oil

72 calories
< 1 g total fat
< 1g saturated
0 cholesterol
495 mg sodium

Condiment

SALSA FRESCA

Ingredients:

1 large ripe fresh tomato, diced
2 large tomitillos
1/4 cup chopped fresh cilantro
1/4 cup chopped onion or green onion
2 T lime juice
2-6 minced fresh, or canned, hot chilies
Salt, to taste

Instructions:

Chop all ingredients in blender and serve.

Equivalent to:

4 Servings
Each =
1/2 c raw
vegetable

30 calories
< 1 g total fat
0 saturated
0 cholesterol
301 mg sodium

Desserts

FROZEN YOGURT

Ingredients:

1 cup plain non-fat yogurt
1/2 tsp Crystal Light Berry Drink Mix
1 cup frozen fruit, must be frozen
Sweetener, to taste
2 T non-fat dry milk, optional

Instructions:

Mix all ingredients in a blender, or food processor, until creamy. Place in the freezer for 15-20 minutes to freeze to proper consistency.

Equivalent to:

1 Serving
Each =
1 dairy
1 fruit serving

189 calories
< 1 g total fat
0 saturated
0 cholesterol
202 mg sodium

BERRY SORBET

Ingredients:

1 envelope Knox Unflavored Gelatin
8 packets sweetener
2 cups Crystal Light Berry Drink prepared according to directions.
2 cups pureed strawberries or raspberries, fresh or frozen (without sugar).
2 T lemon juice

Instructions:

In a medium saucepan, mix unflavored gelatin with berry drink. Let stand 1 minute. Stir over low heat until gelatin is completely dissolved, about 5 minutes. Cool at room temperature; stir in remaining ingredients. Pour into a 9-inch square baking pan; freeze 3 hours or until firm. With food processor, or electric beater, beat mixture until smooth. Return to pan; freeze 2 hours or until firm.

To serve, let thaw at room temperature 15 minutes or until slightly softened.

Serve in dessert dishes, garnish with berries.

Equivalent to:

4 Servings
Each =
1/2 fruit
Scant diet
drink

40 calories
< 1 g total fat
0 saturated
0 cholesterol
3 mg sodium

SPARKLING LEMON-LIME SORBET

Dessert

Ingredients:

1 envelope Knox Unflavored Gelatin
8 packets sweetener
1 cup diet ginger ale
1 cup Diet Sprite
1/2 cup fresh lemon juice (about 3 lemons)
1/2 cup fresh lime juice (about 3 limes)

Instructions:

In a medium saucepan, mix gelatin with diet soda. Let stand 1 minute. Stir over low heat until gelatin is completely dissolved, about 5 minutes. Let cool to room temperature; stir in remaining ingredients. Pour into 9-inch square baking pan; freeze 3 hours or until firm.

With an electric mixer or food processor, beat mixture until smooth. Return to pan; freeze 2 hours or until firm.

To serve, let stand at room temperature 15 minutes. Spoon into dessert dishes; garnish with fresh mint leaves.

Equivalent to:

4 Servings
Each =
Scant diet
drink

25 calories
0 fat
0 saturated
0 cholesterol
21 mg sodium

STRAWBERRY ICE CREAM

Ingredients:

*1 cup frozen strawberries, or frozen fruit of
  your choice*
1 cup skim milk
1/2 cup non-fat cottage cheese
1 scoop vanilla protein powder, optional
*1/2 tsp Crystal Light Berry Drink Mix, or flavor
  of your choice*
1 tsp vanilla
Sweetener, to taste

Instructions:

Mix all ingredients in a blender or food
processor until smooth and creamy.
Serve.

Equivalent to:

1 Serving
Each=
1 fruit
2 dairy
1 additional
food

223 calories
1 g total fat
<1 g saturated
0 cholesterol
137 mg sodium

FRUITY POPS

104

Dessert

Ingredients:

1 envelope Knox Unflavored Gelatin
1/2 cup cold water
1 cup diet soda, or fruit juice, heated to boiling
6 packets Equal
1 T lemon juice
Fruits: Use any of the following, pureed, 1 cup
bananas, blueberries, cantaloupe,
nectarines, strawberries, raspberries, or
fruit of your choice.

Instructions:

In a bowl, sprinkle unflavored gelatine over cold water; let stand 1 minute. Add hot juice and stir until gelatin is completely dissolved, about 5 minutes. Stir in remaining ingredients. Pour into 6 (5 oz) popsicle molds or paper cups. Freeze until partially frozen, about 30 minutes. Insert wooden ice cream sticks; freeze until firm, about 4 hours.
Let stand at room temperature 5 minutes to serve.

Equivalent to:

6 Servings
Each =
1/4 fruit

22 calories
0 fat
0 saturated
0 cholesterol
7 mg sodium

FRUIT SORBET

Ingredients:

1 cup frozen fruit
1 egg white
1/2 tsp Crystal Light Berry Drink Mix
1 tsp vanilla
Enough Diet 7-up to blend

Instructions:

Blend ingredients in a blender or food processor to the consistency of a "slurpee", freeze and use as sorbet.

Equivalent to:

1 Serving
Each =
1 Fruit
1/2 oz protein
1 diet drink

116 calories
0 fat
0 saturated
0 cholesterol
118 mg sodium

FABULOUS FROZEN FRUIT

Dessert

Ingredients:

1 orange, sectioned and diced
1 apple, diced
1/4 cup frozen strawberries
1/4 cup frozen raspberries
1/4 cup blueberries
1/4 cup blackberries
1/2 cup orange juice concentrate

Instructions:

Toss all fruit together, add juice and mix gently. Refrigerate until ready to serve.
Best prepared just before serving to keep fruit frozen.

Equivalent to:

3 Servings
Each=
1 fruit
1 additional
food

89 calories
0 fat
0 saturated
0 cholesterol
3 mg sodium

BLUEBERRIES ROYAL

Ingredients:

2 cups fresh blueberries, washed
1/2 cup orange juice concentrate
2 (5 oz) containers fat-free, sugar-free frozen
yogurt

Instructions:

Equivalent to:

2 Servings
Each =
1 1/2 fruit
1/2 dairy
1 additional
food

194 calories
< 1 g total fat
0 saturated
0 cholesterol
99 mg sodium

In a saucepan, heat orange juice to boiling, add blueberries. Remove from heat and let fruit cool in sauce.

Cutting along sides of plastic containers, remove yogurt and place in serving bowls.
Top with blueberry-orange sauce. Serve immediately.

FRUIT A' LA MODE

Ingredients:

1 peach, peeled and sliced
1 cup strawberries, hulled and halved if large
1/2 orange, sectioned
1/2 cup raspberries or blueberries
2 (5 oz) containers fat-free, sugar-free frozen
  yogurt
Fresh mint leaves, optional for garnish

Instructions:

Slice fruit and place attractively on serving plates.
Using a melon baller, scoop out balls of frozen yogurt and arrange on top of fruit.

Garnish with fresh mint leaves.

Equivalent to:

4 Servings
Each =
1 1/4 fruit
1/4 dairy

90 calories
0 fat
0 saturated
0 cholesterol
47 mg sodium

FAT-FREE MOCHA CAKE (M)

Ingredients:

1 cup all purpose flour
1/3 cup plus 2 T unsweetened cocoa powder
1 tsp instant espresso or instant coffee powder
1 tsp baking powder
1 tsp baking soda
6 large egg whites, room temperature
2/3 cup firmly packed golden brown sugar
1 cup coffee-flavored or chocolate nonfat yogurt
1 tsp vanilla extract

1 tsp powdered sugar
1 tsp ground cinnamon

Equivalent to:

8 Servings
Each =

165 calories
6.4 g protein
34 g
carbohydrate
< 1 g total fat
< 1 g saturated
1.9 mg
cholesterol
mg sodium

Instructions:

Preheat oven to 350 degrees. Line the bottom of a 9-inch-diameter cake pan with waxed paper. Spray pan and paper with vegetable oil spray. Dust pan with four; tap out excess.
Sift 1 cup flour, 1/3 cup plus 1 T cocoa, espresso powder, baking powder and baking soda into medium bowl. Using electric mixer, beat egg whites, brown sugar, yogurt and vanilla in large bowl until blended, about 1 minute. Mix in dry ingredients. Transfer batter to a prepared pan. Bake cake until tester

Instructions:

inserted into center comes out clean, about 35 minutes. Cool in pan on rack for 15 minutes. Cut around pan sides to loosen the cake. Turn out onto a plate. Peel off paper and cool completely.

Combine remaining 1 tsp cocoa powder, powdered sugar and cinnamon in a small bowl. Sprinkle over cake before serving.

Note: The secret to this rich and fudgy cake is good-quality unsweetened cocoa powder, which gives the smooth taste of chocolate without the fat.

STRAWBERRY-ALMOND PARFAIT

Ingredients:

1 package (3.4 oz) sugar-free instant vanilla pudding mix
2 cups skim milk
1/4 tsp almond extract
2 cups strawberries, stemmed and sliced
4 packets Equal
6 graham crackers, crushed
Mint sprigs

Equivalent to:

6 Serving
Each =
1/3 starch
1/2 dairy
1/3 fruit
1 additional
food

175 calories
1.9 g total fat
< 1 g saturated
4 mg
cholesterol
267 mg sodium

Instructions:

In a bowl prepare pudding mix with milk as package directs, mixing in the almond extract; cover and refrigerate.
Add sweetener to strawberries. Spoon about 3 tablespoons into each of six stemmed glasses. Layer each with 3 tablespoons cookie crumbs and 1/2 cup pudding. Top with remaining strawberries and crumbs, dividing equally. Garnish with mint sprigs.

PAPAYA PARFAITS

Ingredients:

1 large papaya
2 T lime juice
1/2 tsp grated lime peel
1 banana, sliced
2 cups fruit; orange segments, sliced
    nectarines, fresh berries
2 containers fat-free, sugar-free frozen yogurt

Instructions:

Peel, halve, and seed papaya. Cut papaya into chunks and place in a blender or food processor along with lime juice and peel. Whirl until smoothly pureed. Cover and refrigerate until cold.

Line each of 6 individual dessert bowls with 1/2 cup fruit mix. Top each with a scoop of frozen yogurt; pour chilled papaya mixture equally over yogurt.

Equivalent to:

6 Servings
Each=
1 fruit
1/4 dairy

94 calories
< 1 g total fat
0 saturated
0 cholesterol
34 mg sodium

Dessert

STRAWBERRY SUNDAES

Ingredients:

1 1-pint basket strawberries, hulled
1 1/2 tsp sweetener
2 T orange juice concentrate
1/2 tsp grated orange peel
2 cups fat-free, sugar-free vanilla frozen yogurt
Fresh mint sprigs

Instructions:

Using a fork, crush half of berries and sweetener in a medium bowl. Slice remaining berries and add to bowl. Add orange juice concentrate and peel and blend well. Let stand 15 minutes. (Can be prepared 6 hours ahead. Cover and refrigerate.)

Divide frozen yogurt between 2 dessert dishes or large goblets. Spoon strawberry sauce over yogurt. Garnish sundaes with fresh mint and serve.

Equivalent to:

2 Servings
Each =
1 fruit
1 dairy

164 calories
< 1 g total fat
0 saturated
0 cholesterol
115 mg sodium

APPLE PIE CAKE

Dessert

Ingredients:

4 cups thinly sliced baking apples
3 T sweetener
1 tsp cinnamon
1/2 cup walnuts, chopped, optional
1/4 cup diet margarine, melted
1/2 cup skim milk and 3 T water
1 egg
1/2 cup fructose
1/2 cup unsweetened applesauce
1/4 tsp salt
1 cup flour
3/4 tsp baking powder
1 tsp baking soda

Instructions:

Mix apples, sweetener & cinnamon, spread in a pie plate sprayed with Pam. Scatter walnuts over the top (if using nuts). In a bowl, combine melted margarine, milk, water & egg. Add the soda to applesauce and stir. Combine salt, flour and baking powder. Blend with liquids. Pour over apples & nuts. Bake 45 minutes 325.

Equivalent to:

10 Servings
Each =
1/4 starch
1 additional
food
1 1/4 oil
1/2 fruit
3/4 nuts-seeds
(if nuts used)

149 or 187
calories
3.2 or 6.7 g
total fat
< 1 g saturated
21 mg
cholesterol
241 mg sodium

TRIPLE BERRY CREAM PIE

Ingredients:

Crust:
9 whole graham crackers, crushed
2 T reduced calorie margarine, melted
1 tsp cinnamon
1-2 packets sweetener
Pam

Filling:
1 1/2 packages (8 oz) fat-free cream cheese
1/2 cup fat-free vanilla yogurt
1/4 cup all fruit raspberry jam
1 1/2-pint basket blackberries or boysenberries
1 1-pint basket strawberries, hulled
1/2 cup fresh blueberries

Equivalent to:

6 Servings
Each =
1/2 fruit
1 starch
1 oil
scant dairy
2 additional
foods

213 calories
4 g total fat
< 1 g saturated
10 mg
cholesterol
508 mg sodium

Instructions:

Crust:
Spray a spring-form pan with Pam, add together ingredients and mix well. Press into spring-form pan and up sides a bit. Compact with a large spoon.
Spray with Pam again and continue pressing into pan.
Bake at 350 degrees for 4-5 minutes.

LEMON CHEESECAKE

Ingredient:

3 oz package lemon sugar free gelatin
1 cup boiling water
6 oz fat-free cream cheese
2 cups non-fat cottage cheese
1-2 tsp grated lemon peel
Cheesecake crust (recipe in Breads)

Instructions:

Prepare cheesecake crust found in "Breads".
In a small bowl, dissolve gelatin in boiling water. Cool to lukewarm.
In a food processor or blender, blend cottage and cream cheese with lemon peel until smooth. Slowly blend in gelatin mixture; pour into crust.
Refrigerate until set, about 2 hours. Garnish with lemon slices and a sprig of mint.

Equivalent to:

6 Servings
Each =
1/3 dairy
2 additional food
Crust =
1 starch
1/2 oil

143 calories
3 g total fat
< 1 g saturated
3 mg cholesterol
195 mg sodium

KEY-LIME PIE

Ingredients:

Equivalent to:

6 Servings
Each =
1 oz protein
1/3 dairy
1/3 fruit
Crust = 1 starch
1/2 oil

Woman Style:
6 Servings
Each =
1/2 legume
1/3 dairy
1/3 fruit
Crust = 1 starch
1/2 oil

166 calories
4 g total fat
0 saturated
0 cholesterol
248 mg sodium

2 packets unflavored gelatin
2 tsp sweetener
1 tsp Crystal Light Lemon-Lime Drink Mix, dry
2 T warm water
1/2 cup freshly-squeezed lime juice
1 tsp vanilla extract
1 package Lite Mori-Nu Firm Tofu, drained
1 cup non-fat cottage cheese
1 tsp grated lime rind
Pinch salt
2 kiwi, peeled and sliced in rounds
Cheesecake crust (recipe in Breads)

Instructions:

Prepare cheesecake crust. Dissolve gelatin and sweetener in warm water. As soon as the mixture is dissolved, add lime juice and vanilla, set aside.

In a food processor or blender, cream tofu and cottage cheese, blend until smooth. Slowly add lime juice mixture, lime rind, sweetener, drink mix, and dash of salt, blend well. Pour into pie crust. Chill and garnish with kiwi slices.

PEACH CHEESECAKE

Ingredients:

1 envelope Knox Unflavored Gelatin
1/4 cup cold water
1 can water packed peaches (16 oz), drained
  and liquid reserved
8 oz Lite Mori-Nu Tofu
2 T loosely packed mint leaves, optional
1 tsp Crystal Lite Citrus Drink Mix
1 tsp sweetener

Instructions:

In a blender, sprinkle unflavored gelatin over water and let stand 2 minutes. In a small saucepan, bring juice to a boil. Add juice to blender and process at low until gelatine is completely dissolved, about 2 minutes.
Add remaining ingredients and process on high until blended.
Prepare crust recipe (given in "Breads").
Pour mixture into 8x9-inch pie pan with crust. Chill until firm, about 3 hours. Garnish with peaches and mint leaves.

Equivalent to:

4 Servings
Each =
2 oz protein
1/2 fruit
Crust = 1
starch
1/4 oil

Woman Style:
4 Servings
Each =
2/3 legume
1/2 fruit
Crust = 1 starch
1/2 oil

220 calories
6 g total fat
1 g saturated
0 cholesterol
300 mg sodium

Dessert

BAKED APPLE

Ingredients:

2 large apples, cored
1 can diet cream soda
1/2 tsp or more sweetener
Cinnamon, nutmeg and allspice, to taste

Instructions:

Place apples in a baking dish, pour soda into hole where core was and over entire apple. Season to taste. Bake in a preheated 350 degree oven for 25-30 minutes.

Microwave Instructions:
Bake uncovered for about 4 minutes.

Equivalent to:

2 Servings
Each =
1 fruit

93 calories
< 1 g total fat
< 1 g saturated
0 cholesterol
2 mg sodium

FRESH STRAWBERRY CHEESECAKE

Ingredients:

Crust:
9 whole graham crackers, crushed
2 T reduced calorie tub margarine
1 tsp cinnamon, optional
Pam

Filling:
10 oz Lite Mori-Nu Tofu
1/2 cup non-fat cottage cheese
1 tsp dry, Crystal Light Lemon or Berry Drink
  Mix
2 tsp butter extract
1/4 tsp salt
1 T sweetener
1 cup fresh strawberries or fruit

Instructions:

Spray glass pie plate with Pam, add graham crust ingredients and mix. Press into pie plate and up sides. Spray with Pam. Bake at 350 for 5 minutes.

Equivalent to

4 Servings
Each =
2 oz protein
Scant fruit &
dairy
Crust = 1 starch
1/2 oil

Woman Style:
4 Servings
Each =
1/2 legume
Scant fruit &
dairy
Crust = 1 starch
1/2 oil

130 calories
4 g total fat
<1 g saturated
0 cholesterol
326 sodium

FRESH STRAWBERRY CHEESECAKE

Instructions Continued:

Drain tofu and wrap in several layers of paper towel and allow to sit 5 minutes. Place all remaining ingredients in blender and mix until smooth. Pour into crust and top with strawberries or preferred fruit.

PEAR FANS WITH ORANGE SAUCE

Ingredients:

1/2 cup orange juice concentrate
1/2 tsp cornstarch
1 T lemon juice
1/2 tsp finely shredded orange or lemon peel
3 medium-size red or yellow pears

Instructions:

Cut pears in half lengthwise. Trim core, stem end, and blossom end from each half; rub cut surfaces with lemon juice to prevent darkening. Slice each pear half lengthwise into 1/4-inch strips, leaving steam end intact; cut from rounded end to within about 1/2 inch of stem end. Drizzle cuts with remaining lemon juice. Place each pear half, cut side down, on a dessert plate. With the palm of your hand, lightly press cut portion down and away from you to fan out sides.

Mix cornstarch in orange juice, heat and stir until thickened; spoon over fruit.

Garnish with orange peel.

Equivalent to:

3 Servings
Each =
1 fruit
1 additional
food

120 calories
< 1 g total fat
0 saturated
0 cholesterol
2 mg sodium

CRISPY MERINGUE DESSERT SHELLS

Ingredients:

4 egg whites
1/2 tsp cream of tarter
1 tsp apple juice concentrate
1/2 tsp vanilla
Sweetener, to taste

Instructions:

Preheat oven to 275 degrees.
Beat egg whites until foamy and soft peaks form. Add cream of tartar and beat until very stiff. Don't under beat. Add apple juice concentrate, vanilla and continue beating until blended in. Divide mixture into six mounds on a cookie sheet sprayed with Pam, and shape mounds into 4 to 5 inch circular shells with a deep dent in the center of each.
Bake approximately 45 minutes until firm to the touch and light brown.
Remove from pan and cool on a wire rack. Fill before serving.

Suggested Fillings: sliced fresh fruit, sugar free
                    pudding, Diet Center
                    Frozen Yogurt.

Equivalent to:

6 Servings
Each =
1/3 oz protein

19 calories
0 fat
0 saturated
0 cholesterol
43 mg sodium

BLUEBERRY COBBLER

Ingredients:

1 fat-free blueberry muffin
1 cup blueberries
cinnamon
Sweetener, to taste

Instructions:

Crumble muffin into microwave safe bowl. Add blueberries, cinnamon and sweetener. Microwave until warmed.

Variation:
For peach cobbler, use apple cinnamon muffin and 1 peach peeled and sliced. Prepare the same way as above.

Equivalent to

1 Serving
Each =
1 starch
1 fruit

192 calories
1.6 g total fat
< 1 g saturated
10 mg cholesterol
209 mg sodium

BAKED CUSTARD WITH FRESH BERRIES

Ingredients:

1 cup skim milk
2 large eggs or 1/2 cup egg substitute, slightly
   beaten
1 tsp sweetener
1 tsp vanilla extract
1/4 tsp nutmeg
1/4 tsp cinnamon
1 cup fresh or frozen berries

Instructions:

Equivalent to

4 Servings
Each=
1/2 oz protein
1/4 fruit
1/4 dairy

77 calories
< 1 g total fat
0 saturated
0 cholesterol
91 mg sodium

Preheat oven to 300 degrees. In a medium-size bowl, gently blend milk, egg or egg substitute, sweetener, vanilla and spices.
Note: avoid whisking or beating mixture.
Divide mixture into 4 custard cups. Fill a glass baking dish with 1/2 inch water. Set custard cups in baking dish and bake for 50-60 minutes. To test, insert a knife near the edge of the cup. If it comes out clean, custard will be solid when cooled. Remove from oven and cool slightly. Chill overnight for best flavor.
Top with fresh berries.

MOIST AND LITE POPPY SEED CAKE

Ingredients:

1 cup flour
1 cup whole wheat flour
2 tsp baking powder
1/4 tsp salt
4 egg whites
1/2 cup fructose
1/4 cup canola oil
1 cup evaporated, skim milk
1 1/2 tsp vanilla extract
2 T poppy seeds

Instructions:

Preheat oven to 350 degrees. Sift both flours together with baking powder and salt, set aside. In a large bowl, lightly beat egg whites. With an electric beater, beat in fructose. Add oil, milk and vanilla, mix well. Gradually add sifted ingredients to liquid mixture and beat at medium speed only until combined. <u>Don't overmix.</u> Fold in poppy seeds. Pour mixture into a 9-13 inch pan sprayed with Pam. Bake 35-40 minutes until cake is golden brown on top and toothpick inserted in center comes out clean.

Equivalent to:

15 Servings
Each =
1/2 starch
1/8 oz protein
3/4 oil
1/4 dairy
1 additional food

126 calories
3.9 g total fat
< 1 g saturated
< 1 g cholesterol
140 mg sodium

LITE LEMON MERINGUE PIE

Ingredients:

Pie Crust: (makes 1)
1 cup all-purpose flour
1/4 tsp salt
3 T canola oil
3 T skim milk
Filling:
1/3 cup fructose
6 T cornstarch
1/2 tsp salt
1 1/2 cups skim milk
3 large egg yolks (reserve whites for meringues)
Zest of 1 lemon (zest lemon before squeezing)
Juice of 1 lemon
Meringue:
3 large egg whites, at room temperature
1/2 tsp cream of tartar
5 T fructose

Equivalent to:

8 Serving
Each=
1/3 oz protein
1/2 starch
1 oil
Scant dairy
1 additional
food

196 calories
7 g total fat
1 g saturated
81 mg
cholesterol
280 mg sodium

Instructions:

To prepare pie shell:
Mix flour and salt in a medium bowl. Mix oil and milk together with a fork. Add flour, mix with hands just until mixed. Add a little cold water if needed. Chill 10 minutes, press dough into a flat circle, with rolling pin, roll dough

LITE LEMON MERINGUE PIE

Instructions Continued:

from center out in one direction, don't roll to and fro. Roll until 1/8 inch thick and large enough for the pie pan. Fold in half, then in half again. Center over pan and unfold. Pierce with a fork in bottom of crust. Bake at 450 for 8-10 minutes. Let cool before filling.

Filling: Mix sugar, cornstarch and salt in a saucepan. Slowly add milk, stirring until it thickens. Beat egg yolks, add 1/2 the hot mixture and stir until smooth. Return egg mixture to pan and cook over med-low heat, stirring for about 2 minutes. Remove from heat; add lemon zest and juice. Let cool in pan while making meringue.

Meringue: Preheat oven to 350 degrees. Beat room temperature egg whites and cream of tartar on high with an electric mixer 1 minute. Gradually add fructose and continue beating until stiff peaks form. Pour filling into pie crust; smooth over with a spatula. Spread meringue over top, making sure meringue touches the edge of the pie shell all around; otherwise it will separate from the shell when baking. Bake at 350 until meringue is golden brown. Remove and cover with wax paper. Chill before serving.

CRUSTLESS APPLE PIE

Ingredients:

3 apples, peeled, sliced and cored
1 cup slim milk
1/3 cup flour
1/2 tsp cinnamon
1/2 tsp nutmeg
1 tsp vanilla
2 T sweetener
2 eggs

Instructions:

Spray a pie plate with Pam, slice apples into pie plate. Blend remaining ingredients and pour over apples. Bake at 350 for 30 minutes.

Equivalent to:

6 Servings
Each =
1/3 oz protein
1/2 fruit
1/4 dairy
1 additional
food

126 calories
2 g total fat
< 1 g saturated
72 mg
cholesterol
44 mg sodium

STRAWBERRY CREPES

Ingredients:

Crepe:
1/4 cup egg substitute or 1 egg, beaten
1 T Diet Center Vanilla Protein Powder
2 T skim milk
2 T unprocessed oat bran

1 cup strawberries, sliced
1 tsp sugar-free fruit preserves
1/2 cup fat-free cottage cheese

Instructions:

Crepe:
Combine ingredients and beat with a wire whisk. In a skillet sprayed with Pam, over medium-high heat, pour and quickly swirl 1/2 of mixture to coat bottom of pan. Cover with a lid for about 30 seconds. Run a spatula around the edge of the crepe, it should start to pull away from the sides of the pan. Continue to cook 30 seconds longer.
Fill crepes with cottage cheese, strawberries and top with strawberry preserves.

Equivalent to:

1 Serving
Each =
1 oz protein
1 fruit
1 dairy
2 additional
foods

225 calories
3 g total fat
< 1 g saturated
5 mg
cholesterol
232 mg sodium

CARROT CAKE

Ingredients:

Equivalent to:

12 Servings
Each =
1 starch
1/4 fruit
1 1/3 oil
1/3 dairy
1 additional
food
(counts icing)

140 calories
1.5 g total fat
< 1 g saturated
0 mg
cholesterol
156 mg sodium

1 1/2 cups sifted unbleached all-purpose flour
2 tsp baking powder
1/2 tsp baking soda
1 tsp cinnamon
1/4 tsp ground cloves
1/4 cup fructose
1/3 cup canola oil
4 egg whites
1/2 cup unsweetened applesauce
1 cup old-fashioned rolled oats
3/4 cup oat bran
1 cup finely grated carrots
1/2 cup raisins
1 recipe Lite Cream Cheese Icing (page 135)

Instructions:

Blend together the flour, baking powder, soda, cinnamon, cloves and fructose. Add the oil, egg whites and applesauce and mix well. Add the rolled oats and oat bran. Stir well. Stir in the carrots and raisins. Spread into a 9x13-inch baking pan sprayed with Pam. Bake 40 minutes at 350 degrees, cool and frost with Lite Cream Cheese Icing.

BANANA BREAD

Ingredients:

3 medium ripe bananas
1 large egg white
3/4 cup frozen unsweetened apple juice
  concentrate, thawed
1/4 cup diet soft tub margarine, melted
2 1/4 cups flour
1 tsp baking powder
1/2 cup chopped walnuts, optional

Instructions:

Mix all ingredients together and place batter in a 8 1/2 by 41/2 inch loaf pan that has been sprayed with Pam.
Bake at 325 degrees for 45 to 50 minutes.
Leave in pan for 10 minutes and remove. Cool. Wrap in plastic wrap overnight so the banana flavor will develop.

Equivalent to:

16 Servings
Each=
1/2 fruit
3/4 oil
1 additional
food
1/2 nut-seed (if
walnuts used)

125 or 149
calories
2 g or 4.2 g
total fat
< 1 g saturated
0 cholesterol
60 mg sodium
(higher values
reflect when
walnuts used)

PUMPKIN BARS

Ingredients:

3 T canola oil
1 large egg white
1 tsp vanilla
1 cup canned pumpkin
1 cup frozen unsweetened apple juice
  concentrate, thawed
2 cups flour
1 cup quick cooking rolled oats
1 tsp baking soda
1 tsp cinnamon
1/2 cup golden raisins

Equivalent to:

Instructions:

24 Servings
Each =
1/2 starch
1/2 fruit
1/4 oil

94 calories
2.2 g total fat
< 1 g saturated
0 cholesterol
39 mg sodium

Mix all ingredients together until fully incorporated. Bake at 375 degrees for 20 to 25 minutes in a 7 by 11 inch baking pan sprayed with vegetable coating.

BANANA MOUSSE WITH RASPBERRY SAUCE

Ingredients:

1 T unflavored gelatin
1/3 cup water
2 medium bananas
1 1/2 T sweetener
1 tsp grated lemon rind
1 T lemon juice
1/2 cup fat-free, sugar-free vanilla yogurt
1/2 cup skim milk
1 cup fresh or thawed frozen raspberries

Instructions:

Mix gelatin with the water and allow to soak for 5 minutes. Put over hot water and stir until dissolved.
Peel and cut bananas, put into a blender with gelatin, sweetener, lemon rind, lemon juice, milk and yogurt. Whirl until smooth.
Pour into a souffle dish or a mold and chill until set.
Place raspberries into the blender and blend until smooth.
Unmold the banana mousse and serve with the pureed raspberries.

Equivalent to:

3 Servings
Each =
1 1/2 fruit
1/3 dairy
1 additional
food

141 calories
< 1 g total fat
< 1 g saturated
0 cholesterol
43 mg sodium

LITE CREAM CHEESE ICING

Dessert

Ingredients:

1 1/2 cup fat-free ricotta cheese
1/2 cup fat-free cream cheese
6 T Equal
1 tsp vanilla

Instructions:

Blend all ingredients in a blender, or food processor, until smooth and creamy.

Equivalent to:

8 Servings
Each =
1/3 dairy
1 additional
food

50 calories
0 fat
0 saturated
2.5 mg
cholesterol
117 mg sodium

COCONUT GRANOLA SNACKS   (M)

Dessert

Ingredients:

1/2 cup coconut
1 cup quick cooking rolled oats
2 T firmly packed brown sugar
1/4 cup chopped pitted prunes
1/4 cup chopped pitted apricots
2 T sesame seed
1 T oil
2 T honey
1/4 cup seedless raisins

Instructions:

Mix coconut with oats, brown sugar, prunes, apricots and sesame seeds in a large bowl. Combine oil and honey in saucepan and bring to a boil over medium heat. Pour over cereal mixture and stir to coat well. Spread evenly in 13x9-inch pan. Bake at 325 degrees for 20 minutes, stirring several times to toast evenly. Sprinkle with raisins and spread out on a tray to cool. Break into small pieces and store in airtight container.

Equivalent to:

12 Servings
Each =
116 calories
2.6 g protein
19.6 g carbohydrate
4 g total fat
1.5 g saturated
0 cholesterol
1.6 g fiber
12 mg sodium

TRAIL BARS   (M)

Ingredients:

2 ripe, medium bananas
8 ounces dried figs
8 ounces dried apricots
8 ounces pitted dates
8 ounces raisins
2 cups granola
8 ounce chopped nuts
1 cup flaked coconut

Instructions:

Equivalent to:

12 Servings
Each=
341 calories
11 g total fat
4 g saturated
0 cholesterol
114 mg sodium
6.3 g protein
58 g
carbohydrate
4 g fiber

Coarsely chop bananas, figs, apricots, dates, raisins and granola in food processor. Stir in nuts. Press mixture into a 13x9-inch baking dish sprayed with Pam. Sprinkle with coconut. Cover; refrigerate 24 hours to allow flavors to blend. Cut into squares.

PINA COLADA DESSERT RING (M)

Dessert

Ingredients:

2 envelopes unflavored gelatin
2 1/4 cups pineapple juice, unsweetened
1 package (8 oz) Neufchatel cheese
10 packets Equal Sweetener
1 tsp grated orange rind
1 tsp grated lemon rind
1 1/2 tsp rum extract
1/2 cup non-fat dry milk
1/2 cup ice water
2 T lemon juice
1/2 cup toasted flaked coconut
Fresh fruit

Instructions:

Soften gelatin in pineapple juice; heat to dissolve. Pour into blender. Add cheese, sweetener, and rum extract. Cover; blend until smooth. Pour into a large bowl. Chill until mixture mounds from a spoon. Place milk, ice water, and lemon juice in mixing bowl. Beat on high until stiff peaks form, 4-6 minutes. Fold into gelatin mixture. Spoon into 6-cup ring mold. Chill until firm. Unmold onto serving plate, sprinkle with coconut and fresh fruit.

Equivalent to:

8 Servings
Each =
158 calories
2.2 g total fat
1.8 g saturated
6.5 mg cholesterol
218 mg sodium
9.7 g protein
24 g carbohydrate

BANANA-CRUNCH POPS

Ingredients:

8 oz fat-free, sugar-free yogurt
15 wooden sticks
3 bananas, peeled and cut into 5 pieces each
1 1/2 cup Grape Nut Cereal

Instructions:

Place yogurt in a shallow dish, insert a wooden stick into each banana piece, roll banana pieces in yogurt, covering entire piece of banana. Place the cereal in a small shallow dish. Roll the banana pieces in cereal. Place on wax paper lined baking sheet. Place in the freezer, when frozen wrap each in freezer wrap.
Let stand at room temperature for 10 minutes before serving.

Equivalent to:

15 Servings
Each =
1/2 starch
1/2 fruit
Scant dairy

50 calories
< 1 g total fat
< 1 g saturated
0 cholesterol
46 mg sodium

CREAMY LOW-CAL RICE PUDDING

Dessert

Ingredients:

1 package (4 servings) Jell-O Sugar-Free
   Vanilla Pudding
3 cups skim milk
1/2 cup Minute Rice
1/4 cup raisins
1/8 tsp ground cinnamon
Sweetener, to taste

Instructions:

Combine all ingredients in medium saucepan, Bring to a boil over medium heat, stirring constantly. Pour into 1-quart casserole or individual dessert dishes. Place plastic wrap directly on surface of hot pudding. Chill 30 minutes; remove plastic wrap. Sprinkle with additional cinnamon, if desired.

Equivalent to:

4 Servings
Each =
1/2 starch
1/2 fruit
1/4 dairy
1 additional
food

184 calories
< 1 g total fat
< 1 g saturated
3 mg
cholesterol
147 mg sodium

OATMEAL SPICE COOKIES

Ingredients:

Mix together to make a brown sugar mixture:
1 cup fructose
3 T vanilla

Then Add:
1 cup unsweetened applesauce
2 egg whites
2 cups flour
3 cups oatmeal
1 tsp baking soda
1/2 tsp baking powder
Dash salt
2 tsp cinnamon
1/2 tsp nutmeg
3/4 cup raisins

Yield:

3 dozen
cookies
Each =
1/4 fruit
1 starch
1 additional
food

88 calories
< 1 g total fat
< 1 g saturated
0 cholesterol
41 g sodium

Instructions:

Mix all ingredients together. On a cookie sheet sprayed with Pam, bake in a 350 degree oven for 8-10 minutes.

EASY STRAWBERRY SHORTCAKE   (M)

Ingredients:

1 angel food cake
1 1/2 pints fresh strawberries, hulled and sliced
1/3 cup orange juice concentrate
1 T fructose sweetener or 3 packages Equal
1 cup fat-free, sugar-free vanilla yogurt

Instructions:

Place strawberries in a bowl.
Combine orange juice and sweetener; pour over strawberries and mix to coat. Cover with plastic wrap and refrigerate, stirring occasionally to coat berries.

To Serve:
Cut cake into slices, spoon strawberries and sauce over cake. Top with yogurt.

Equivalent to:

8 Servings
Each =
178 calories
<1 g total fat
0 saturated
0 cholesterol
166 mg sodium
5 g protein
39 g carbohydrate
1 g fiber

APPLE CRUNCH

Ingredients:

1 1/4 cup quick rolled oats
1/3 cup flour
1 tsp cinnamon
1/3 cup diet soft tub margarine
3 cups apple, chopped
1 T flour
1 tsp cinnamon
1 1/2 T orange juice
1/4 cup fructose or sweetener

Equivalent to:

6 Servings
Each =
1 starch
1/2 fruit
1 oil
1 additional
food

183 calories
5.6 g total fat
< 1 g saturated
0 cholesterol
84 mg sodium

Instructions:

Combine the flour, oats, 1 tsp cinnamon and margarine; mix until crumbly in texture.
Place 1/2 of mixture in bottom of a baking dish.
Combine apples and flour, cinnamon, juice and sweetener. Pour into the pan over oatmeal mixture. Top with remaining oatmeal mixture; bake at 350 for 40 to 45 minutes.

BLUEBERRY AND PAPAYA CAKES (M)

Ingredients:

6 slices angel food cake or 6 angel food cake
   cups
1/2 papaya
1 1/2 cup blueberries
1/2 cup orange juice concentrate
1 container fat-free, sugar-free vanilla yogurt
Grated lemon rind

Instructions:

Slice papaya in half, lengthwise. Seed, peel,
and dice. Place papaya in saucepan with orange
juice, cook 3 minutes. Stir in blueberries and
lemon rind; bring to a boil again. Pour into a
bowl and refrigerate until cold.
Fill cakes with yogurt, spoon fruit and sauce
over top, letting it drip down sides of the cake.
Top with more yogurt if desired.

Equivalent to:

6 Servings
Each =
199 calories
< 1 g total fat
0 saturated
0 cholesterol
173 mg sodium
5.7 g protein
45 g
carbohydrates
1.9 g fiber3

FROZEN YOGURT POPS

Ingredients:

1 can (6 oz) frozen orange, grape or apple
  juice concentrate
3/4 cup water
1 cup non-fat sugar free yogurt

Instructions:

In a blender or food processor, whirl juice
concentrate, water, and yogurt until well
blended.
Divide mixture equally among eight 3 oz paper
drink cups. Cover cups and freeze until firm
(about 3 hours).

Equivalent to:

8 Servings
Each =
1/2 fruit
Scant dairy

23 calories
0 fat
0 saturated
0 cholesterol
15 mg sodium

Main Dish

SOUR CREAM ENCHILADAS

Main Dish

Ingredients:

1 1/2 cans (7 3/4 oz) chicken, turkey, or
   8 oz chicken cooked and shredded
1/2 cup green onion
1/2 can green chilies, or 1 hot chili,
   chopped
4 oz fat-free cheddar cheese, shredded
1/4 tsp Teton Valley Nice n Spicy or Season All
1/2 tsp Mexican seasoning
3/4 cup fat-free sour cream
Mexican Salsa (recipe in Condiments) or
   Picante sauce
2 fat-free flour or corn tortillas

Instructions:

Mix chicken, onion, and chilies together. If
using raw chilies; roast, peel and chop.
Mix seasonings into sour cream. Use 1/2 of
sour cream to chicken mixture. Fill tortilla with
chicken mixture and 1/2 of cheese. Roll and
place in a baking dish sprayed with Pam. Top
enchiladas with remaining sour cream mixture
and cheese. Bake at 350 degrees until warmed
and cheese is melted. Serve on a bed of
shredded lettuce and tomatoes. Top with salsa.

Equivalent to:

2 Servings
Each =
3 1/2 oz
protein
1 1/3 dairy
1 starch
Scant cooked
vegetable

317 calories
2.3 g total fat
< 1 g saturated
69 mg
cholesterol
951 mg sodium

Main Dish

CHILI VERDE

Ingredients:

12 oz chicken breast or extra lean pork loin
3 T flour
2 tsp olive oil
3 bunches green onions, sliced
3 large cans diced green chilies
1 large (8 oz) can low-sodium tomato sauce
1/2 tsp garlic powder
1/2 tsp oregano
6 corn or fat-free flour tortillas
4 oz fat-free cheddar cheese, shredded

Equivalent to:

6 Servings
Each =
2 oz protein
1 starch
1/3 dairy
1/3 cup cooked
vegetable
1 add. food

207 calories
3 g total fat
< 1 g saturated
41 mg
cholesterol
520 mg sodium

Instructions:

Flour and brown meat in olive oil. Add remaining ingredients and cook until tender. If mixture seems too thick, a little water or chicken broth can be added.

Serve Chili Verde in tortilla and top with cheese.

BEEF ENCHILADAS

Ingredients:

Beef Filling:
8 oz super lean ground round beef
3 oz fat-free cheddar cheese, shredded
1/2 cup onion, chopped
1 clove garlic, minced
1 can green chilies; or fresh hot chilies,
* chopped*
1/2 tsp Mexican seasoning
1/4 tsp Teton Valley Nice n Spicy or Season All
1/8 tsp cumin
1 tsp cilantro, chopped
3 corn or fat-free flour tortillas
1 can Enchilada sauce

Instructions:

Heat skillet sprayed with Pam to med-high heat. Cook beef, onion and garlic. Add remaining ingredients, (except cheese, tortillas, and 1/2 cup of enchilada sauce). Simmer 10 minutes. Fill tortillas with meat mixture and roll. Place in a baking dish sprayed with Pam, seam side down. Top with remaining enchilada sauce and cheese. Bake at 350 degrees for 10 minutes or until warmed through and cheese is melted.

Equivalent to:

3 Servings
Each =
2 oz protein
1/2 dairy
1 starch
1 additional
food

278 calories
6 g total fat
1.3 g saturated
52 mg
cholesterol
872 mg sodium

CHICKEN CROQUETTES

Ingredients:

2 T diet soft tub margarine
3 T flour
1 cup skim milk
12 oz finely chopped chicken
1/2 cup each, onion and mushrooms, chopped
1/4 cup green pepper, chopped
2 T parsley, chopped
1 tsp dry mustard
1/2 cup dry bread crumbs
2 egg whites
1/2 tsp Teton Valley Nice n Spicy or Season All
1/2 tsp salt
1/4 tsp pepper and garlic powder

Equivalent to:

6 Servings
Each=
3 oz protein
1/2 starch
1/2 oil
Scant dairy

158 calories
3.4 g total fat
< 1 g saturated
34 mg
cholesterol
371 mg sodium

Instructions:

Make a roux of margarine and flour, don't brown. Gradually add milk, whisk until smooth over med-low heat, about 15 minutes, stirring constantly. Remove from heat. In a skillet sprayed with Pam, over med-high heat, saute mushrooms, onion and green pepper for about 3 minutes, over med-high heat. Add chicken and seasoning, blend well. Chill 45 minutes. Shape chicken mixture into cones, roll in egg whites, then crumbs. Bake 30 minutes at 350.

MEXICAN CASSEROLE

Main Dish

Ingredients:

8 oz extra lean ground round beef
1 onion, chopped
1/2 cup each celery & mushrooms, chopped
1 medium green pepper, diced
1/2 to 1 tsp Mexican seasoning
1/2 tsp Season All
1/4 tsp herb garlic seasoning
1 cup canned tomatoes & 2 T tomato paste
2/3 cup kidney beans
2 oz non-fat cheddar cheese, shredded
(1 oz) baked low-fat tortilla chips
1 can green chilies, chopped
2 T cornstarch, mixed with 1/3 cup cold water

Instructions:

In a skillet sprayed with Pam, cook beef and chopped vegetables until browned. Add the tomatoes, paste, seasonings, beans, and thickening; simmer 10 minutes. Place in a casserole dish, adjust seasonings. Top with cheese and chips. Microwave on high for 3-5 minutes or until warmed and cheese is melted.

Equivalent to:

2 Servings
Each =
31/2 oz protein
2 starch
1 1/2 cup
cook vegetable
1/2 dairy

Woman Style:
2 Servings
Each =
1/3 legume
31/2 oz protein
1 1/2 cup
cook vegetable
1/2 dairy
1 starch

429 calories
8 g total fat
2 g saturated
75 mg
cholesterol
885 mg sodium

Main Dish

BEEF FAJITAS

Ingredients:

1/4 cup lime juice
2 tsp oil
1 clove garlic, minced
1/2 tsp Fajita seasoning
8 oz eye of round steak, sliced thin
2 corn or fat-free flour tortillas
Garnishes:
Shredded lettuce, chopped tomato, chopped
green onion, shredded non-fat cheddar
cheese, fat-free sour cream, Pace
Picante Sauce

Equivalent to:

2 Servings
Each =
31/2 oz protein
1 starch
1/2 oil

298 calories
9 g total fat
2 g saturated
72 mg
cholesterol
507 mg sodium

Instructions:

In a small bowl, combine lime juice, oil,
seasoning and garlic; pour over meat.
Refrigerate 6 hours or overnight, turning
occasionally.
Warm tortillas in microwave a few seconds.
Grill or broil* meat as desired, basting
frequently with marinade. Place meat on
tortillas.
Top with desired garnishes, count garnishes
used accordingly.

* You may also stir-fry meat in a skillet.

CHICKEN FAJITAS

Ingredients:

1/2 lb skinless, boneless chicken breast
2 T fresh lime juice
1/2 tsp salt, or to taste
1/4 tsp Mexican seasoning
1/4 cup non-fat plain yogurt
1 T chopped fresh cilantro
1/4 tsp minced jalapeno pepper, or to taste
1/8 tsp cumin
1 large onion, thinly sliced
1 cup shredded lettuce
1 ripe tomato, sliced thinly
2 corn or fat-free flour tortillas

Instructions:

Preheat the broiler. Put chicken breasts in a shallow dish and sprinkle with lime juice and seasonings. Let marinate in refrigerator for 15 minutes. In a small bowl whisk together yogurt, cilantro, jalapeno and cumin. Season with salt and set aside. In a baking dish sprayed with Pam, broil chicken and onions 4 minutes. Turn chicken and stir onions. Cut chicken into strips; fill tortilla with chicken, onions, lettuce and tomato. Top with yogurt mixture and serve.

Equivalent to:

2 Servings
Each =
31/2 oz protein
1 cup raw
vegetable
1 starch
Scant dairy

252 calories
2.9 g total fat
<1 g saturated
68 mg
cholesterol
287 mg sodium

Main Dish

CHICKEN FAJITA

Ingredients:

6 T Mexican Salsa (recipe in condiments) or
   Picante sauce
7 oz chicken breast, sliced in thin strips
1/2 tsp Teton Valley Nice N Spicy or Season All
1/2 tsp Mexican seasoning
Salt, to taste
1 green pepper, sliced
1 red pepper, sliced
1/2 onion, sliced
1/2 cup mushrooms, sliced
2 oz fat-free cheddar cheese, grated
2 corn or fat-free flour tortillas

Equivalent to:

2 Servings
Each=
31/2 oz protein
1 cup cooked
vegetable
1/2 dairy
1 starch

249 calories
3.2 g total fat
< 1 g saturated
62 mg
cholesterol
731 mg sodium

Instructions:

Marinate chicken strips in salsa for 2-3 hours.
In a skillet sprayed with Pam, combine chicken
and marinade with all other ingredients and stir-
fry until done, about 5-7 minutes. Put fajita
mixture into tortilla; add 1-2 T more salsa and
cheese on top.

MEXICAN STUFFED POTATOES

Main Dish

Ingredients:

*8 oz extra lean ground round beef or chicken
1/2 onion, chopped
1/4 tsp herb garlic seasoning
1/2 tsp Mexican seasoning
Pinch hot red pepper flakes, optional
4 T tomato paste
1/2 cup Pace Picante Sauce
2 oz fat-free cheddar cheese, shredded
1 tomato, diced
1 green onion, sliced
1/2 cup fat-free sour cream
2 medium baked potatoes

Instructions:

In a skillet spayed with Pam, cook beef, onion and seasonings until browned; drain off any fat. Add tomato paste, picante sauce, and enough water to make a sauce consistency out of tomato paste, adjust seasonings. To assemble: cut potato in half, top with meat mixture, sour cream, tomatoes, onions and cheese. If desired, top with more picante sauce.

* Woman Style: Add 1 cup cooked beans and reduce beef to 4 oz.

Equivalent to:

4 Servings
Each =
2 oz protein
1/3 dairy
1 starch
1/2 cup
vegetable

Woman Style:
4 Servings
Each =
1 oz protein
1/2 legume
1 starch
1/3 dairy
1/2 cup cooked
vegetable

255 calories
4 g total fat
< 1 g saturated
37 mg
cholesterol
391 mg sodium

Main Dish

CHICKEN TACOS

Ingredients:

3 1/2 oz shredded chicken, or canned chicken
1 corn or fat-free flour tortilla
1 oz fat-free cheddar cheese, shredded
1/4 tsp Mexican seasoning
1 tomato, chopped
Shredded lettuce
2 T Pace Picante Sauce
2 T non-fat sour cream

Instructions:

Warm chicken and season to taste. Place on tortilla with lettuce, cheese and tomatoes.
Top with picante sauce and sour cream if desired.

Equivalent to:

1 Serving
Each =
31/2 oz protein
1 starch
1/2 dairy
1/2 cup raw
vegetable

259 calories
3.7 g total fat
< 1 g saturated
62 mg
cholesterol
818 mg sodium

BEEF TACOS

Ingredients:

*8 oz extra lean ground round beef or 7 oz
   cooked shredded top round beef
1/4 red pepper, chopped
1/4 green pepper, chopped
Green chili pepper, chopped, to taste
1/8 tsp garlic powder
1/2 tsp Mexican seasoning
Cayenne pepper, optional, to taste
1 oz fat-free cheddar cheese, shredded
Shredded lettuce
Chopped tomatoes
Pace Picante Sauce
2 corn or fat-free flour tortillas

Instructions:

Saute beef and vegetables until tender in a
skillet sprayed with Pam, then add cooked beef;
season to taste. Fill tortillas with meat, lettuce,
tomato, cheese and picante sauce.

* Woman Style: Add 1/2 cup cooked red or
kidney beans & reduce beef to 4 oz.

Equivalent to:

2 Servings
Each=
31/2 oz protein
1 starch
1/2 cup cooked
vegetable
1/2 dairy

Woman Style:
2 Servings
Each=
1 3/4 oz
protein
1/2 legume
1 starch
1/2 dairy
1/2 cup cooked
vegetable

292 calories
7.7 g total fat
2 g saturated
75 mg
cholesterol
777 mg sodium

Main Dish

CHILI MACARONI

Ingredients:

*12 oz extra lean ground round beef or
cooked shredded top round*
1 cup onion, chopped
1/2 cup sliced mushrooms
1/2 cup sliced celery
*2 cups small shell macaroni or elbow
macaroni, cooked*
*1/2 tsp Mexican seasoning, or chili powder to
taste*
1/8 tsp herb garlic seasoning
1/8 tsp cayenne pepper, optional
1/2 tsp Teton Valley Nice n Spicy or Season All
8 T tomato paste
Water or beef broth

Equivalent to:

4 Servings
Each =
2 1/2 oz
protein
1/2 cup cooked
vegetable
1 starch

257 calories
4.9 g total fat
1.5 g saturated
52 mg
cholesterol
69 mg sodium

Instructions:

Spray skillet with Pam, brown beef with other
ingredients except macaroni, and simmer 1
hour. In the last 15 minutes of cooking add
macaroni and more water if necessary.

CHICKEN TORTILLA PIES

Main Dish

Ingredients:

8 oz chicken breasts, cut in thin strips
1/2 cup zucchini
1/2 cup onion, chopped
1/2 green onion, chopped
1/4 cup green pepper, chopped
1/2 tsp Mexican seasoning
1/4 tsp cumin
1/3 cup salsa
2 oz fat-free cheddar cheese
2 corn or fat-free flour tortilla
2 T fat-free sour cream

Instructions:

Place tortilla in a custard cup sprayed with Pam. Place a small square of cheese in each cup, grate remaining cheese.

In a skillet sprayed with Pam, saute chicken, zucchini, onion and pepper. Add seasonings and salsa; simmer 3-5 minutes. Spoon into tortilla

*Woman Style: use 5 oz chicken and 1/2 cup cooked beans.

Equivalent to:

2 Servings
Each=
31/2 oz protein
2/3 cup cooked
vegetable
1 starch
1/2 dairy
1 add. food

Woman Style:
2 Servings
Each=
2 oz protein
1/2 legume
1/2 dairy
2/3 cup cooked
vegetable
1 add. food

264 calories
4 g total fat
<1 g saturated
71 mg
cholesterol
840 mg sodium

CHICKEN TORTILLA PIES

Instructions Continued:

and sprinkle top with cheese.
Bake at 350 degrees for 15 minutes.
Add sour cream, more salsa, and top with green onion just before serving.

TOSTADA WITH CHICKEN FILLING

Ingredients:

*8 oz chicken breast, cooked and shredded
1/4 cup onion
4 T tomato paste
1 cup water
1/2 tsp sweetener
1/2 tsp Teton Valley Nice n Spicy or Season All
1/4 tsp Mexican seasoning
2 corn or fat-free flour tortillas
Chopped lettuce
Chopped tomato
1 oz shredded fat-free cheddar cheese

Instructions:

Saute onion until tender, then add chicken. Stir in remaining ingredients, (not lettuce, tomato, or cheese), simmer 20-30 minutes until thoroughly heated and flavors are well blended, stirring often. On a cookie sheet, heat tortilla in a 350 degree oven for 5 minutes, or until crisp. Serve filling in tortilla, topped with lettuce, tomato and cheese.

* Woman Style reduce chicken to 5 oz and add 1/2 cup cooked beans.

Equivalent to:

2 Servings
Each =
31/2 oz protein
1 starch
1/4 dairy

Woman Style:
2 Servings
Each =
2 oz protein
1/2 legume
1 starch
1/4 dairy

257 calories
2.9 g total fat
<1 g saturated
68 mg cholesterol
474 mg sodium

CHICKEN CHILI-CHEESE QUESADILLA

Ingredients:

2 fat-free flour tortillas (80 calories or under)
3 oz thinly sliced cooked chicken breast
1 red bell pepper, roasted, peeled and sliced into strips
1 poblano chili, roasted, peeled, seeded and cut into strips
2 oz fat-free cream cheese
4 oz fat-free jack cheese
2 T chopped green onion

Equivalent to:

2 Serving
Each =
1 1/2 oz
protein
1 starch
1 dairy
1 additional
food

255 calories
2.2 g total fat
< 1 g saturated
39 mg
cholesterol
929 sodium

Instructions:

On tortillas, spread cream cheese over 1/2 of surface. Divide the chili and pepper slices evenly over the cream cheese. Top with sliced chicken and green onion, then sprinkle halves with jack cheese. Fold the tortillas over pressing to seal. Heat a non-stick skillet over medium heat and toast the folded tortillas until the cheese melts and they are brown on one side. Cut each quesadilla into four wedges.

CHICKEN, BEAN & CHEESE BURRITOS

Ingredients:

7 oz chicken breast, cut into 1/2-inch strips
1 tsp olive oil
2 cloves garlic, minced
1/4 tsp Mexican seasoning
1/2 small onion, chopped
1/2 cup pinto beans, rinsed and drained
Hot pepper sauce, (such as Tabasco)
2 oz fat-free jack cheese, shredded
2 corn or fat-free flour tortillas

Chunky Salsa:
2 cup diced tomatoes
1/2 cup diced seeded peeled cucumber
1/2 cup diced red onion
2 T chopped fresh cilantro
1 small jalapeno chili, seeded, minced

Instructions:

Combine chicken, oil, and 1 garlic clove in medium bowl. Season generously; refrigerate 1 hour. In a skillet sprayed with Pam over high

Equivalent to:

2 Servings
Each =
3 oz protein
2 starch
1 oil
1/2 dairy

Woman Style:
2 Servings
Each =
3 oz protein
1/2 legume
1 starch
1/2 dairy

Salsa: Recipe =
3 cups raw
  vegetable

294 calories
4.9 g total fat
< 1 g saturated
62 mg
cholesterol
916 mg sodium

CHICKEN, BEAN & CHEESE BURRITO

Instructions Continued:

high heat, cook chicken mixture, about 4 minutes. Transfer chicken to plate. In same skillet, cook onion until very tender over medium heat. Stir in remaining garlic, cook 1 minute more. Mix in beans, remove from heat and season to taste with hot pepper sauce. Mix in cooked chicken.

Preheat oven to 350 degrees. Spoon 1/4 of filling down center of tortilla; roll up and top with 2 T salsa; roll up burrito. Place in baking dish sprayed with Pam, seam side down. Repeat with remaining ingredients. Sprinkle with cheese, cover and bake until burritos are heated through, about 15 minutes.

Serve with remaining salsa.

Salsa:
Combine all ingredients in a small bowl. Season to taste with salt. Cover and refrigerate.

PASTA WITH MARINARA SAUCE

Main Dish

Ingredients:

1 medium red onion, diced
2 cloves garlic, minced
2 T fresh parsley, chopped
1 tsp rosemary
1 tsp thyme
1/4 cup fresh basil leaf
1/4 cup fresh oregano
48 oz diced tomatoes
6 oz low-sodium tomato sauce
3 oz tomato paste
2 T honey or sweetener
1 tsp salt or to taste
1/2 tsp pepper
3 cups pasta

Instructions:

Saute onions and garlic, add all other ingredients and simmer 2 hours. Add water if it starts to thicken.
Serve over fresh pasta of your choice.

Equivalent to:

6 Servings
Each =
1 starch
1 cup cooked
vegetable

221 calories
1 g total fat
< 1 g saturated
0 cholesterol
438 mg sodium

PEPPER STEAK

Ingredients:

1 pound top round steak
1 T diet soft tub margarine
1 T flour
10 oz canned tomatoes
1 medium onion
1/2 cup low-sodium beef broth
1 green pepper
Salt and pepper to taste
1 1/3 cup cooked rice

Equivalent to:

4 Servings
Each =
31/2 oz protein
1 starch
1/3 fat/oil
1/2 cup cooked
vegetable

295 calories
9 g total fat
2.9 g saturated
68 mg
cholesterol
229 mg sodium

Instructions:

Cut round steak into 1 inch strips and brown in skillet with margarine. Stir in flour. Drain tomatoes reserving liquid; add enough water to liquid from tomatoes and broth to make 4 cups total. Add liquid; reserve tomatoes. Chop onion and add to skillet, stir. Cover and cook over low heat for 1 hour or until meat is tender. Stir occasionally. Cut green pepper into thin strips; add with reserved tomatoes. Cover and heat for 5 minutes.

Serve over cooked rice.

STUFFED GREEN PEPPERS

Main Dish

Ingredients:

8 oz extra lean ground round beef
1/2 cup mushrooms, chopped
1/2 onion, chopped
1/4 cup celery, chopped
1/4 cup green pepper, chopped
1 small can tomato paste
1/2 cup canned tomatoes
2/3 cup cooked rice
2 whole green peppers, seeded
1/2 tsp Teton Valley Nice n Spicy or Season All
1/2 tsp garlic herb seasoning
2 oz fat-free cheddar cheese, sliced

Instructions:

Steam green peppers about 10 minutes or until just tender. In a skillet sprayed with Pam, cook beef and vegetables until done. Mix tomato paste with water to get consistency of tomato sauce, add rice, adjust seasonings. Fill peppers with meat mixture and top with cheese. Bake in a 350 degree oven for 15 minutes or microwave until warmed through and cheese is melted.

Equivalent to:

2 Servings
Each =
3 1/2 oz protein
1 cup cooked
vegetable
1 starch
1/2 dairy

346 calories
6.5 g total fat
2 g saturated
75 mg
cholesterol
505 mg sodium

Main Dish

STUFFED ZUCCHINI

Ingredients:

8 oz extra lean ground round beef
1/2 cup mushrooms, chopped
1/2 onion, chopped
1/4 cup green pepper, chopped
1 small can tomato paste, mixed with water to
  a sauce consistency
2/3 cup cooked rice
1/2 tsp Teton Valley Nice n Spicy or Season All
1/4 tsp garlic herb seasoning
1/2 tsp Italian seasoning
2 oz fat-free cheddar cheese, sliced
2 zucchini

Equivalent to:

2 Servings
Each=
31/2 oz protein
1/2 dairy
1 cup cooked
vegetable
1 starch

382 calories
6 g total fat
2 g saturated
75 mg
cholesterol
494 mg sodium

Instructions:

Microwave zucchini for 7 minutes on high, or until soft. Cut each zucchini in half, scoop out pulp and seeds. In a skillet sprayed with Pam, cook beef with vegetables until done. Add other ingredients, except cheese. Fill zucchini and top with cheese. Bake at 350 for 15 minutes.

CHICKEN-STUFFED PEPPERS

168

Main Dish

Ingredients:

4 large green, peppers
2 cans chicken or 9 oz chicken breast, skinned,
  boned and cut in cubes
8 Sesame Ryvita Crackers, crushed
1/2 cup mushrooms, sliced
1 small onion, chopped
1/2 cup celery, chopped
1/2 cup green pepper, chopped, (use tops)
1 egg, beaten
1/2 tsp Teton Valley Good Stuff or chicken
  seasoning
1/4 tsp garlic herb seasoning
1/2 tsp lemon pepper
1/2 tsp poultry seasoning
2 oz fat-free mozzarella cheese, sliced

Instructions:

Cut tops off of green peppers and remove seeds. Steam until just tender, about 8-10 minutes.
In a skillet sprayed with Pam, saute chicken with vegetables until chicken is done. Add cracker crumbs to egg and mix with other ingredients, add seasonings to taste.

Equivalent to:

4 Servings
Each =
2 oz protein
1 cup cooked vegetable
1 starch
1/2 dairy

214 calories
2.5 g total fat
<1 g saturated
931 mg cholesterol
312 mg sodium

CHICKEN-STUFFED PEPPERS

Instructions Continued:

In a oven proof dish sprayed with Pam, place steamed peppers. Fill each pepper full of stuffing mixture. Cover and bake in at 350 degree oven for approximately 35 minutes. In last 10 minutes add cheese to melt.

MEATY MANICOTTI

Ingredients:

8 oz extra lean ground round beef or chicken
1/2 cup chopped onions
3/4 cup non-fat cottage cheese
4 manicotti shells, cooked
3 oz fat-free mozzarella cheese, grated
1 egg, slightly beaten
2 Ryvita Sesame Crackers, crushed
1/4 tsp lemon pepper
1/2 tsp Italian seasoning
1/2 tsp Teton Valley Nice n Spicy or Season All
4 T tomato paste, thinned with water to a sauce
    consistency, or prepared Lite Spaghetti sauce

Instructions:

In a skillet sprayed with Pam brown beef and onions. Add egg, cracker crumbs, cottage cheese, seasonings and 1/3 of grated mozzarella. Fill manicotti shells with stuffing, being careful not to split shells. Place in a casserole dish sprayed with Pam, top with thinned tomato sauce and remaining cheese. Bake in a 350 degree oven, covered, for about 20-25 minutes.

Equivalent to:

4 Servings
Each=
2 oz protein
1 1/4 starch
1/3 dairy

250 calories
4 g total fat
1.3 g saturated
93 mg
cholesterol
377 mg sodium

EASY OVERNIGHT LASAGNA

Main Dish

Ingredients:

8 oz extra lean ground round beef
16 oz lite prepared spaghetti sauce
1/2 cup water
8 oz fat-free ricotta cheese
3 T chopped fresh chives
1/2 tsp oregano leaves
2 egg whites or equivalent in egg substitute
4 oz lasagna noodles, uncooked
8 oz fat-free mozzarella cheese, shredded
2 T grated Parmesan cheese

Equivalent to:

6 Servings
Each =
1 oz protein
1 starch
scant oil
1 dairy
1 additional
food

236 calories
6.3 g total fat
2.2 g saturated
22 mg
cholesterol
474 mg sodium

Instructions:

In a skillet, brown ground beef, drain. Add spaghetti sauce and water; blend well. Simmer 5 minutes. In a bowl, combine ricotta cheese, chives, oregano and egg; mix well. In a square baking dish, spread 1/2 of meat sauce; top with 1/2 of uncooked noodles; 1/2 of ricotta cheese mixture, and 1/2 of mozzarella cheese. Repeat layers; top with remaining meat sauce. Sprinkle with Parmesan cheese. Cover and refrigerate overnight.
Bake at 350, uncovered, for 50-60 minutes, until noodles are tender and casserole is bubbly. Let stand 15 minutes before serving.

MANICOTTI ITALIAN STYLE

Main Dish

Ingredients:

4 manicotti shells
1 egg, beaten
1 green onion, sliced
1 T chopped onion
4 oz fat-free mozzarella cheese
1 cup fat-free cottage cheese
1/2 package (9 oz) frozen chopped spinach,
  thawed, squeezed to drain
1/2 small can tomato paste, thinned with water
  to sauce consistency, or lite spaghetti sauce
1/2 tsp Teton Valley Nice n Spicy or Season All
1/4 tsp garlic herb seasoning
1/2 tsp Italian seasoning
Pepper

Instructions:

Cook manicotti shells, drain; place in cold water. In a medium bowl combine eggs, onions, cottage cheese, 1/2 of the cheese, spinach and seasonings, mix well. Fill manicotti shells with cheese mixture. Place side by side in baking dish sprayed with Pam. Place tomato sauce on top, then the rest of the cheese.
Bake at 350 for 35-40 minutes.

Equivalent to:

4 Servings
Each =
1/4 oz protein
1 starch
2/3 dairy
Scant vegetable

210 calories
2 g total fat
< 1 g saturated
61 mg
cholesterol
484 mg sodium

BEEF GOULASH

Ingredients:

8 oz top round, cut in 1-inch cubes
1 small onion, sliced
1 small clove garlic, minced
1/2 tsp Teton Valley Nice n Spicy or Season All
1/4 tsp dried marjoram leaves
1/4 tsp dried thyme leaves
2 dashes Tabasco pepper sauce
1/2 bay leaf
3/4 cup tomatoes, undrained, cut into pieces
1 tsp paprika
1/2 cup beef broth

Equivalent to:

2 Servings
Each =
31/2 oz protein
1/2 cup cooked
vegetable

221 calories
6 g total fat
2 g saturated
70 mg
cholesterol
93 mg sodium

Instructions:

In a skillet sprayed with Pam, brown cubes of meat, remove. Spray pan again and saute onions and garlic about 3-5 minutes. Stir in other ingredients, return meat to skillet. Cover and simmer, stirring occasionally 1 1/2 to 2 hours.
Serve over noodles or rice.

BEEF LASAGNA

Ingredients:

8 oz extra lean ground round beef or chicken
1/2 cup sliced mushrooms
1/2 cup chopped onion
1/2 cup chopped green pepper
1 cup cooked wide egg noodles
1/2 cup non-fat cottage cheese
4 T tomato paste
1 cup stewed tomatoes
1/2 tsp oregano
1/2 tsp basil
1/4 tsp garlic herb seasoning
1/2 tsp Nice and Spicy or Season All
1/3 cup beef broth or water
1 oz fat-free cheddar cheese, grated

Instructions:

Make a sauce with tomato paste and beef broth or water, stirring to thin. Add seasonings to sauce. In a skillet sprayed with Pam, saute beef and vegetables until done. Add tomatoes, season to taste with same seasonings.

Equivalent to:

2 Servings
Each =
3 1/2 oz
   protein
1 starch
1/2 oil
1/2 dairy

373 calories
7 g total fat
2 g saturated
75 mg
cholesterol
279 mg sodium

BEEF LASAGNA

Instructions Continued:

In a microwave safe dish sprayed with Pam, layer noodles, meat mixture, cottage cheese, tomato sauce mixture, and top with cheese.
Heat until warmed through and cheese is melted.

SPAGHETTI WITH MEAT SAUCE

Main-Dish

Ingredients:

8 oz extra lean ground round beef
1/2 cup sliced mushrooms
1/2 cup chopped onion
1/2 cup chopped green pepper
1/2 cup chopped celery
4 T tomato paste
1 cup stewed tomatoes
2/3 cup beef broth, defatted, or water
Salt, pepper
1/2 tsp Teton Valley Nice n Spicy or Season All
1/2 tsp herb garlic seasoning
1/2 tsp Italian seasoning
1/2 tsp oregano
1/2 tsp basil
1 cup cooked spaghetti
1 oz fat-free cheddar cheese, grated

Instructions:

In a skillet sprayed with Pam, cook beef, vegetables and seasonings until done. In a small bowl mix tomato paste, beef broth until smooth and the consistency of tomato sauce, adding italian spices to sauce.

Equivalent to:

2 Servings
Each serving=
31/2 oz protein
1 starch
1/2 cup cooked
vegetable
1/4 dairy

353 calories
6.7 g total fat
2.1 saturated
<1 mg
cholesterol
347 mg sodium

Instructions Continued:

Add tomatoes to mixture and to vegetables in skillet and continue to simmer. Adjust seasonings and serve over spaghetti or you may stir pasta into sauce mix and serve that way. Top with grated cheese. Heat until cheese is melted and serve.

CHEESY CHICKEN TETRAZZINI

Main Dish

Ingredients:

8 oz chicken breast, skinned and boned, cut in
  1-inch pieces
3/4 cup sliced mushrooms
1/2 red bell pepper, cut into julienne strips
1/2 cup green onion, sliced
3/4 cup chicken broth
1/3 cup buttermilk or skim milk
1/3 cup plain non-fat yogurt
1/4 tsp lemon pepper
1/8 tsp dried thyme, crushed
1 T chopped fresh parsley
2 oz fat-free mozzarella cheese
2 T cornstarch
1 cup tri-colored corkscrew pasta, cooked

Instructions:

In a skillet sprayed with Pam, brown chicken over medium-high heat. Add mushrooms; cook and stir until tender. Add red pepper and green onion; cook several minutes, stirring occasionally.

Equivalent to:

2 Servings
Each =
31/2 oz protein
3/4 cup cooked vegetable
1 starch
1/2 dairy

346 calories
3 g total fat
< 1 g saturated
72 mg cholesterol
606 mg sodium

CHEESY CHICKEN TETRAZZINI

Instructions Continued:

Add cornstarch to chicken broth and mix well. Stir in broth, milk and yogurt to skillet and cook until slightly thickened, stirring constantly.
Add seasonings and adjust to taste. Toss with pasta. Place in a casserole dish sprayed with Pam and top with grated cheese. Microwave or bake until cheese is melted.

CHICKEN CASSEROLE

Ingredients:

7 oz canned or cooked chicken breast, cubed
1/2 cup mushrooms, sliced
1/4 cup celery, chopped
1 1/3 cup zucchini, chopped
1/2 cup onion, chopped
1/3 cup green pepper, chopped
1/2 tsp Teton Valley Nice n Spicy or Season All
1/4 tsp garlic herb seasoning
4 Wasa Crisp or Ryvita, crushed
1 egg, whipped

Instructions:

Stir-fry chicken and vegetables with spices. Add water as needed to keep moist. Transfer chicken-vegetable mixture into bowl; add crushed Wasa and raw egg. Mix well, put mixture into a 9x13 inch pan sprayed with Pam. Bake at 350 degrees for 30 minutes.

Equivalent to:

2 Servings
Each =
3 1/2 oz protein
1 starch
1/2 cup cooked
vegetable

246 calories
4 g total fat
1 g saturated
164 mg
cholesterol
137 mg sodium

VEGETARIAN PIZZA

Ingredients:

2 tsp olive oil
1 medium zucchini, diced
1 medium-size yellow crookneck squash, diced
1/2 c mushrooms, sliced
1/8 tsp dried crushed red pepper
1 16-oz Boboli baked pizza crust,
8 oz mushroom pizza sauce
3 garlic cloves, minced
1 c fat-free mozzarella cheese, (4 oz)
1/2 cup sun-dried tomatoes, thinly sliced
1/3 cup grated Parmesan cheese

Equivalent to:

8 Servings
Each =
2 starch
1/3 oil
1/2 dairy
1/2 cup cooked
vegetable

229 calories
4.5 g total fat
1.7 g saturated
10 mg
cholesterol
242 mg sodium

Instructions:

Preheat oven to 450 degrees. Heat oil in heavy medium skillet over medium heat. Add zucchini, yellow squash, mushrooms, garlic and crushed red pepper; saute until vegetables are almost tender, about 5 minutes.
Place pizza crust on a baking sheet. Spread mushroom sauce over. Sprinkle with mozzarella. Top with squash mixture and tomatoes. Sprinkle with Parmesan cheese.
Bake pizza until cheese melts and crust is crisp, about 13 minutes. Cut into 8 pieces and serve.

PITA PIZZA

Ingredients:

2 whole wheat pita breads (1 oz each)
2 T tomato paste, thinned with water
1 tsp Italian seasoning
1/2 tsp Teton Valley Nice n Spicy or Season All
1/4 tsp lemon pepper
6 mushrooms, sliced
1/2 green pepper, chopped
4 oz chicken breast, cooked and cubed
1 tomato, chopped
1/2 small onion, chopped
2 oz fat-free mozzarella cheese, grated
1 oz fat-free cheddar cheese, grated

Instructions:

Preheat oven to 425 degrees.
Place pita on a cookie sheet sprayed with Pam.
Add Italian spice to tomato paste. Spread on pita. In a skillet sprayed with Pam, saute chicken, onion and seasonings together until chicken is done. Place a layer of cheese, vegetables, meat mixture, then another layer of cheese on top of pita.
Bake 10 minutes.

Equivalent to:

2 Servings
Each =
1 starch
1/2 cup cooked vegetable
2 oz protein
3/4 dairy

267 calories
1.9 g total fat
< 1 g saturated
40 mg cholesterol
854 mg sodium

MINI CHEESE PIZZAS

Ingredients:

1 English Muffin, sliced
3 oz canned, or cooked chicken or beef
2 T chopped green pepper
2 mushrooms, sliced
4 T Lite Spaghetti sauce or tomato sauce
1/2 tsp Italian seasoning
1/8 tsp oregano
2 oz fat-free cheddar cheese
Dash Teton Valley Nice n Spicy or Season All

Equivalent to:

2 Servings
Each =
11/2 oz protein
1/2 dairy
1 starch

183 calories
1.3 g total fat
< 1 g saturated
29 mg
cholesterol
658 mg sodium

Instructions:

Mix tomato sauce with seasonings. Spoon 1 T sauce over muffin and spread. Top with meat, vegetables and cheese.
In a preheated 400 degree oven, bake pizza until warmed through and cheese is melted.

DINNER CREPES

Ingredients:

Basic Crepe:
1 large egg
1 T Diet Center Vanilla Protein Powder
2 T skim milk
2 T unprocessed oat bran

Crepe Filling:
1 cup mixed vegetables: celery, mushrooms,
  green onion, red and green bell pepper, onion
2 1/2 ounce canned chicken, cooked turkey or
  beef, (shrimp or crab may also be used)
2 drops low-sodium soy sauce
1/8 tsp garlic herb seasoning
1/4 tsp Teton Valley Nice n Spicy or Season All
1/4 tsp paprika
Salt, optional
1/8 tsp lemon pepper
1 oz fat-free cheddar cheese, shredded

Instructions:

Crepe:
Combine ingredients and beat with a wire whisk. Prepare a pan by spraying with Pam and

Equivalent to:

1 Serving
Each =
4 oz protein
1 cup cooked
vegetable
1/2 additional
food

311 calories
6.8 g total fat
1.8 g saturated
259 mg
cholesterol
699 mg sodium

DINNER CREPES

Instructions Continued:

heating over medium-high heat. When pan is hot, pour and quickly swirl 1/2 of egg mixture to coat bottom of pan. Return pan to heat again, cover with a lid and cook for 30 seconds. Crepe should begin to curl away from the sides of the pan. Run a spatula around the edge of crepe to loosen, may turn and brown other side or continue cooking with lid on until completely cooked, about 30 seconds.

Filling:
Saute vegetables until crisp-tender. Season to taste, add meat to vegetables and heat thoroughly. Spoon 1/2 mixture onto each crepe, roll up edges, top with cheese and serve. May heat under broiler until cheese is melted.

CHICKEN DINNER IN A DISH

Main Dish

Ingredients:

8 oz chicken breast, skinned and boned
1 medium potato, quartered
1/2 cup carrot, sliced
1/2 onion, sliced
1/2 cup mushroom, sliced
1/3 cup chicken broth
1 bay leaf
1/2 tsp Teton Valley Good Stuff Seasoning or
  any chicken seasoning
1/4 tsp lemon pepper
1/8 tsp garlic herb seasoning
1/8 tsp dill
8 oz package frozen cut green beans, thawed,
  drained

Instructions:

Preheat oven to 350 degrees.
In a casserole dish sprayed with Pam, arrange chicken, potatoes, carrots, and onion. Pour broth over chicken; add bay leaf and seasonings. Cover and bake at 350 for 45 minutes. Add beans and continue cooking another 10-15 minutes, or until chicken is thoroughly cooked and vegetables are tender.

Equivalent to:

2 Servings
Each =
31/2 oz protein
1 Starch
1 cup cooked vegetable

256 calories
2.5 g total fat
<1 g saturated
66 mg cholesterol
116 mg sodium

Main Dish

CABBAGE ROLLS

Ingredients:

4 large cabbage leaves
1 pound extra lean ground round beef or
  chicken
1 clove garlic, minced
1 small onion, finely chopped
1 egg, slightly beaten
2/3 cup cooked rice
1/2 tsp thyme
1/2 tsp dill weed
1/4 tsp lemon pepper
1/2 tsp Teton Valley Nice n Spicy or Season All
1 tomato, chopped
Lemon juice

Equivalent to:

4 Servings
Each =
31/2 oz protein
1/2 cooked
  vegetable
1/2 starch

237 calories
6.9 g total fat
2.3 g saturated
  123 mg
  cholesterol
75 mg sodium

Instructions:

Microwave whole cabbage for 5 to 7 minutes on full power, until leaves fall off easily. Sprinkle four cabbage leaves with lemon juice. Set aside. Combine beef, garlic, onion, rice, egg, thyme, dill, salt and pepper. Mix thoroughly, then place one-fourth of meat mixture in each cabbage leaf and roll up. Secure with toothpicks.

CABBAGE ROLLS

Instructions Continued:

Arrange rolls in a microwave-safe dish. Sprinkle with chopped tomatoes and season to taste.

Cover and microwave for approximately 30 minutes, on 70% power until cabbage is soft and meat is cooked.

Occasionally baste with juices to keep cabbage moist.

Main Dish

HAWAIIAN HAYSTACK

Ingredients:

7 oz cooked chicken breast, cubed
1 green onion, chopped
1/3 cup green pepper, chopped
1/3 cup celery, sliced
1 can pineapple chunks, drained
2/3 cup cooked rice
1 oz fat-free cheddar cheese, grated
4 T water chestnuts
1 tomato, sliced
2/3 cup chicken broth
1-2 T cornstarch

Equivalent to:

2 Servings

Each=
3 oz protein
1 starch
3/4 cup raw
vegetable
1/3 fruit
1/4 dairy

279 calories
2.6 g total fat
< 1 g saturated
61 mg
cholesterol
344 mg sodium

Instructions:

Chop vegetables and prepare other ingredients and place in small bowls. Mix cornstarch into chicken broth and heat until thickened to gravy consistency.
To assemble haystacks: layer rice, chicken, vegetables, pineapple, cheese and top with gravy. Serve immediately.

BEEF SLOPPY JOES

Main Dish

Ingredients:

8 oz extra lean ground beef or chicken breast
1/4 cup beef broth or water
2 T dry onion flakes
1/4 tsp Teton Valley Nice and Spicy or Season
  All
1/4 tsp herb garlic seasoning
2 tsp prepared mustard
1/4 tsp Liquid Smoke
2-3 T tomato paste, (may use up to 4 T),
  depending on personal taste.
2/3 cup cooked rice, optional
1 oz fat-free cheddar cheese, grated

Instructions:

Brown ground meat with seasonings. Mix all
ingredients together, stir well. Add rice and
seasonings then adjust to taste. Serve on a
whole wheat roll, english muffin, bread or
crackers. Top with grated cheese.
Also great on salad greens as a taco salad meat
mixture.

Equivalent to:

2 Servings
Each =
4 oz protein
1 starch
1/4 dairy

255 calories
6 g total fat
1.9 g saturated
72 mg
cholesterol
349 mg sodium

JAMBALAYA

Ingredients:

2 tsp diet soft tub margarine
1 medium onion, chopped
1 medium green pepper, chopped
1 pound large shrimp, shelled
2 cups canned tomatoes, cut up
1 cup chicken broth
6 oz can tomato paste
1/2 cup rice
1 tsp sweetener
1 tsp thyme leaves
1/2 tsp garlic powder
1/8 tsp pepper
1 bay leaf
1/2 tsp Teton Valley Nice n Spicy or Season All

Equivalent to:

4 Servings
Each =
2 oz protein
1 cup cooked
vegetable
1 starch
1/4 oil

252 calories
4.5 g total fat
< 1 g saturated
174 mg
cholesterol
251 mg sodium

Instructions:

In a large dutch oven melt margarine, saute onion for 2-3 minutes or just until tender. Stir in remaining ingredients, except shrimp, blend well. Cover, simmer 20-30 minutes until rice is tender and liquid absorbed, stir occasionally. Add shrimp last 5 minutes of cooking time. Remove bay leaf. Serve.

TIN FOIL DINNERS

Main Dish

Ingredients:

4 oz chicken breast or fish fillet
2 thick slices onion
1 small potato, sliced
1/2 cup carrot, sliced
1/2 small zucchini, sliced
1/2 small crookneck, sliced
2 rings green pepper
5 asparagus spears, optional
3 mushrooms, sliced
1/4 cup broccoli florets
1/4 cup cauliflower florets
1/2 tsp Teton Valley Nice n Spicy or Season All
Dash of garlic seasoning
1/8 tsp lemon pepper

Instructions:

Using heavy weight aluminum foil, sprayed with Pam, assemble dinners with onion on bottom, meat, then vegetables on top. Fold and completely seal the foil. Wrap again, having sealed edges on opposite sides. Place on grill or in 350 oven for about 25 minutes each side, being careful not to puncture foil when turning.

Equivalent to:

1 Serving
Each =
31/2 oz protein
2 cups cooked vegetable

250 calories
2.3 g total fat
< 1 g saturated
66 mg cholesterol
106 mg sodium

Main Dish

SUKIYAKI

Ingredients:

8 oz beef top eye of round or sirloin steak
1/3 cup beef broth
2 tsp low-sodium soy sauce
1/2 tsp sweetener
3 cups thinly sliced bok choy
1 cup green onion, bias sliced 1-inch pieces
1/2 cup bias sliced celery
8 oz Lite Mori-Nu Extra Firm Tofu, cubed
1 cup fresh bean spouts or 1 cup canned
6 T bamboo shoots, drained
6 T water chestnuts, drained and sliced
1/2 cup thinly sliced mushrooms
1/2 tsp Oriental seasoning

Equivalent to:

3 Servings
Each =
31/2 oz protein
2 cup cooked
vegetable

Woman Style:
3 Servings
Each =
21/3 oz protein
2/3 legume
2 cup cooked
vegetable

220 calories
4.9 g total fat
1.3 g saturated
46 mg
cholesterol
165 mg sodium

Instructions:

Partially freeze beef, slice thin across grain into thin stirps. Mix soy sauce, broth and sweetener together. In a wok or skillet sprayed with Pam, add beef and stir-fry 2 minutes or until browned. Add celery, bamboo shoots, water chestnuts, mushrooms, green onions, bok choy, add tofu then stir-fry 3-5 minutes, stir in broth mixture. Stir-fry until beef is done and vegetables are crisp-tender, Serve immediately.

SHRIMP CREOLE

Ingredients:

1 medium green pepper, cut into thin strips
2 medium onions, thinly sliced
1/2 cup chopped celery
1 garlic clove, minced
1/4 cup chopped fresh parsley
1 tsp sweetener
1/4 cup Pace Picante Sauce
1 bay leaf
1/4 tsp lemon pepper
1/4 tsp thyme leaves
1/4 tsp curry powder
1 tsp lemon juice
1/4 to 1/2 tsp hot pepper sauce
2 cups whole tomatoes, cut up
1 lb shrimp, peeled and deveined
1 1/3 cups hot cooked rice

Instructions:

In a large skillet sprayed with Pam, saute green pepper, onion, celery and garlic until tender. Add remaining ingredients except shrimp. Cover; simmer 40 minutes. Add shrimp, simmer 10 minutes. Serve with rice.

Equivalent to:

4 Servings
Each =
2 oz protein
1 starch
1 cup cooked
  vegetable

244 calories
2.9 g total fat
< 1 g saturated
173 mg
cholesterol
229 mg sodium

FAST BEEF STIR-FRY

Ingredients:

1 (16 oz) package frozen vegetable blend
8 oz beef, eye of the round or sirloin steak,
  sliced thin
*1/4 cup chopped onion and mushrooms
2/3 cup chinese style pasta or rice, cooked
1/2 tsp Teton Valley Nice n Spicy or Season All
1/4 tsp Oriental seasoning
1/8 tsp garlic powder
1/2 tsp low-sodium soy sauce
1-2 T red wine vinegar, to taste
Dash Worcestershire sauce

Equivalent to:

2 Servings
Each =
31/2 oz protein
1 cup cooked
vegetable
1 starch

343 calories
6.4 g total fat
2 g saturated
70 mg
cholesterol
154 mg sodium

Instructions:

Pierce bag of vegetables and microwave on high for 5-7 minutes; drain. In a skillet sprayed with Pam, saute onion and mushrooms over high heat for 1 minute. Add other ingredients except, pasta. Stir-fry until beef looks done, about 4 minutes. Add pasta, stir well; warm thoroughly and serve.
* May add any vegetables desired to those not in frozen mix.

SHRIMP STIR-FRY

Main Dish

Ingredients:

12 oz shrimp, shelled
1/2 medium green pepper, chopped
1/2 cup onion, chopped
1/2 cup chopped celery, sliced on the diagonal
4 T water chestnuts
4 T bamboo shoots
1/2 cup broccoli florets
1/2 cup chicken stock
2 tsp low-sodium soy sauce
1/2 tsp Teton Valley Nice n Spicy or Season All
1/2 tsp Oriental seasoning
1/4 tsp garlic herb seasoning

Instructions:

Spray a wok or skillet with Pam, heat on medium-high. Starting with densest vegetables, stir-fry until all are crisp-tender. Add broth while stirring to keep vegetables from scorching. In the last 2-3 minutes, add shelled shrimp and cook until shrimp turns pink, don't overcook.

Equivalent to:

2 Servings
Each =
3 oz protein
1 1/4 cup cooked vegetable

234 calories
3.7 g total fat
< 1 g saturated
260 mg cholesterol
343 mg sodium

CHICKEN CHOW MEIN

Ingredients:

12 oz chicken breast, cubed
1 cup chopped celery, cut on the diagonal
2/3 cup onion, chopped
1 green pepper, cut in strips
1 cup bean sprouts, rinsed and drained
1 cup mushrooms, sliced
2 T pimento, chopped, optional
2 T water
1 cup chicken stock
1 T cornstarch
2 T low-sodium soy sauce
1/2 tsp Oriental seasoning
1/2 tsp Teton Valley Nice n Spicy or Season All
1/2 tsp garlic herb seasoning

Equivalent to:

3 Servings
Each =
31/2 oz protein
1 cup cooked
vegetable

211 calories
2.6 g total fat
< 1 g saturated
66 mg
cholesterol
203 mg sodium

Instructions:

Combine celery, onion, green pepper and water in a 2 quart microwave safe casserole dish. Cover and microwave on high 6-7 minutes or until vegetables are crisp-tender. Add bean sprouts, mushrooms, pimento and chicken; set aside. Combine chicken stock, tofu, seasonings and soy sauce in a 4 cup measure, mix well. Microwave on high uncovered 5-6 minutes or until mixture boils and thickens.

Instructions Continued:

Stir once or twice during last half of cooking time. Add all together and microwave on high 5-7 minutes or until heated through, stir once.

BEEF AND VEGETABLE STIR-FRY

Main Dish

Ingredients:

8 oz beef top eye of round or sirloin steak
1 cup broccoli, cut into one-inch pieces
1/2 cup carrot, sliced bias
1 T cornstarch
1 tsp low-sodium soy sauce
1/2 cup chicken broth
1 T red wine vinegar
1/2 tsp Oriental seasoning
1 medium onion, cut in thin wedges
2/3 cup frozen peas, thawed
4 T water chestnuts, drained and thinly sliced
4 T bamboo shoots, halved lengthwise
2/3 cup cooked rice

Equivalent to:

2 Servings
Each =
31/2 oz protein
1 1/4 cup
cooked
vegetable
2 starch

390 calories
7.4 g total fat
2.3 g saturated
71 mg
cholesterol
148 mg sodium

Instructions:

Partially freeze beef; slice thin across the grain into strips. In a skillet, or wok sprayed with Pam, stir-fry carrots and broccoli for 2 minutes then add onions cooking another 2 minutes. Next add beef and cook 2-3 minutes or until browned. Last add peas, chestnuts, and bamboo shoots. Mix cornstarch, broth, soy sauce, and vinegar. Combine mixtures, cooking until slightly thickened. Serve over rice.

PEPPERY CRAB WITH ASPARAGUS

200

Main Dish

Ingredients:

8 oz crab meat, cooked and shelled or 1 (6 oz)
  package frozen crab meat
3/4 cup chicken broth
1-2 T cornstarch
2 tsp sow-sodium soy sauce
1/2 tsp sweetener
1/2 tsp crushed red pepper
1 tsp grated ginger root
2 cups asparagus, bias-sliced into 1-inch
  lengths
1/4 cup green onion, sliced

Instructions:

Cut crab into bite-size pieces. Blend chicken broth and cornstarch. Add soy sauce, sweetener, and red pepper. In a wok or skillet sprayed with Pam, over high heat, stir-fry ginger root 30 seconds. Add asparagus, cook 1 minute; add green onion, stir-fry 1 minute. Remove asparagus and green onion. Add crab to skillet or wok, cook 1 minute, then add broth mixture to crab and cook until slightly thickened. Combine with asparagus and green onion, cover and cook 2-3 minutes. Serve.

Equivalent to:

2 Servings
Each =
2 oz protein
1 cup cooked
vegetable

209 calories
2.8 g total fat
<1 g saturated
02 mg
cholesterol
446 mg sodium

Main Dish

TUNA ASPARAGUS CASSEROLE

Ingredients:

6 1/2 oz can tuna, drained and flaked
2/3 cup cooked egg noodles
1/2 cup chopped green pepper
1/2 cup sliced mushrooms
1/2 onion, chopped
2 oz fat-free cheddar cheese
1 cup cooked asparagus spears
1/2 tsp Teton Valley Nice n Spicy or Season All Salt, to taste
1/4 tsp lemon pepper
1/4 tsp garlic herb seasoning
1/2 cup plain non-fat yogurt
1/2 cup buttermilk or skim milk
1-2 T cornstarch

Equivalent to:

2 Servings
Each =
31/4 oz protein
1 starch
1 1/2 cup cooked vegetable
1 dairy

356 calories
3.9 g total fat
1.6 g saturated
47 mg cholesterol
824 mg sodium

Instructions:

Saute all vegetables in a skillet sprayed with Pam until crisp-tender. Add all other ingredients except cheese and mix well. Top casserole with cheese and bake in a microwave, or oven, until hot and sauce is thickened. Then in a 350 degree oven, cover and bake about 20-25 minutes.

Meats

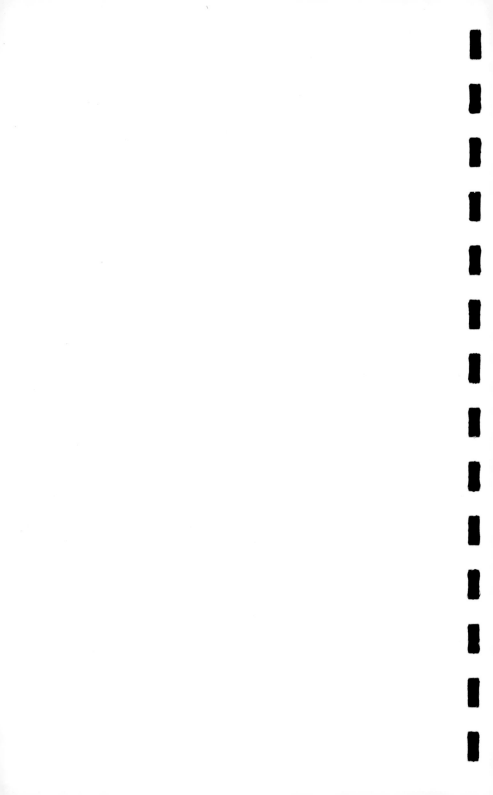

MEXICAN MEAT LOAF ROLL

Ingredients:

1 pound extra lean ground round beef
4 crushed Ryvita Crackers
1/2 cup chopped onion
1 egg, slightly beaten
1/2 tsp Worcestershire sauce
1/2 tsp pepper
1/2 tsp Mexican seasoning
3/4 cup non-fat cottage cheese
1 (4 oz) can green chilies, chopped and drained
1/2 cup Pace Picante Sauce

Instructions:

Combine meat, crackers crumbs, egg, seasonings and mix well. On wax paper, press meat mixture into a rectangle. Combine cottage cheese and chilies. Spread cheese mixture over meat to within 1 inch of outer edge. Roll jelly roll style, starting at narrowest end. Place in a baking dish and bake at 350 degrees for 40 minutes. Top with salsa, continue to cook 10 minutes more. Let stand 10 minutes before serving.

Equivalent to:

4 Servings
Each =
31/2 oz protein
1/2 starch
1/3 dairy
Scant vegetable

249 calories
7.6 g total fat
2.2 g saturated
125 mg cholesterol
207 mg sodium

TURKEY-SPINACH MEAT LOAF

Ingredients:

1 pound turkey breast, ground
1 10-ounce package frozen chopped spinach, thawed and drained well
4 Ryvita Crackers, crushed
1 small onion, finely chopped
1/4 tsp garlic herb seasoning
1/2 tsp lemon pepper
1/4 tsp salt
1/2 tsp dill weed
1 tsp low-sodium Worcestershire Sauce
1 egg
1 large tomato, chopped

Equivalent to:

4 Servings
Each=
31/2 oz protein
1/4 cup cooked
vegetable
1/2 starch

209 calories
3 g total fat
<1 g saturated
119 mg
cholesterol
152 mg sodium

Instructions:

In a food processor, combine all ingredients except tomatoes, process until very well blended. In shallow 8 or 9-inch microwave safe dish, form meat mixture into a 6x4 inch loaf. Evenly distribute tomato in dish around meat loaf. Microwave on high 10 minutes, rotating once or twice. Let stand 3 minutes.
To serve: Transfer meatloaf to serving dish; stir tomato pieces and pan juices together and spoon over top of meat loaf.

BEEF MEAT LOAF

Ingredients:

1 pound extra lean ground round beef
1/2 onion, chopped
1 tsp Teton Valley Nice n Spicy or Season All
1/2 tsp herb garlic seasoning
1/2 tsp barbecue seasoning
1/2 tsp Liquid Smoke
4 Ryvita Crackers, crushed
4 T tomato sauce or catsup, (use this on top of
   meat loaf as a sauce).
1 egg, beaten
1/4 tsp sweetener

Instructions:

Spray loaf pan with Pam, mix all ingredients,
except the tomato sauce or catsup. Place in pan
and top with tomato sauce. Bake at 350 degrees
for 50 minutes, or until loaf starts to pull away
from the sides of the pan.

Equivalent to:

4 servings
Each=
31/2 oz protein
1/2 starch

230 calories
6.8 g total fat
2 g saturated
123 mg
cholesterol
85 mg sodium

MINI-MEAT LOAF MUFFINS

Ingredients:

1 medium potato, peeled and grated fine
1/2 cup grated carrots
1 pound extra lean ground round beef
2 egg whites
1 medium onion, chopped and sauted 3-4
 minutes
1/4 tsp allspice
1/2 tsp Mexican seasoning
Salt, to taste
Pepper

Equivalent to:

4 Servings
Each =
31/2 oz protein
1/2 starch
1/3 cup cooked
vegetable

199 calories
5.5 g total fat
1.8 g saturated
70 mg
cholesterol
63 mg sodium

Instructions:

Combine carrots and potatoes in large bowl.
Add beef and mix together well. Add remaining
ingredients and mix until thoroughly
incorporated. Press mixture into cups of muffin
ring sprayed with Pam. Microwave 5 minutes
uncovered. Remove and let cool slightly before
serving.

TEXAS STYLE CHILI

Ingredients:

1 pound top round steak, cut into 1-inch cubes
1 onion, chopped
1/2 cup green pepper, chopped
1/2 cup celery, chopped
1 clove garlic, minced
2 cups canned tomatoes, cut up, undrained
1 cup beef broth or water
1 small can tomato paste
2 tsp chili powder, or to taste
1 tsp ground cumin
1/2 tsp oregano
1/2 tsp sweetener
1/2 tsp Teton Valley Nice n Spicy or Season All

Instructions:

In a large pan sprayed with Pam, brown meat chunks. Add onion, garlic and green pepper; cook and stir until tender. Add remaining ingredients, cover and bring to a boil. Reduce heat; simmer 1 1/2 hours or until meat is tender.
Serve with shredded non-fat cheddar cheese if desired.

Equivalent to:

4 Servings
Each =
31/2 oz protein
1 cup cooked vegetable

241 calories
6.5 g total fat
2 g saturated
70 mg cholesterol
114 mg sodium

SAUSAGE

Ingredients:

1 pound raw ground chicken or turkey breast
1/2 tsp sage
1/4 tsp poultry seasoning
1/2 tsp pepper
1 tsp liquid smoke
1/2 tsp Teton Valley Nice n Spicy or Season All

Instructions:

Mix all ingredients and form 8 patties. Cook in a pan sprayed with Pam, until browned on both sides.

Equivalent to:

4 Servings
Each =
31/2 oz protein

127 calories
1.4 g total fat
< 1 g saturated
66 mg
cholesterol
80 mg sodium

ORIENTAL STEAK KABOBS

Ingredients:

8 oz beef top eye of round or sirloin steak, cut
in 1-inch chunks
2 packets Diet Center Italian Dressing or 4 T of
reduced calorie Italian dressing
1 T low-sodium soy sauce
1 tsp sweetener
1/4 tsp ground ginger
2 T green onion, sliced
6 large mushrooms
1 cup broccoli florets
1/2 red pepper, cut in chunks

Instructions:

In a large shallow baking dish, combine Italian
dressing, soy sauce, sweetener, ginger and
onion. Add beef and vegetables; turn to coat.
Cover and marinate in refrigerator, stirring
occasionally, 4 hours or overnight. Remove
beef and vegetables, reserving marinade.
Onto large skewers, alternately thread beef with
vegetables. Grill or broil, turning and basting
frequently with reserved marinade, about 10
minutes or until done as preferred.

Equivalent to:

2 Servings
Each =
31/2 oz protein
1 cup cooked
vegetables
1 oil

256 calories
9.8 g total fat
2.4 g saturated
70 mg
cholesterol
274 mg sodium

GRILLED PEPPER STEAK

Ingredients:

9 oz top eye of round or sirloin steak
2 tsp oil
4 tsp red wine vinegar
1 tsp Dijon mustard
1/2 tsp herb garlic seasoning or 1 clove
 garlic, minced
1/2 green onion, chopped
1/2 tsp coarsely ground pepper
1/2 minced fresh thyme or 1 tsp dried,
 crumbled
1/2 tsp minced fresh rosemary or 1 tsp dried,
 crumbled

Equivalent to:

2 Servings:
Each =
4 oz protein
1 tsp oil

233 calories
10 g total fat
2.7 g saturated
78 mg
cholesterol
90 mg sodium

Instructions:

Whisk all ingredients, except steak, in a medium bowl to blend. Place steak in a single layer in a large baking dish. Pour marinade over and turn steaks to coat. Cover and refrigerate overnight. Prepare barbecue to medium-hot coals. Remove steak from marinade and season all sides with pepper. Grill steak about 4 minutes per side for medium-rare. Thinly slice steak diagonally across grain. Arrange slices on a platter and serve.

SZECHUAN BEEF AND SNOW PEAS

Ingredients:

7 oz boneless sirloin beef steak or top loin
2 T cornstarch
3 T low-sodium soy sauce, divided
1 T dry sherry
1 clove garlic, minced
3/4 cup water
1/4 to 1/2 tsp crushed red pepper
1 tsp oil
6 oz fresh snow peas, trimmed
1 medium onion, cut in chunks
1 medium tomato, cut in chunks
Hot cooked rice

Instructions:

Slice beef across grain into thin strips. Mix 1 T each cornstarch and soy sauce with sherry and garlic in a small bowl; add beef. Let stand 15 minutes. Next, combine water, 2 T soy sauce, 1 T cornstarch, and red pepper; set aside. Heat oil in hot wok or skillet over high heat. Add beef and stir-fry 1 minute; remove. Add snow peas and onion; stir-fry 3 minutes. Add beef, soy sauce mixture and tomato. Cook until sauce thickens and tomato is heated through.
Serve with rice.

Equivalent to:

2 Servings
Each =
3 oz protein
1 cup cooked
vegetable
1 additional
food

290 calories
9.5 g total fat
2.9 g saturated
64 mg
cholesterol
174 mg sodium

TERIYAKI KABOBS

Ingredients:

12 oz eye of round or sirloin steak, or chicken
  breast, skinned and boned
1 1/2 cup chunk pineapple, in it's own juice
10 medium mushrooms
1 green pepper, cut in chunks
1/2 red onion, cut in chunks

Marinade:
3 T low sodium soy sauce
1 T honey
1 T red wine vinegar
1 T oil
1 clove garlic, minced
1/2 tsp ginger

Equivalent to:

3 Servings
Each =
31/2 oz protein
1/2 cup cooked
vegetable
1/2 fruit
1 tsp oil

248 calories
6.5 g total fat
< 1 g saturated
66 mg
cholesterol
218 mg sodium

Instructions:

Mix all marinade ingredients together in a
shallow dish & marinate meat covered, 4-6
hours in refrigerator. Soak bamboo skewers in
water for 15 minutes. Thread meat, pineapple,
and vegetables on skewers, filling to the end.
Prepare grill, fire should be medium-hot. As
kabobs cook, baste with marinade mixture.
Grill 6 minutes on each side.

BEEF STROGANOFF

Ingredients:

1 pound beef sirloin, cut in 1/4 inch strips
1 T flour
1/2 tsp salt
2 T diet soft tub margarine
1 cup sliced mushrooms
1/2 cup chopped onions
1 clove garlic, minced
2 T cornstarch
1/2 tsp pepper
1 T Worcestershire sauce
1 (10 oz) can low-sodium beef broth
1 cup fat-free sour cream or yogurt
2 T cooking sherry, optional
3 cups cooked noodles

Instructions:

Dredge beef strips in flour and salt, brown in melted margarine. Add mushrooms, onions and garlic, cook until vegetables are tender. Mix beef broth with cornstarch, add and stir until mixture thickens. Simmer 5 minutes, add sherry and sour cream just before serving, stirring to mix well.
Serve over cooked noodles.

Equivalent to:

6 servings
Each =
2 1/3 oz
protein
1 starch
1/2 oil
1 additional
food

169 calories
5.9 g total fat
1.9 g saturated
45 mg
cholesterol
318 mg sodium

STEAK WITH MUSTARD MARINADE

Ingredients:

8 oz eye of round or sirloin steak
2 T Dijon-style mustard
1 tsp low-sodium soy sauce
1 tsp cooking sherry, optional
1 tsp sweetener
1 tsp oil
1/4 tsp garlic powder
1/8 tsp Tabasco pepper sauce

Instructions:

Equivalent to:

2 Servings
Each =
31/2 oz protein

210 calories
8 g total fat
2 g saturated
68 mg
cholesterol
244 mg sodium

In a medium bowl, combine mustard, soy sauce, sherry, sweetener, oil, garlic and Tabasco sauce; mix well.
Place steak in a shallow dish or plastic bag; add marinade. Cover, and refrigerate at least 5 hours; turn meat occasionally.
Remove meat from marinade, place on grill about 5 inches from source of heat. Brush with marinade. Grill 10 minutes or until desired doneness.

STUFFED ROUND STEAK

Ingredients:

1 pound top round, flank, or sirloin steak

Marinade:
1 T oil
1/4 cup red wine vinegar
1 T low-sodium soy sauce
1/2 tsp Teton Valley Nice n Spicy or Season All
1/4 tsp thyme leaves, crushed
1/4 tsp lemon pepper
1/8 tsp herb garlic seasoning

Filling:
1/2 cup chopped onion
1/2 cup shredded carrots
2 oz shredded cheddar cheese
9 oz package frozen chopped spinach, thawed
 and well drained
1 tsp Dijon mustard
1/8 tsp lemon pepper
1/4 tsp Teton Valley Nice n Spicy or Season All

Instructions:

Score steak diagonally in a criss-cross pattern;

Equivalent to:

4 Servings
Each =
4 oz protein
3/4 oil
1/2 cup cooked
vegetable
1/4 dairy

249 calories
9 g total fat
2 g saturated
72 mg
cholesterol
337 mg sodium

STUFFED ROUND STEAK

Instructions Continued:

pound meat lightly with a meat mallet or rolling pin. Place in shallow glass dish. In a small bowl, combine marinade ingredients and pour over meat. Cover; marinate in refrigerator 8-12 hours. Heat oven to 325.

In a medium skillet, sprayed with Pam, saute onion until tender. Remove from heat. Stir in remaining filling ingredients; blend well. Remove meat from marinade; discard marinade. Spoon filling evenly over meat, roll tightly starting with narrow end; tie securely with string. Place beef roll in 10x6-inch (1 quart) baking dish sprayed with Pam*. Roast at 325 degrees for 1 1/2 hours or until desired doneness. Cover and let stand 5-10 minutes before slicing.

TIP* Stuffed Steak can be made ahead. To make ahead, prepare as above to *; cover and refrigerate no longer than 8 hours. Bake as directed above.

SALISBURY STEAK

Ingredients:

1 lb extra lean ground round beef
4 Ryvita crackers, crushed
2 egg whites, beaten
1/2 cup plain non-fat yogurt
1/2 cup chopped onion
1/2 cup sliced mushrooms
1/2 tsp Teton Valley Nice and Spicy or Season
   All
1/4 tsp garlic herb seasoning
1/8 tsp lemon pepper
1 cup beef broth
1-2 T cornstarch

Instructions:

In a bowl, mix beef, cracker crumbs, egg, onion, seasonings and half of yogurt. Shape firmly into 6 patties. In a skillet over medium heat, cook patties until browned on both sides. Add mushrooms. Mix beef broth with cornstarch, stir in remaining yogurt. Pour over meat, reduce heat to low and simmer 20 minutes, turning occasionally.
Serve over rice or pasta.

Equivalent to:

4 Servings
Each=
33/4 oz protein
1/2 starch
1 additional food
Scant dairy

232 calorie
5.5 g total fat
1.9 g saturated
70 mg cholesterol
123 mg sodium

TURKEY & BROCCOLI STROGANOFF

Meat

Ingredients:

1 T diet soft tub margarine
1 pound white turkey or chicken, cut into strips
2 cups fresh mushrooms, thinly sliced
1/2 cup onion, chopped
1/3 cup red pepper, chopped
3/4 cup low-sodium chicken broth
1 tsp Teton Valley Nice n Spicy or Season All
1/2 tsp salt
1/2 tsp pepper
3 T flour
1 cup plain non-fat yogurt
1 cup cooked broccoli florets
2 T dry white wine, optional
3 cups cooked noodles

Equivalent to:

6 Servings
Each =
2 1/2 oz
protein
1/4 oil
1/2 cup cooked
vegetable
Scant dairy
1 additional
food

261 calories
3.3 g total fat
< 1 g saturated
47 mg
cholesterol
302 mg sodium

Instructions:

Melt margarine in a skillet. Saute turkey, mushrooms, onion & pepper until tender, about 5 minutes. Add chicken broth and seasonings, bring to a boil. Reduce heat and simmer 5 minutes. Combine yogurt and flour until thick. Stir into turkey mixture. Bring to boil, cook 1 minutes stirring constantly. Stir in broccoli, wine and heat through. Serve over noodles.

ITALIAN-STYLE SALISBURY STEAK

Ingredients:

1 lb extra lean ground round beef
2 crushed Ryvita Sesame Crackers
2 egg whites, slightly beaten
1/4 tsp lemon pepper
2 packets Diet Center Italian Dressing or 4 T of
 reduced calorie Italian dressing
2 cups finely chopped onion
2 cups finely chopped mushrooms
1/2 (4 oz) can tomato paste
1/2 tsp basil leaves

Instructions:

Combine ground beef, bread crumbs, egg and seasonings. Shape into 4 oval patties, then place in a 1 1/2 quart oblong baking dish; set aside. In a skillet sprayed with Pam, heat Italian dressing and cook onions and mushrooms over medium heat, stirring occasionally, for 5 minutes. Add water to tomato paste to make the consistency of tomato sauce, add basil. Spoon mixture over patties and bake 30 minutes at 350 degrees.

Equivalent to:

4 Servings
Each =
31/2 oz protein
1/4 starch
1/2 oil
1/2 cup cooked
vegetable

257 calories
7 g total fat
2 g saturated
70 mg
cholesterol
178 mg sodium

SWISS STEAK

Ingredients:

1 pound top round steak
1 tsp olive oil
1/4 tsp pepper
1/2 tsp Teton Valley Nice n Spicy or Season All
1/4 tsp garlic seasoning
1/2 large onion, sliced
8-oz can tomatoes, undrained and cut up
4 T tomato paste, thinned to tomato sauce
  consistency with water
4 T flour

Equivalent to:

4 Servings
Each =
31/2 oz protein
1/4 cup cooked
vegetable
1/2 oil
1 additional
food

225 calories
6.8 g total fat
2 g saturated
70 mg
cholesterol
61 mg sodium

Instructions:

Cut meat into serving pieces.
In a small bowl, combine oat bran with seasonings, dredge meat in this. In a skillet heat oil, place meat in skillet and brown. Add remaining ingredients. Cover and simmer 1 1/4 to 1 1/2 hours or until meat is tender. More water may need to be added during cooking time to keep sauce at right consistency.

Poultry

SPICY BARBECUED CHICKEN

Ingredients:

8 oz chicken breasts, skinned and boned
1 small clove garlic, minced
2 T tomato paste
1 tsp sweetener
1 tsp chili powder
2 T vinegar
1 to 2 drops hot pepper sauce
1 small tomato, peeled and chopped

Instructions:

In a small saucepan sprayed with Pam, saute onion and garlic until tender. Stir in remaining ingredients. Bring to a boil; simmer 5 minutes stirring occasionally. Brush chicken with sauce. Place chicken on grill 4-5 inches from medium coals. Cook 8 minutes, turn and baste with sauce. Cook an additional 8 minutes or until chicken tests done. Serve with remaining sauce.

Oven Method:
Place chicken in a casserole dish sprayed with Pam, brush with sauce. Bake at 350 for 20-25 minutes, or until tender, basting chicken twice.

Equivalent to:

2 Servings
Each =
31/2 oz protein
1/4 cup cooked vegetable

160 calories
1.9 g total fat
<1 g saturated
66 mg cholesterol
94 mg sodium

HOT & SPICY CHICKEN

Ingredients:

8 oz chicken breasts, skinned and boned
2 T Durkee Red Hot Sauce, or any Louisiana
  hot sauce, (not Tabasco sauce unless you
  really like it <u>hot</u>).
2 tsp diet soft tub margarine

Instructions:

Mix hot sauce and margarine together and warm. Coat chicken with sauce. Cook chicken on grill over medium heat for approximately 5 minutes on each side, or until chicken tests done. Baste often with sauce.

Oven Method: Baste chicken with sauce and bake in a 350 degree oven about 20 minutes.

Equivalent to:

2 Servings
Each =
31/2 oz protein
1 oil

147 calories
3.9 g total fat
1 g saturated
66 mg
cholesterol
149 mg sodium

LEMON CHICKEN KABOBS

Ingredients:

8 oz chicken breasts, cut in chunks
16 mushroom caps
1 yellow pepper, cut in large chunks
2 tsp oil
4 tsp wine vinegar
1 T chopped fresh tarragon
2 broccoli stalks, peeled, and cooked
1/2 red onion, cut in large pieces
Juice of one lemon
1/2 tsp Teton Valley Good Stuff Seasoning or
    chicken seasoning
1/4 tsp lemon pepper

Instructions:

Mix oil, vinegar, tarragon and other seasonings
in a bowl. Add chunks of chicken and mix to
coat evenly, refrigerate 35 minutes or longer.
Drain and reserve marinade. Alternate chicken,
mushrooms, yellow pepper, broccoli and onion
on skewers.
Cook over medium hot coals for 12 minutes,
turn skewers once and baste with marinade
while cooking.

Equivalent to:

2 Servings
Each =
3 1/2 ounce
protein
1 oil
1 cup cooked
vegetable

242 calories
7 g total fat
<1 g saturated
66 mg
cholesterol
95 mg sodium

BARBECUED CHICKEN BREASTS

Ingredients:

8 oz chicken breasts, skinned and   boned

Marinade:
1/3 cup unsweetened apple juice
1 tsp oil
1/4 tsp garlic herb seasoning
1/8 tsp tarragon
1 tsp sweetener

Instructions:

Preheat barbecue to medium heat. Bring marinade ingredients to a boil in a small saucepan. Continue cooking for 2 minutes more.
Pour over chicken and marinate 25 minutes.
Place chicken breasts on hot grill and cook 4 to 5 minutes on each side. Baste and season twice.

Equivalent to:

2 Serving
Each =
31/2 oz protein
1/2 oil

169 calories
3.7 g total fat
< 1 g saturated
66 mg
cholesterol
75 mg sodium

FRESH HERB GRILLED CHICKEN

Ingredients:

1 lb chicken breasts, skinned, boned and
  pierced with a fork
1/3 cup lemon juice
2 tsp oil
2 tsp chopped fresh rosemary
1 1/2 tsp chopped thyme
1 clove garlic, minced
1/2 tsp lemon pepper
Salt, to taste

Instructions:

In a baking dish, arrange chicken breasts. In a small bowl combine remaining ingredients and pour over chicken. Cover and refrigerate 6-8 hours. Grill on barbecue, using marinade to baste as you grill.
Variation: Broil about 4 inches from heat for 8 minutes, brush frequently with sauce. Turn chicken, continue broiling, basting frequently for 6-8 more minutes or until chicken is tender. Serve warm or cold.

Equivalent to:

4 Servings
Each =
3 1 2 oz protein
1/2 oil

154 calories
3.9 g total fat
< 1 g saturated
66 mg cholesterol
150 mg sodium

SESAME CHICKEN BREASTS

Ingredients:

8 oz chicken breasts
1 T sesame seeds, toasted
1 T light mayonnaise
1 T fat-free mayonnaise
2 T plain non-fat yogurt
1/2 tsp Oriental seasoning
1/8 tsp lemon pepper

Instructions:

Mix mayonnaise, yogurt, and seasonings together. Place chicken on a rack of broiler pan; brush with half of mayonnaise mixture. Broil 5 to 7 inches form heat for 8 minutes. Turn; brush with remaining mixture and broil about 8 minutes longer.
Sprinkle with sesame seeds.

Equivalent to:

2 Servings
Each =
31/2 oz protein
1 oil

208 calories
8.6 g total fat
1.6 g saturated
68 mg
cholesterol
160 mg sodium

CURRY SKILLET CHICKEN

Ingredients:

8 oz chicken breasts or turkey breasts
1 T curry powder
1/2 tsp salt
1/2 tsp paprika
1/4 tsp ginger
1 small onion, chopped
1/2 apple, cored and cut into bite-size pieces
1 small garlic clove, minced
3/4 cup chicken broth
1 T cornstarch
2/3 cup cooked rice

Instructions:

Place chicken in freezer for 30 minutes until firm but not frozen; slice thinly across grain of meat. In a skillet sprayed with Pam, saute onions, garlic and apple until tender. Remove from pan and set aside. Saute chicken and seasonings until browned. Add cornstarch to broth then add to chicken. Add apple mixture to pan stirring constantly, cook until sauce thickens.
Serve over cooked rice.

Equivalent to:

2 Servings
Each=
31/2 oz protein
1/3 cup cooked vegetable
1 Starch
1/4 Fruit

297 calories
3 g total fat
<1 g saturated
66 mg cholesterol
121 mg sodium

SHREDDED CHICKEN

Ingredients:

1 pound chicken breasts, boned and skinned
3 cups water
1 small onion, quartered
1 bay leaf
1/4 tsp lemon pepper
1/2 tsp Mexican seasoning
1/4 tsp garlic powder

Instructions:

Put all ingredients together in a pan and bring to a boil. Reduce heat and simmer 30 minutes or until chicken is tender. Let chicken cool in its broth, then shred finely.
(May save broth and freeze for stir-fry or soup use.)

Equivalent to:

4 Servings
Each =
31/2 oz protein

136 calories
1.5 g total fat
< 1 g saturated
66 mg
cholesterol
79 mg sodium

CHICKEN VEGETABLE RATATOUILLE

Ingredients:

8 oz chicken breast, skinned and boned
1 green pepper, cut in rings
1 small zucchini, sliced
1 small crookneck squash, sliced
1 onion, chopped
2 tomatoes, cut in wedges
2 cloves garlic, minced
1 1/2 tsp dried oregano
1 1/2 tsp dried basil
2 T lemon juice
pepper

Instructions:

Cut chicken into crosswise strips. Saute onion and pepper rings in a skillet sprayed with Pam, over medium-high heat until soft, about 3 minutes. Add zucchini, crookneck and tomato; cook until it begins to brown, 3-4 minutes. Cook chicken with seasonings until done and liquid evaporates, about 5 minutes. Combine all ingredients adding lemon juice and adjusting seasonings.

Equivalent to:

2 Servings
Each =
31/2 oz protein
2 cup cooked
vegetable

218 calories
2.6 g total fat
< 1 g saturated
66 mg
cholesterol
97 mg sodium

CHICKEN CORDON BLEU

Ingredients:

16 oz chicken breasts, skinned and boned
4 slices fat-free swiss cheese
4 thin slices extra lean ham or turkey ham
2 tsp Dijon mustard
1/2 tsp Teton Valley Nice n Spicy or Season All
1/4 tsp garlic herb seasoning
2 egg whites
1/3 cup bread crumbs
2 tsp diet soft tub margarine
Pepper

Instructions:

Pound chicken between two pieces of plastic wrap until flattened. Spread chicken with mustard then season, placing a slice of ham, and cheese on top. Roll up breast and secure ends by pressing together, season again if desired. Dip chicken breast in egg wash then bread crumbs, refrigerate 1 hour.

In a skillet with margarine, brown chicken breasts until golden brown, about 2 minutes. Transfer chicken to a baking dish. Bake at 350 degrees for 25 minutes.

Equivalent to:

4 Servings
Each =
4 oz protein
1/2 dairy
1/4 oil
1 additional
food

248 calories
3.9 total fat
1 g saturated
82 mg
cholesterol
932 mg sodium

CHICKEN SUPREME

Ingredients:

8 oz skinned, boned chicken breasts
Grey Poupon mustard
Red onion slices
1 oz fat-free mozzarella cheese, sliced
Dash lemon pepper

Instructions:

Place chicken in a oven proof dish sprayed with Pam. Rub chicken breasts with Grey Poupon mustard and season with lemon pepper. Layer onion then cheese on top of chicken. Cover with foil and bake at 350 degree oven for 20-25 minutes.

Equivalent to:

2 Servings
Each=
31/2 oz protein
1/4 dairy

155 calories
1.5 g total fat
<1 g saturated
68 mg
cholesterol
465 mg sodium

CHICKEN DIJON

Ingredients:

8 oz chicken breasts, skinned and boned
2 T dijon mustard
1 cup chicken broth, or water
1 clove garlic, minced or garlic powder
2 tsp lemon juice
1/4 tsp lemon pepper

Instructions:

In a non-stick skillet sprayed with Pam, brown chicken on both sides.
Add remaining ingredients together for sauce. Pour sauce over chicken and simmer 10 minutes or until chicken tests done.

Equivalent to:

2 Servings
Each=
31/2 oz protein

179 calories
3.2 g total fat
< 1 g saturated
67 mg
cholesterol
316 mg sodium

CHICKEN STRIPS IN ORANGE MARINADE

Ingredients:

8 oz chicken breast cut in strips

Marinade:
1/4 cup orange juice
2 T lime juice
1 tsp apple cider vinegar
1/2 tsp Teton Valley Nice n Spicy or Season All
1/8 tsp salt
Dash lemon pepper

Instructions:

Place chicken in marinade for 2 hours.
Grill on a barbecue at medium-high or under a broiler, approximately 3-4 minutes on each side.
Baste with sauce to keep moist.

Equivalent to:

2 servings
Each =
31/2 oz protein

148 calories
1.4 g total fat
< 1 g saturated
66 mg
cholesterol
361 mg sodium

ITALIAN CHICKEN & MUSHROOMS

Ingredients:

1 lb. chicken breasts, skinned and boned
1 cup mushrooms, sliced
1/3 cup green onions, sliced
1 lemon, juiced
3 packets Diet Center Italian Dressing or 4 T
* reduced calorie Italian dressing*
1 tsp Teton Valley Good Stuff Seasoning or
* chicken seasoning*
1/2 tsp lemon pepper
1/2 tsp Italian seasoning

Equivalent to:

4 Servings
Each =
31/2 oz protein
1/4 cup cooked
vegetable
2/3 oil

168 calories
4.6 g total fat
< 1 g saturated
66 mg
cholesterol
203 mg sodium

Instructions:

Marinate chicken breasts in dressing at least 1 hour covered, in refrigerator. In a skillet sprayed with Pam, saute chicken breasts until browned. Remove from pan. Add dressing and lemon juice to mushrooms.

Return chicken to skillet, spooning mixture over chicken while heating.

May also place all ingredients in a baking dish and bake at 350 degrees for 25-30 minutes.

SPICY CHICKEN MEATBALLS

Ingredients:

8 oz raw chicken
1 egg beaten
2 tsp parsley, chopped
1 stalk celery, finely chopped
3 T chopped onion
4-8 drops Tabasco Sauce, may use less if
   milder taste desired
Dash Mexican seasoning
1/2 tsp Teton Valley Nice n Spicy or Season All
1/2 tsp lemon pepper
5 mushrooms, chopped
2 Ryvita Crackers, finely crushed

Instructions:

Place all ingredients into a food processor and mix until smooth. To easily form meatballs from the chicken mixture more easily, rinse your hands in cold water. Brown spice balls in a non-stick skillet sprayed with Pam. Place meatballs into a baking dish and bake at 350 degrees for 15 minutes.

Equivalent to:

2 Servings
Each=
31/2 oz protein
1/2 starch

217 calories
4.3 g total fat
1.2 g saturated
172 mg cholesterol
144 mg sodium

CHICKEN SCHNITZEL

Ingredients:

7 oz chicken breast, skinned and boned
2 egg whites, whipped
4 Ryvita crackers, crushed well or bread
  crumbs
1/2 tsp Teton Valley Nice n Spicy or Season All
1/4 tsp salt
1/4 tsp garlic powder
Pepper

Instructions:

Equivalent to:

2 Servings
Each =
31/2 oz protein
1 starch

190 calories
1.2 g total fat
< 1 g saturated
57 mg
cholesterol
427 mg sodium

Add seasoning to crumbs. Whisk egg in small bowl. Place chicken breasts between 2 sheets of wax paper or plastic wrap. Pound chicken flat with a mallet or rolling pin. Cut in long strips and dip in egg wash, then crumbs. In a frying pan, over med-high heat, melt margarine. Cook chicken until browned on one side then turn. Chicken will cook fast because it is very thin, don't overcook.
Wonderful cold or hot. Use any dressing as dipping sauce.
May be frozen to serve later.

CHICKEN CACCIATORE

Ingredients:

8 oz chicken breast, skinned and boned
1/2 small onion, sliced
1/2 cup green pepper, sliced
1/2 tsp Italian seasoning
1 packet sweetener
1/2 tsp salt
1/2 tsp Teton Valley Nice n Spicy or Season All
1/4 tsp pepper
8-oz tomatoes, cut up
1 cup cooked noodles

Instructions:

In a skillet sprayed with Pam, over medium-high heat, cook chicken until browned on both sides. Add remaining ingredients, except noodles; mix well. Cover and simmer 15-20 minutes, stirring occasionally until chicken is fork tender. Serve over hot noodles.

Equivalent to:

2 Servings
Each=
31/2 oz protein
1 cup cooked
vegetable
1 starch

266 calories
2.6 g total fat
<1 g saturated
66 mg
cholesterol
84 mg sodium

CHICKEN WITH CHILI CREAM SAUCE

Ingredients:

1 anaheim chili
3/4 cup skim milk
1/2 small red onion, thinly sliced
2 T chopped cilantro
1/2 tsp herb garlic or 1 clove garlic, minced
1/4 tsp salt
1 tsp Teton Valley Nice n Spicy or Season All
12 oz boneless chicken breasts
1 large tomato, peeled and chopped

Instructions:

Char chili over gas flame or under broiler until blackened on all sides. Wrap in a paper bag, let stand 10 minutes to steam. Peel, seed, and chop. Combine chili, milk, onion, cilantro and garlic in a heavy saucepan over medium heat. Simmer until slightly thickened, about 7 minutes, stirring constantly.
Prepare barbecue or preheat broiler.
Season chicken and grill until springy to the touch, about 5 minutes per side. Cut chicken diagonally into thin slices. Add tomato to sauce and bring to simmer. Season to taste with seasonings. Spoon sauce onto plates, fan chicken on top of sauce and serve.

Equivalent to:

3 Servings
Each =
31/2 oz protein
1/4 cup cooked
vegetable
1/4 dairy

167 calories
1.6 g total fat
< 1 g saturated
67 mg
cholesterol
304 mg sodium

ROSEMARY CHICKEN

Ingredients:

14 oz chicken breasts, skinned and boned
2 tsp diet soft tub margarine
1/2 tsp lemon pepper
1/2 tsp Season All
1/4 tsp dried rosemary leaves, crushed
2 T lemon juice
Fresh rosemary sprigs and lemon slices for
  garnish

Instructions:

In a skillet over medium-high heat, melt margarine. Place chicken in skillet and season. Cook until golden brown, about 5 minutes. Turn chicken; reduce heat to medium, cooking chicken until juices run clear when pierced with a knife. Remove to platter and keep warm.
Add lemon juice and 1/4 cup water to skillet. Cook over medium heat boiling and stirring occasionally to loosen brown bits from bottom of skillet. Pour drippings over chicken on platter. Garnish with fresh rosemary and lemon slices.

Equivalent to:

4 Servings
Each =
3 oz protein
1/4 oil

120 calories
2 g total fat
< 1 g saturated
57 mg
cholesterol
372 mg sodium

LEMON CHICKEN AND ZUCCHINI

Ingredients:

8 oz chicken breast, cut in 1-inch pieces
3/4 cup chicken broth
1 T cornstarch
2 tsp low-sodium soy sauce
1/2 tsp sweetener
1/2 tsp grated ginger root
2 cups sliced zucchini
1 T lemon juice
1/2 tsp lemon pepper
1/2 tsp Oriental seasoning
2/3 cup rice

Equivalent to:

2 Servings
Each=
31/2 oz protein
1 cup cooked
vegetable
1 starch

277 calories
3 g total fat
< 1 g saturated
66 mg
cholesterol
144 mg sodium

Instructions:

Blend chicken broth, cornstarch, soy sauce and sweetener. In a wok or skillet sprayed with Pam, cook ginger root 30 seconds. Add chicken and stir-fry 2 minutes or until done. Add zucchini and stir-fry 2-3 more minutes. Stir broth mixture into chicken and zucchini, cook and stir until slightly thickened. Add lemon juice and seasonings, cook 1 minute more. Serve with cooked rice.

THAI CHICKEN STRIPS

Ingredients:

3 packets Diet Center Italian Dressing or 6 T
  reduced calorie Italian dressing
2 T red wine vinegar
1 1/2 tsp sweetener
1 T low-sodium soy sauce
1 T finely chopped cilantro or parsley
1/2 tsp ground ginger
1/2 tsp ground cumin
1/4 tsp paprika
1/4 cup sesame seeds, well toasted
1 pound boneless chicken breasts, cut into
  lengthwise strips

Instructions:

In a food processor or blender, process Italian
dressing, vinegar, sweetener, soy sauce and
seasonings until well blended.
In a shallow baking dish, combine dressing
mixture, sesame seeds and chicken. Cover and
marinate in refrigerator, stirring occasionally,
at least 3 hours.
Bake at 350 degree oven for 20 minutes. Serve
with rice or oriental noodles.

Equivalent to:

4 Servings
Each =
31/2 oz protein
3/4 oil

196 calories
6.7 g total fat
1 g saturated
65 mg
cholesterol
222 mg sodium

CHICKEN & BROCCOLI

Ingredients:

*1 pound chicken breasts, skinned and boned,
  cut in bite-size pieces
3 cups broccoli florets, cooked
1 T low-sodium soy sauce
2 cups fresh mushrooms, sliced
1 T fresh lemon juice
1 T red wine vinegar
1 T chopped pimento, optional
1 1/3 cup cooked rice*

Equivalent to:

4 Servings
Each =
31/2 oz protein
1 1/4 cup
cooked
vegetable
1 starch (rice)

232 calories
2.2 g total fat
< 1 g saturated
66 mg
cholesterol
114 mg sodium

Instructions:

In a medium bowl, combine soy sauce, lemon juice and vinegar. Marinate chicken in mixture for 1 hour, reserve marinade. In a skillet sprayed with Pam, brown chicken, remove. Add mushrooms; cook and stir until tender. Then add chicken, broccoli, and remaining ingredients, except rice; add marinade. Heat through.
Serve with rice.

TANDOORI-STYLE CHICKEN KABOBS

Ingredients:

8 oz plain non-fat yogurt
4 packets Diet Center Italian Dressing or 8 T
  reduced calorie Italian dressing
1 T chopped fresh ginger or 1/2 tsp ground
  ginger
1 tsp cumin seeds or 1/2 tsp ground cumin
1 tsp coriander seeds, optional
1/2 tsp lemon pepper
1/4 tsp Italian seasoning
1/2 tsp paprika
1 pound chicken breasts, skinned and boned

Instructions:

In a food processor or blender, process all ingredients, except chicken. In a large shallow baking dish sprayed with Pam, combine chicken with dressing mixture. Cover and marinate in refrigerator, stirring occasionally, at least 3 hours. Reserve marinade.
Soak bamboo skewers in water for 15 minutes. On skewers, thread chicken, then grill or broil, turning and basting occasionally with reserved marinade, 5 minutes or until chicken is done.

Equivalent to:

4 Servings
Each =
31/2 oz protein
1/2 oil
1/4 dairy

201 calories
5.5 g total fat
< 1 g saturated
66 mg
cholesterol
284 mg sodium

SPINACH & PESTO STUFFED CHICKEN

Ingredients:

*2 packets Diet Center Italian Dressing or 4 T
reduced calorie Italian dressing*
*2 T chopped fresh basil leaves, or 1 1/2 tsp
dried basil leaves*
1/8 tsp lemon pepper
Salt, to taste
1/4 tsp Italian seasoning
*1/2 package (10 oz) frozen chopped spinach,
cooked and squeezed dry, or 1/2 pound fresh*
2 Sesame Ryvita Crackers, crushed
8 oz chicken breasts, skinned and boned
2 oz fat-free mozzarella cheese

Equivalent to:

2 Servings
Each =
31/2 oz protein
1 oil
1/2 starch
1/2 cup cooked
vegetable
1/2 dairy

265 calories
5.7 g total fat
< 1 g saturated
71 mg
cholesterol
786 mg sodium

Instructions:

In a food processor, blend dressing with
seasonings. Add cheese and blend well. In a
medium bowl combine dressing mixture with
spinach and cracker crumbs.
With a knife parallel to cutting board, cut 3-
inch long cut in the center of each breast to
form a pocket. Evenly stuff pockets with
spinach mixture. Place chicken In a baking dish
sprayed with Pam; brush with Italian dressing.
Broil, turning once, about 7 minutes or until
chicken is done.

STUFFED TURKEY ON SKEWERS

Ingredients:

1 shallot, finely chopped
8 oz turkey breast, sliced thin and pounded flat
1/8 tsp tarragon
1 cup mushrooms, finely chopped
1 tsp parsley, chopped
1 1/2 T plain yogurt
1/4 red onion, in pieces
1 green pepper, cut in bite-size pieces
2 tsp lemon juice
1/4 tsp lemon pepper
1/4 tsp salt, to taste

Instructions:

Preheat oven to 400 degrees.
In a skillet sprayed with Pam, cook shallots and tarragon for 2 minutes. Add mushrooms and parsley; continue to cook 4 minutes over medium-high heat. Season generously. Mix in yogurt, and remove from heat; cool slightly.
Lay turkey slices flat, fill with 1 T mushroom mixture. Fold both sides so they overlap slightly, then roll.
Soak skewers 15 minutes in water.
Alternate turkey rolls with onions and green peppers on skewers. Drizzle with lemon juice

Equivalent to:

2 Servings
Each=
31/2 oz protein
1 cup cooked
vegetable

160 calories
1.1 g total fat
< 1 g saturated
70 mg
cholesterol
358 mg sodium

STUFFED TURKEY ON SKEWERS

Instruction Continued:

and season well.
Change oven setting to Broil and cook 12 minutes 6-inches from top element. Turn skewers over once and baste occasionally.

MANDARIN CHICKEN WITH BROCCOLI

Ingredients:

14 oz skinned, boned chicken breasts
1/4 tsp salt
1/4 tsp pepper
1/2 cup chopped onion
1/2 tsp paprika
1/2 tsp Season All
1 clove garlic, minced
1 bunch fresh broccoli, cooked and drained
1 can mandarin oranges, drained
1 cup plain non-fat yogurt
1/2 tsp Molly McButter
2 T light mayonnaise
2 oz grated fat-free mozzarella cheese

Instructions:

Sprinkle chicken with salt and pepper. In a large fry pan sprayed with Pam, saute onion and garlic for 3 minutes. Stir in seasonings, add chicken to onion mixture, turning to coat. In a shallow baking pan sprayed with Pam, place chicken in single layer. Bake at 375 degrees 35 minutes, or until fork can be inserted in chicken with ease. Remove chicken from oven and

Equivalent to:

3 Servings:
Each =
31/2 oz protein
Scant fruit
1 cup cooked
vegetable
1/2 dairy
2 oil

324 calories
8 g total fat
1.8 g saturated
83 mg
cholesterol
666 mg sodium

MANDARIN CHICKEN WITH BROCCOLI

Instructions Continued:

place broccoli around chicken; add mandarin oranges. In a medium mixing bowl, mix together yogurt and mayonnaise, spoon over chicken, broccoli and oranges. Sprinkle with cheese and return to oven, uncovered. Bake about 6 minutes longer.

CHICKEN-ASPARAGUS BAKE

Ingredients:

1 pound chicken breasts, cut in 1/2-inch strips
8 sprigs fresh rosemary, or 2 tsp dried
1/4 tsp garlic herb seasoning
1/2 tsp Teton Valley Nice and Spicy or Season All
1/4 tsp lemon pepper
12 to 16 fresh asparagus stalks, cut on diagonal into 1-inch pieces
12-16 mushrooms, sliced
1 large onion, sliced
4 T water
2 tsp lemon juice

Instructions:

Place 1/4 of chicken strips on the lower half of a 12-18 inch sheet of aluminum foil. Season with 1 sprig or 1/2 tsp rosemary, sprinkle with other seasonings. Top with a quarter of the vegetables. Add another sprig of rosemary and more seasonings. Sprinkle with a little water and 1/2 tsp lemon juice. Fold foil, allowing some head room for expansion. Repeat with other 3 packets. Place on a cookie sheet and bake at 450 degrees for 20-22 minutes.

Equivalent to:

4 Servings
Each =
31/2 oz protein
1 cup cooked vegetable

173 calories
2 g total fat
<1 g saturated
66 mg cholesterol
83 mg sodium

CHICKEN STIR-FRY

Ingredients:

12 oz chicken breast, or raw shrimp
1/2 cup zucchini, cut on the bias
1 rib celery, cut on the bias
1/2 cup sliced mushrooms
1/2 cup green pepper, chopped
1/2 cup bean sprouts, washed and drained
1/2 cup chinese cabbage, cut up
1/2 cup onion
Low-sodium soy sauce
1/2 tsp Oriental seasoning
1/2 tsp garlic herb seasoning
1/2 tsp chicken seasoning

Equivalent to:

3 Servings
Each =
31/2 oz protein
1 1/4 cup
cooked
vegetables

155 calories
1.6 g total fat
< 1 g saturated
66 mg
cholesterol
98 mg sodium

Instructions:

Cut up all vegetables and chicken. If using fresh shrimp, wash, remove shell. Spray a skillet or wok with Pam . Starting with celery and green pepper, stir-fry 1-2 minutes. Add other vegetables, stir-fry 3-4 minutes longer. Save the chinese cabbage until the very last. Add chicken and stir-fry 3-4 more minutes, until done. If it seems a little dry, you may add homemade chicken stock or water. Season to taste, add cabbage, cook until warmed.

CHICKEN & SMOKEY RED ONION SAUCE

Ingredients:

1 pound chicken breasts

Rub:
2 T chili powder
1 T cumin
1 T cracked black pepper
Salt

Smokey Red-Onion Sauce:
1 small red onion, cut into 4 slices
1 tomato, cut into 4 slices
6 T fresh lime juice
1/4 cup fresh cilantro
4 to 10 dashes red pepper sauce
Salt and cracked pepper, to taste

Instructions:

Make salsa: Grill onion and tomato slices 2 minutes per side. Chop coarsely and transfer to bowl. Stir in remaining ingredients. Makes 2 cups.

Combine ingredients for rub together. Rub all over chicken. Grill chicken over med-hot coals until cooked through, 4-5 minutes per side. Top with sauce.

Equivalent to:

2 Servings
Each =
31/2 oz protein
1/2 cup
vegetable

170 calories
2.6 g total fat
<1 g saturated
66 mg
cholesterol
411 mg sodium

GRILLED TURKEY BREAST

Ingredients:

1 T oil
1/2 cup Diet 7-Up
2 T low-sodium soy sauce
1/8 tsp marjoram leaves
1/8 tsp basil leaves
1/8 tsp thyme
8 oz fresh turkey breast

Instructions:

In a small bowl combine all ingredients except turkey; mix well. Place turkey in a baking dish; pour marinade over turkey. Cover; refrigerate 2 to 4 hours, turning occasionally.
When ready to barbecue, place turkey on grill 4 to 6 inches from medium-hot coals. Cook about 10 minutes or until no longer pink, turning once.

Equivalent to:

2 Servings
Each =
31/2 oz protein
1 1/2 oil

201 calories
7.7 g total fat
< 1 g saturated
70 mg cholesterol
131 mg sodium

TURKEY WITH GINGER LIME SAUCE

Ingredients:

8 oz boneless turkey breast
2 Sesame Ryvita Crackers, crushed
2 egg whites, slightly beaten
1 packets Diet Center Italian Dressing or 2 T
   reduced calorie Italian dressing
1/3 cup chopped green onion
1/3 cup chicken broth
1 tsp lime juice
1/8 tsp ground ginger
1/8 tsp lemon pepper
1/8 tsp salt
1/8 tsp Oriental seasoning

Instructions:

Dip turkey into egg, then into cracker crumbs. In a large skillet sprayed with Pam, cook turkey with Italian dressing over medium heat, turning once, about 5 minutes or until done; remove and keep warm. Into skillet, add green onions and cook 1 minute. Stir in remaining ingredients then bring to a boil to heat through. Serve over turkey.

Equivalent to:

2 Servings
Each=
3 3/4 oz protein
1/2 oil
1/2 starch

212 calories
3.2 g total fat
< 1 g saturated
71 mg cholesterol
369 mg sodium

ASPARAGUS-CHICKEN ROLL-UPS

Ingredients:

1 lb chicken breasts, skinned and boned
20 asparagus spears
1/2 pound fresh mushrooms, sliced
Salt, to taste
1/2 tsp Teton Valley Nice n Spicy or Season All
1/2 tsp lemon pepper

Instructions:

Equivalent to:

4 Servings
Each =
31/2 oz protein
1 cup cooked
vegetable

316 calories
3.8 g total fat
1 g saturated
131 mg
cholesterol
442 mg sodium

Between two sheets of wax paper or plastic wrap, pound chicken breasts until flat. Sprinkle with seasonings. Place 5 spears of asparagus on each breast, then add a few slices mushrooms. Roll up each breast and fasten with a toothpick. Sprinkle with seasonings again if desired.
* Place roll-ups in a microwave safe dish sprayed with Pam. Top with remaining mushrooms. Bake at 350 degrees for 25 to 30 minutes.

* You may also do separate foil pouches with each breast if desired.

Salads

CITRUS BEEF AND SPINACH SALAD

Ingredients:

Salad:
Juice of 4 limes
1 small jalapeno pepper, minced or 1 small can green chilies
1 clove garlic, minced
1 T sweetener
10 oz top round, flank or sirloin steak
1 (10 oz) bag spinach, cleaned and torn in bite size pieces
1 (11 oz) can mandarin oranges, drained
1/2 small red onion, sliced
3 T orange juice concentrate
2 T Lime Poppy Seed Dressing

Lime Poppy Seed Dressing:
Juice of one lime or lemon
2 T white wine vinegar
3 T poppy seeds
1 T dijon mustard
Salt
lemon pepper
2/3 cup corn oil
Makes 1 1/4 cup--2 T= Serving

Equivalent to:

2 Servings
Each =
4 oz protein
3 cups raw
vegetable
2 oil
1/4 fruit

Salad =
347 calories
10 g total fat
3.9 g saturated
92 mg
cholesterol
165 mg sodium

Dressing =
130 calories
14 g total fat
1.8 g saturated
0 cholesterol
77 mg sodium

CITRUS BEEF AND SPINACH SALAD

Instructions:

Salad:
Combine lime juice, jalapeno or chilies, garlic, and sweetener in small bowl. Stir together with fork until blended. Pour over steak in shallow bowl. Cover and refrigerate overnight. Grill or cook steak until done as prefered. Meanwhile, toss together spinach, onion, and oranges; top with lime-poppy seed dressing and orange sauce. Serve beef with spinach salad.

Alternate method: for complete dinner salad, thinly slice cooled beef and toss with spinach, oranges and onion.

Dressing:
Combine lime juice, vinegar, sweetener, mustard and salt and pepper in a blender or food processor. Slowly add oil, blend until creamy. Stir in poppy seeds.
Yield: 10 Servings--Each= 2 T

TACO SALAD

Ingredients:

7 oz extra lean ground round beef
1 small onion, chopped
1/2 tsp Mexican seasoning
Pinch red pepper flakes, optional
1/8 tsp garlic herb seasoning
1/2 cup red kidney beans, rinsed
1 tomato, chopped
1/2 green pepper, chopped
Chopped lettuce
2 green onions, sliced
2 oz fat-free cheddar cheese, shredded
2 tortillas

Instructions:

In a skillet sprayed with Pam, combine beef, onion, and seasonings. Cook until browned over medium-high heat; drain any fat.
In a salad bowl, combine lettuce, tomato, green pepper, kidney beans, green onions, and cheese. Add cooked beef mixture; toss gently. Top with your favorite Diet Center Dressing, or picante sauce.
TACO BOWL: Spray a microwave safe bowl with Pam, fold tortilla into bowl shape and microwave 2 minutes on high. Let cool & fill.

Equivalent to:

2 Servings
Each =
3 1/2 oz protein
2 starch
3 cups raw
vegetable
1/2 dairy

Woman Style:
2 Servings
Each =
3 1/2 oz protein
1/2 legume
3 cups raw
vegetable
1/2 dairy

352 calories
6.5 g total fat
1.8 g saturated
66 mg
cholesterol
867 mg sodium

CALYPSO SHRIMP SALAD

Ingredients:

1/2 cantaloupe, peeled and cut in rings
8 oz salad shrimp
1 orange, peeled and sliced
2 kiwi, peeled and sliced
1/2 cup red grapes, cut in clusters
Banana Dressing

Banana Dressing:
1 banana
1 T light mayonnaise
1 T fat-free mayonnaise
1/2 cup plain non-fat yogurt
1/4 tsp Crystal Light Lemon Drink Mix, dry

Equivalent to:

2 Servings
Each =
2 oz protein
2 fruit
1 tsp oil
1/4 dairy

373 calories
8 g total fat
1.6 g saturated
175 mg
cholesterol
300 mg sodium

Instructions:

Arrange each cantaloupe ring on lettuce lined plate. Fill centers with shrimp. Arrange sliced fruit around cantaloupe. Serve with Banana Dressing.

Dressing:
Put all ingredients in food processor or blender and blend until smooth and creamy. Refrigerate covered until ready to serve.

SUPER SHRIMP SALAD

Salads

Ingredients:

1 pound shrimp, cooked, shelled and deveined
1 stalk celery, chopped
2 T chopped scallions or chives
1 T fresh dill
*1-2 packets Diet Center Italian Dressing or 2 T
  reduced calorie Italian dressing*
4 cups lettuce
Tomato wedges

Instructions:

Mix shrimp, celery, scallions or chives, dill and salad dressing. Chill in refrigerator for 1 hour or longer.
Serve on a bed of lettuce and garnish with tomato wedges.

Equivalent to:

4 Servings
Each =
2 oz protein
1/2 oil (if 2 packets used)
1 cup vegetable

129 calories
3.2 g total fat
< 1 g saturated
173 mg cholesterol
227 mg sodium

CRAB AND SHRIMP PASTA SALAD

Ingredients:

3 cups cooked pasta
6 oz crab or 1 (6 oz) can crabmeat, drained
6 oz shrimp or 1 (6 oz) can shrimp, drained
  and rinsed
1 can water chestnuts, sliced
3/4 cup celery, chopped
1/2 cup green pepper, chopped
1/4 cup green onion, sliced
1/2 cup red pepper, chopped
1 T onion, chopped fine
2 T light mayonnaise
1 packet Diet Center Ranch Dressing or 2 T
  reduced calorie Ranch dressing
1/2 cup plain non-fat yogurt
1-2 T lemon juice
1/4 tsp lemon pepper
1/8 tsp garlic herb seasoning
1/2 tsp Teton Valley Nice n Spicy or Season All
1/8 tsp salt

Equivalent to:

6 Servings
Each =
1 oz protein
1/3 cup raw
vegetable
1 starch
1 1/2 oil
Scant dairy

264 calories
8.4 g total fat
1.6 g saturated
72 mg
cholesterol
275 mg sodium

Instructions:

Mix all ingredients together, adding shrimp last. Adjust seasonings and chill to mix flavors.

JAPANESE CUCUMBER & CRAB SALAD

Ingredients:

4 cucumbers, sliced thin, unpeeled
1/2 tsp salt
6 oz crab or 1 can (6 oz) crab

Dressing:
1 T low-sodium soy-sauce
1/8 cup rice wine vinegar
1 1/2 tsp sesame seed oil
1 packet sweetener

Instructions:

Mix the cucumbers with salt. Place in a colander, and the salt and water will drain off. Drain for about 45 minutes. Mix with the crab. Prepare dressing and toss with crab mixture.

Equivalent to:

2 Servings
Each=
1 1/2 oz protein
3/4 oil
1 1/2 cup raw vegetable

214 calories
5.2 g total fat
<1 g saturated
76 mg cholesterol
908 mg sodium

CRAB LOUIE

Ingredients:

1/2 head iceberg lettuce
1 1/2 cup finely shredded cabbage
8 oz flaked cooked crab, chilled
1 hard boiled egg, peeled and quartered
2 packets Diet Center Thousand Island Dressing
    or 4 T reduced calorie dressing of your choice
1/4 tsp lemon pepper
1/8 tsp salt

Instructions:

Equivalent to:

2 Servings
Each =
21/2 oz protein
3 cups raw
vegetable
1 oil

221 calories
8.4 g total fat
1.6 g saturated
207 mg
cholesterol
744 mg sodium

Arrange lettuce and cabbage on 2 salad plates.
Arrange crab on lettuce; surround with egg.
Just before serving top with dressing.

CRAB SALAD

Ingredients:

6 oz crab or 6 1/2 oz can crab meat, drained
  and flaked
1/2 cup celery, finely chopped
1/2 cup green pepper, finely chopped
1 green onion, chopped
4 T water chestnuts
1 packet Diet Center Ranch Dressing or 2 T
  reduced calorie Ranch dressing
1 T light mayonnaise
1 T fat-free mayonnaise
2 T plain non-fat yogurt
1/4 tsp white wine vinegar
1/2 tsp Season All
1/8 tsp salt
1 oz fat-free cheddar cheese, shredded

Instructions:

Mix all ingredients together and refrigerate 2-3
hours to combine flavors.

*This is great in pita bread, on whole grain
rolls, rice cakes, etc.

Equivalent to:

2 Servings
Each =
1 1/2 oz
protein
1 1/2 tsp oil
1/4 dairy
1/2 cup raw
vegetable

210 calories
8 g total fat
1.4 g saturated
81 mg
cholesterol
789 mg sodium

CHEF SALAD

Ingredients:

2 cups torn salad greens
2 1/2 oz cooked chicken breast, cut into thin strips; or canned chicken, flaked
1 oz fat-free cheddar cheese
1 small tomato, cut in wedges
1/4 green pepper, cut into rings
1 hard boiled egg, quartered
1 package Diet Center Dressing or 2 T reduced calorie dressing of choice

Instructions:

On a bed of lettuce arrange chicken, cheese strips, tomato wedges and top with green pepper rings. Top with dressing of your choice.

Equivalent to:

1 Serving
Each =
31/2 oz protein
1 oil
3 cups raw
vegetable

286 calories
10 g total fat
2.4 g saturated
259 mg
cholesterol
731 mg sodium

SEAFOOD SALAD

Ingredients:

7 oz crab
1/2 cup sliced celery
1 hard cooked egg
2 T sliced green onion
2 tsp lemon juice
1/2 tsp dry mustard
2 tsp light mayonnaise
2 T fat-free mayonnaise
1 T plain non-fat yogurt
1/8 tsp lemon pepper
1/8 tsp salt
1 tomato, sliced

Instructions:

Mix crab, egg, celery, mayonnaise, yogurt, onion, seasonings and lemon juice.
Mix together and chill until ready to serve.
If desired, serve on a bed of lettuce with sliced tomatoes on the side.

Equivalent to:

2 Servings
Each =
2 oz protein
1 oil
1 additional food

187 calories
5.8 g total fat
1.4 g saturated
195 mg cholesterol
656 mg sodium

FRUIT AND TUNA SALAD

Ingredients:

3 1/2 oz water packed tuna
1/4 cup red grapes, halved
1/4 cup shredded cabbage
1/4 cup shredded carrot
2 1/2 cups mixed salad greens
1/2 cup fat-free, sugar-free lemon yogurt
Garnishes: peach slices and red grapes

Instructions:

Combine drained tuna, grapes, cabbage, carrot and yogurt. Scoop salad onto a plate lined with mixed salad greens.
Serve with peach slices and more grapes.

Equivalent to:

1 Serving
Each =
31/2 oz protein
3 cups raw
vegetables
1/2 oz dairy
1 fruit

241 calories
3 g total fat
< 1 g saturated
56 mg
cholesterol
476 mg sodium

MARINATED SHRIMP AND VEGETABLES

Ingredients:

8 oz medium shrimp, cooked and deveined
1/2 cup fresh cauliflower, cut in florets
4 oz fresh whole mushrooms
1/2 cup zucchini
1/2 red or green bell pepper, cut in chunks
2 T lemon juice
1 T chopped green onion
1 tsp sweetener
1/4 tsp salt
1/4 tsp garlic herb seasoning
1/2 tsp lemon pepper
3 drops hot pepper sauce
4 T low-fat Italian dressing or half fat-free and half regular Italian dressing

Instructions:

Place shrimp and vegetables in a shallow dish. Add dressings and seasonings, mix well. Cover and refrigerate 6 hours or overnight, stirring occasionally.
Serve on a bed of lettuce.

Equivalent to:

2 Servings
Each =
2 oz protein
2 cups raw vegetable
1 oil

206 calories
7.6 g total fat
1 g saturated
173 mg cholesterol
754 mg sodium

GREEN SALAD WITH TUNA

Ingredients:

Equivalent to:

1 Serving
Each =
4 oz protein
1 starch
3 cups raw
vegetable
1 oil

Woman Style:
1 Serving =
1 legume
3 oz protein
1 oil
3 cups raw
vegetable

347 calories
3.2 g total fat
< 1 g saturated
53 mg
cholesterol
779 mg sodium

1/2 cup frozen lima beans
1/2 cup frozen green beans
1/2 cup cucumber, chopped
3 oz tuna, drained
1 cup fresh spinach, washed and dried
1 cup lettuce greens
2 green onions, sliced
1 package Diet Center Vinaigrette Dressing or
    2 T reduced calorie Vinaigrette dressing
1 oz fat-free jack cheese, shredded

Instructions:

Cook frozen vegetables and drain if necessary.
Pour vinaigrette dressing over vegetables and
tuna in separate bowls. Cool and toss
occasionally. Cover and chill in refrigerator.
Reserve some of spinach leaves for lining bowl.
Tear remaining spinach and lettuce into pieces
and put in salad bowl with onions, green beans
and cheese.
Line edge of bowl with reserved spinach. Top
with lima beans and tuna.

TROUT-MACARONI SALAD

Ingredients:

1 can (7 3/4 oz) trout, drained
2 cups zucchini, sliced and cooked
1 1/2 cup cooked macaroni
1/4 cup green onions
1/4 cup celery
1/4 cup green pepper
6 T water chestnuts
1 tomato, sliced
1 hard cooked egg, diced
1 T light mayonnaise
3 T fat-free mayonnaise
2 T non-fat plain yogurt
1/2 tsp Teton Valley Nice n Spicy or Season All
1/2 tsp lemon pepper
1/2 tsp salt, or to taste
1/4 tsp garlic herb seasoning
1 T lemon juice

Equivalent to:

3 Servings
Each=
2 oz protein
1 cup cooked
vegetable
2/3 oil
1 starch
1 additional
food

246 calories
8 g total fat
< 1 g saturated
2 mg
cholesterol
607 mg sodium

Instructions:

Saute zucchini until crisp-tender in a skillet sprayed with Pam, cool. Add remaining ingredients and adjust seasonings. Chill at least 2 hours to blend flavors.

SLIM SALAD

Ingredients

2 cups shredded lettuce
1/4 cup chopped green onion
1/2 cup sliced celery
1 cup cherry tomatoes, halved
1/2 pound cooked chicken breast
1 small banana
1 pink grapefruit, peeled and sectioned

Dressing:
1/4 cup lime juice
1 T olive oil
1 tsp sweetener
1/2 tsp paprika
1/4 tsp salt
1/4 tsp dry mustard

Equivalent to:

2 Servings
Each=
1 1/2 cup
vegetable
1 fruit
2 oil

321 calories
9 g total fat
1.5 g saturated
66 mg
cholesterol
402 mg sodium

Instructions:

In medium size bowl, combine lettuce and onion. On 2 salad plates, arrange bananas, grapefruit, tomatoes and celery around chicken. Top with dressing.

Dressing: In a screw top jar, combine ingredients, shake well.

SESAME TURKEY SALAD

Ingredients:

3 oz cooked turkey breast, cut in thin strips
1/2 head romaine lettuce, torn into bite-size
  pieces
1/2 cucumber, peeled and cut in rounds
2 celery stalks, sliced
1/2 red or yellow pepper, cut in strips
2 T balsamic, red wine, or rice wine vinegar
1 tsp toasted sesame seeds

Instructions:

Toss turkey and vegetables in a bowl with vinegar. Arrange on a chilled plate, sprinkle with sesame seeds.

Equivalent to:

1 Serving
Each =
3 oz protien
3 cups raw
vegetable

190 calories
3 g total fat
< 1 g saturated
53 mg
cholesterol
141 mg sodium

SPANISH CHICKEN & RICE SALAD

Ingredients:

2 tsp olive oil
1 small onion, chopped
2 cups par boiled rice
1 tsp tumeric
salt, to taste
14 oz chicken breasts, cut in chunks
2 T chili powder
2 (15 oz) cans red kidney beans, rinsed
1 (4oz) can green chilies, chopped
2 T cider vinegar
2 T fresh chopped cilantro

Equivalent to:

6 Servings
Each =
2 oz protein
3 starch
1/3 oil

Woman Style:
6 Servings
Each =
1 1/3 legume
1 starch
2 oz protein
1/3 oil

297 calories
2.7 g total fat
< 1 g saturated
38 mg
cholesterol
778 mg sodium

Instructions:

In a saucepan, heat 1/2 oil, cook onion until tender. Stir in rice, turmeric, and 4 cups water. Heat to boiling, reduce heat, cover and cook 20 minutes.

In a skillet, heat the rest of oil, cook chicken until browned, stirring in chili powder. Add beans, chilies, and cook until chicken is done.

In a large bowl, mix rice, chicken mixture, vinegar, cilantro until blended.

Serve warm or cover and refrigerate to serve cold.

BLACK BEAN & CORN SALAD

Ingredients:

1/3 cup bottled or fresh lime juice
2 T water
1 T olive oil
2 cloves garlic, finely minced
1/2 tsp salt
1/4 tsp sweetener
1/4 tsp ground cumin
1/8 tsp cayenne
1 (17 oz) can whole kernel corn, drained
1 (15 oz) can black beans, drained and rinsed
1/2 cup each chopped green and red bell
  pepper
1/2 cup chopped celery
1 T finely chopped jalapeno pepper, or to taste
1/4 cup chopped cilantro
Lettuce or cabbage leaves

Instructions:

Mix all ingredients together and cool in refrigerator before serving.

Equivalent to:

6 Servings
Each =
2/3 oz protein
1 2/3 starch
1/2 oil
Scant raw
vegetable

Woman Style:
6 Servings
Each =
2/3 legume
1 starch
1/2 oil
Scant raw
vegetable

135 calories
5 g total fat
0 cholesterol
440 mg sodium

CITRUS CHICKEN SALAD

Ingredients:

5 oz cooked breast, cubed or same amount canned chicken
2/3 cup rice, cooked
1/2 cup chopped celery
1/2 cup chopped green pepper
1/4 chopped green onion
1 package Diet Center Caesar Dressing or 2 T reduced calorie Caesar dressing
1 T light mayonnaise
2 T fat-free mayonnaise
1/8 tsp garlic herb seasoning
1/4 tsp lemon pepper
1/4 tsp Oriental seasoning
1/4 tsp salt
1 cup mixed salad greens; bean sprouts, mushrooms, etc.
4 T water chestnuts
1 orange, peeled and sliced

Equivalent to:

2 Servings
Each=
21/2 oz protein
1 starch
1 cup raw
vegetables
1/2 fruit
1/2 oil
1 additional
food

289 calories
8.5 g total fat
1 g saturated
27 mg
cholesterol
579 mg sodium

Instructions:

In a medium bowl, combine rice, green pepper, celery, green onion and chicken. Combine dressing, mayonnaise and seasonings. Toss lightly with other ingredients.

CHINESE CHICKEN SALAD

Salads

Ingredients:

7 oz chicken breast, cooked and sliced
1 tsp fresh chopped ginger
1 clove garlic, smashed and chopped
1 tsp low-sodium soy sauce
2 cups shredded radicchio
1/2 cup cooked green peas
1 cup bean sprouts
1 yellow pepper, thinly sliced
2 green onions, sliced
2 tsp sesame oil
3 T red wine vinegar
1/4 tsp Oriental seasoning
1 tsp sesame seeds, toasted

Instructions:

Place chicken, ginger, garlic, soy sauce, radicchio and green peas in bowl. Season well. Add bean sprouts, yellow pepper and green onions. Pour in wine vinegar and oil. Toss, adjust seasonings and serve. Top with sesame seeds.

Equivalent to:

2 Servings
Each =
3 oz protein
1/4 starch
2 1/4 cups raw vegetable
1 oil

219 calories
7 g total fat
1 g saturated
57 mg cholesterol
94 mg sodium

CHICKEN & FRUIT SPINACH SALAD

Ingredients:

12 oz chicken breast, cut into thin 2-inch strips
1/3 cup orange juice concentrate
6 cups torn fresh spinach leaves or assorted
   greens
1 cup fresh raspberries, (may use other berries)
Savory or napa cabbage, optional
1 papaya, peeled, seeded and cut into thin
   slices or 2 medium nectarines or peaches.

Dressing:
1/4 cup raspberry vinegar or white wine
   vinegar
3 tsp oil
4 packets sweetener
1/2 tsp finely shredded orange peel
1/4 tsp lemon pepper
1/4 tsp salt

Instructions:

Dressing:
Combine all ingredients together in a screw top
jar. Shake well. Chill dressing until needed.

Equivalent to:

3 Servings
Each =
31/2 oz protein
1 fruit
2 cups raw
vegetable
1 oil

330 calories
7.5 g total fat
< 1 g saturated
66 mg
cholesterol
520 mg sodium

CHICKEN & FRUIT SPINACH SALAD

Instructions Continued:

In a microwave-safe dish sprayed with Pam, combine orange juice, 2 T water and chicken. Microwave on high 4-6 minutes or until chicken is tender and no longer pink. Drain, discard cooking liquid. In a large bowl combine warm chicken and spinach. Add dressing and raspberries; toss gently.

Line dinner plates with cabbage, if desired.

Divide salad among the plates. Top each salad with several papaya, peach or nectarine slices, arrange them in a fan.

MIAMI CHICKEN SALAD

Ingredients:

6 oz chicken breast, cooked and diced or same
  amount canned
1/2 cup grapefruit sections
1 orange, peeled and sliced 1/4-inch thick
1/2 cup diced celery
1/8 tsp grated lime peel
1 T lime juice
1 T light mayonnaise
1 T fat-free mayonnaise
1/4 cup fat-free, sugar free vanilla yogurt
1/8 tsp salt
1/8 tsp lemon pepper
Endive

Equivalent to:

2 Servings
Each =
21/2 oz protein
3/4 fruit
2 oil
Scant dairy
3 c raw
vegetable

236 calories
6.4 g total fat
1 g saturated
52 mg
cholesterol
460 mg sodium

Instructions:

Mix together grapefruit, chicken and celery.
Add the lime peel, lime juice and yogurt to the
mayonnaise; add seasonings.
Beat until mixed and fluffy. Fold into chicken
mixture.
Line a salad bowl with snipped endive. Place
the chicken salad in the center; arrange the
orange slices around the outside edge over
endive. Chill in the refrigerator for 1 hour.

CURRY CHICKEN SALAD

Ingredients:

5 oz chicken breasts, cooked and cubed or same
   amount canned
1/2 cup celery, diced
1/2 cup chopped green onion
1/2 cup diced green pepper
4 T water chestnuts
1 cup red or green grapes
1/2 tsp curry powder
1 T light mayonnaise
3 T fat-free mayonnaise
1/2 cup plain non-fat yogurt
1 T lemon juice
1/2 tsp sweetener
1 tsp Nice n Spicy or Season All
1/2 tsp lemon pepper
Salt, to taste
1/4 tsp garlic herb seasoning
1 cup cooked shell pasta

Instructions:

Mix all ingredients together and adjust
seasonings to your taste. Salad needs to be
refrigerated 2-3 hours to combine flavors.

Equivalent to:

2 Servings
Each =
21/2 oz protein
1 starch
1/2 fruit
1 cup raw
vegetable
1 oil
1 additional
food

237 calories
6.5 g total fat
1 g saturated
52 mg
cholesterol
594 mg sodium

WALDORF CHICKEN SALAD

Ingredients:

5 oz chicken, cooked and sliced or same
    amount canned
3 stalks celery, sliced
1 large apple, diced
1 T light mayonnaise
1 T fat-free mayonnaise
1/2 tsp Teton Valley Nice n Spicy or Season All
1/4 tsp lemon pepper
1/4 tsp salt
1 packet sweetener
Endive

Equivalent to:

2 Servings
Each =
21/2 oz protein
1/2 fruit
3/4 oil
1 cup raw
vegetable

202 calories
6.5 g total fat
1.3 g saturated
52 mg
cholesterol
472 mg sodium

Instructions:

Toss all ingredients together. Place on a bed of lettuce and serve.

MELON AND CHICKEN SALAD

Ingredients:

1 cantaloupe
7 oz cooked chicken breast, diced
3/4 cup celery, chopped
1/4 cup green pepper, chopped
1 green onion, sliced
4 T water chestnuts, sliced
1 T light mayonnaise
1 T fat-free mayonnaise
2 T plain non-fat yogurt
1/4 tsp salt
1/4 tsp lemon pepper
1/2 tsp Teton Valley Nice n Spicy or Season All

Instructions:

Cut cantaloupe in half and remove seeds. Combine remaining ingredients in a large bowl. Adjust seasonings. Spoon salad equally into cantaloupe halves.

Equivalent to:

2 Servings
Each =
31/2 oz protein
1 fruit
3/4 oil
1/2 cup raw vegetable
1 additional food

292 calories
7 g total fat
1.4 g saturated
60 mg cholesterol
502 mg sodium

CHICKEN SALAD SUPREME

Ingredients:

7 oz chicken breast, cooked and cubed
1/2 cup seedless grape halves
1 small can mandarin oranges, packed in water
1/2 cup celery, chopped
4 T water chestnuts, chopped
1/8 tsp ground nutmeg
1 T lime juice
1 1/2 T light mayonnaise
1 T fat-free mayonnaise
2 T non-fat plain yogurt
1/4 tsp salt

Equivalent to:

2 Servings
Each =
31/2 oz protein
1/2 fruit
1 oil
1 additional
food

229 calories
6.5 g total fat
1.4 g saturated
60 mg
cholesterol
465 mg sodium

Instructions:

In a bowl combine mayonnaise, lime and seasonings.
Add remaining ingredients; mix well.
Chill. Serve on lettuce leaves.

WILD RICE AND CHICKEN SALAD

Ingredients:

1 can (15 oz) chicken broth
1/2 cup wild rice
9 oz cooked chicken, diced
1 large celery stalk, diced
1/2 large crisp red apple, diced
1 green onion, thinly sliced
2 T minced fresh tarragon or 2 tsp dried
2 T olive oil
1 1/2 T tarragon vinegar
1 tsp Dijon mustard
1 packet sweetener
1/2 tsp lemon pepper
1/4 tsp salt

Instructions:

Combine broth and wild rice in a small saucepan. Bring to a boil. Cover and simmer over medium-low heat until rice is tender and liquid is absorbed, about 50 minutes. Transfer to medium bowl. Cover and refrigerate until well chilled. Add chicken, celery, apple, green onion and tarragon to wild rice. Whisk remaining ingredients to blend. Pour over mixture, toss well and adjust seasonings.

Equivalent to:

3 Servings
Each=
1 starch
3 oz protein
Scant fruit
2 oil

234 calories
6 g total fat
< 1 g saturated
51 mg cholesterol
341 mg sodium

BROCCOLI & CHICKEN SALAD

Ingredients:

4 cups broccoli
8 oz chicken breasts
1/4 cup chopped parsley
1/4 tsp salt
1/2 tsp Oriental seasoning
2 packages Diet Center Dressing or 4 T
  reduced calorie dressing

Instructions:

Equivalent to:

2 Servings
Each =
31/2 oz protein
2 cups raw
vegetable
1 oil

207 calories
5.9 g total fat
< 1 g saturated
66 mg
cholesterol
568 mg sodium

Clean broccoli, peel and trim off the toughest parts of the stems. Cut the upper parts of the stems and the tops into small pieces.
Blanch in boiling water. Simmer for about 5 minutes, then drain and plunge into cold water. Drain and chill.
Cook chicken breast, cut up and chill.
Assemble the salad, add parsley, onion and seasonings.
Toss salad with dressing.

TURKEY AND SWISS MARINATED SALAD

Ingredients

1 cup elbow macaroni, cooked
7 oz turkey breast, cooked and cut in cubes
2 oz fat-free swiss cheese, cut julienne
1/4 cup sliced carrots
1/2 cup celery, sliced
1/2 cup green pepper, sliced
2 green onions, sliced
2 oz jar pimento, drained
4 package Diet Center Italian Dressing or 8 T
  reduced calorie Italian dressing
1/4 tsp lemon pepper
1/8 tsp garlic herb seasoning
Lettuce leaves

Instructions:

In a large bowl, combine all remaining ingredients; toss gently. Cover; refrigerate to blend flavors.
To serve, spoon into lettuce-lined serving bowls.

Equivalent to:

2 Servings
Each =
31/2 oz protein
2 oil
1 starch
3/4 cup raw vegetable
1/2 dairy

385 calories
9.5 g total fat
1.3 g saturated
67 mg cholesterol
954 mg sodium

TURKEY SALAD IN PITA BREAD

Ingredients:

7 oz chicken breast, cooked and cubed
1/2 cup plain non-fat yogurt
1 green onion, sliced
1/4 tsp garlic herb seasoning
1/2 tsp Teton Valley Nice n Spicy or Season All
1/2 medium cucumber, sliced thin
1/2 small red onion, cut into thin slices
1 tomato, sliced
6 mushrooms, sliced thin
Lettuce leaves
2 (1 oz) pita bread

Equivalent to:

2 Servings
Each =
31/2 oz protein
1 cup raw
vegetable
1 starch
1/4 dairy

272 calories
1.7 g total fat
< 1 g saturated
62 mg
cholesterol
245 mg sodium

Instructions:

Blend yogurt, green onions and seasonings in a medium bowl. Add turkey and vegetables (except lettuce). Toss to combine.
Fill pita bread halves with turkey mixture, top with lettuce and serve as sandwiches.

DELICIOUS TURKEY SALAD

Ingredients:

1 cup cooked turkey breast, cubed
4 T grated carrots
1/4 cup finely chopped onion
1 green onion, chopped
1 cup celery, diced
1/2 cucumber, peeled, seeded and sliced
1 cup mushrooms, sliced

Dressing:
3 T non-fat cottage cheese
3 T plain non-fat yogurt
2 T lime juice
2 tsp oil
1 mint leaf, chopped
1/2 tsp wine vinegar
Few drops Worcestershire sauce
1/4 tsp lemon pepper
1/8 tsp salt

Instructions:

Place all vegetables in a large salad bowl.
In a blender or food processor, mix together
remaining ingredients until smooth. Pour
dressing over salad and serve.

Equivalent to:

2 Servings
Each =
3 1/2 oz protein
1 1/2 cup raw
vegetable
1/2 dairy
1 oil

225 calories
5.7 g total fat
< 1 g saturated
63 mg
cholesterol
274 mg sodium

SPINACH SALAD

Ingredients:

2 1/2 cups fresh spinach, washed and stems
   removed
1/2 cup fresh bean sprouts, rinsed and drained
1/4 red onion, sliced
1 hard cooked egg, chopped
1/2 cup mushrooms, sliced
2 T imitation bacon bits, optional
1 packet Diet Center Caesar Dressing or other
   low-fat caesar dressing
1/2 tsp Teton Valley Nice n Spicy
1/4 tsp garlic seasoning
Salt, to taste

Instructions:

Mix all salad ingredients together and toss. Add
enough of dressing to personal taste.
Adjust seasonings and serve.

Equivalent to:

1 Serving
Each =
3 cups raw
vegetable
1 oil
1 oz protein

254 calories
9 g total fat
2 g saturated
213 mg
cholesterol
832 mg sodium

SPINACH SALAD WITH RASPBERRY DRESSING

Ingredients:

1/2 cup plain non-fat yogurt
1/4 cup fresh or frozen red raspberries, thawed
  if frozen
1 T skim milk
1 1/2 tsp chopped fresh mint or 1/2 tsp dried
  mint, crushed
6 cups fresh spinach, washed, drained and
  trimmed
2 large fresh mushrooms, sliced
1 T sesame seeds, toasted
4 to 6 red onion rings

Instructions:

Carefully combine yogurt, raspberries, milk and mint in a small bowl; set aside. Combine spinach, mushrooms and sesame seeds in a medium bowl, mix well.

Arrange spinach mixture evenly on 2 individual salad plates, top with red onion rings. Drizzle yogurt dressing over salads. Garnish with fresh raspberries and mint sprig, if desired.

Equivalent to:

2 Servings
Each =
1/4 oz dairy
3 cups raw
vegetable
Scant fruit

198 calories
3.9 g total fat
< 1 g saturated
< 1 mg
cholesterol
426 mg sodium

CUCUMBER SALAD & YOGURT DRESSING

Ingredients:

1 cucumber peeled and sliced
2 stalks celery, sliced
1 large tomato, cut in wedges
4 T water chestnuts, sliced
1 T chopped parsley
1/4 cup plain non-fat yogurt
1/4 tsp dry mustard
1 tsp red wine vinegar
2 T fresh lemon juice
1 packet sweetener
1/4 tsp Teton Valley Nice n Spicy or Season All
1/4 tsp salt
Pinch of paprika
Alfalfa sprouts, for decoration

Instructions:

Place cucumber, celery, tomatoes, water chestnuts and parsley in salad bowl. Toss gently. Mix remaining ingredients, except alfalfa sprouts and paprika. Pour dressing over salad and toss to coat evenly.

Arrange servings on small bed of alfalfa sprouts and sprinkle with paprika.

Equivalent to:

2 Servings
Each =
2 cups raw
vegetable
Scant dairy

77 calories
< 1 g total fat
< 1 g saturated
0 cholesterol
357 mg sodium

VEGETABLE SALAD & ORANGE DRESSING

Ingredients:

SALAD:
1/2 small head cauliflower, cut in florets
1/2 lb green beans, cut into 1 inch long pieces
1 large bunch broccoli, cut into florets
1 lb asparagus, trimmed, cut into 1 inch pieces
1 (8 oz) can water chestnuts, drained and sliced

ORANGE DRESSING:
1/2 cup sunflower oil
1/3 cup red wine vinegar
1/3 cup orange juice
2 tsp orange peel, grated
1/4 tsp salt
Orange peel, (orange part only), cut in strips
1/4 tsp almond extract

Instructions:

Salad: Bring a large pot of water to boil, add green beans and cook until crisp-tender, about 5 minutes. Take beans out and put in ice water

Equivalent to:

3 Servings
Each =
1 1/2 cup
cooked
vegetable
2 oil

184 calories
8 g total fat
< 1 g saturated
0 cholesterol
328 mg sodium
(totals include
dressing)

VEGETABLE SALAD &
ORANGE DRESSING

Instructions Continued:

and let cool. Drain beans. Cook broccoli, cauliflower and asparagus until crisp-tender, about 3-5 minutes. Drain well and transfer to bowl of ice water and cool. Drain all vegetables thoroughly. Combine all vegetables in a large bowl, (can be prepared 1 day ahead, cover and chill).

Dressing:
Whisk all ingredients in a small bowl. Pour dressing over salad and toss gently.
Garnish with orange peel strips and serve.
Serving= 1 1/2 T= 2 oil

VEGETABLE & CHICK PEA SALAD

Instructions:

1 cup chick peas, drained
1 cup cooked green beans
1 1/2 cup cauliflower, lightly steamed
1 red pepper, diced
1 cup yellow wax beans
1 T chopped parsley
1/2 tsp tarragon
2 packets Diet Center Italian Dressing or 4 T
   low-calorie Italian dressing
1 tsp chopped fresh mint
Few drops lemon juice
Tabasco sauce, to taste
Lemon pepper, to taste
1/8 tsp salt

Instructions:

Place chick peas, beans, cauliflower, parsley and red pepper in large salad bowl.
Add remaining ingredients to salad, toss and adjust seasonings. Refrigerate at least 4 hours before serving.

Equivalent to:

4 Servings
Each =
1 starch
1 cup cooked
vegetable
1/2 oil

Woman Style:

4 Servings
Each =
1 legume
1/2 oil
1 cup cooked
vegetable

123 calories
2.9 g total fat
< 1 g saturated
0 choleterol
581 mg sodium

THREE BEAN SALAD

Ingredients:

1 can (16 oz) cut green beans, drained
1 can (16 oz) wax yellow beans, drained
1 can(16 oz) red kidney beans, drained and
* rinsed*
1/2 cup slivered green pepper
1/4 cup raw onion rings
1 tsp sweetener
2 packets Diet Center Italian Dressing or 4 T
* low-calorie Italian dressing*
1/4 tsp lemon pepper
1/4 tsp Italian seasoning

Instructions:

Combine beans, green pepper and onion rings.
Combine sweetener, seasonings and dressing.
Toss ingredients together.
Let stand, covered, in refrigerator overnight.

Equivalent to:

4 Servings
Each =
1 oz protein
1 starch
1 cup raw
vegetable
1/2 oil

Woman Style:
4 Servings
Each =
1 legume
1 cup raw
vegetable
1/2 oil

160 calories
2.6 g total fat
< 1 g saturated
0 cholesterol
768 mg sodium

MULTI-VEGETABLE & BEAN SALAD

Ingredients:

1 small zucchini, chopped fine
3/4 cup celery, chopped fine
1/2 cup garbanzo beans
1/2 cup kidney beans
1/2 cup peas
1/2 cup corn
1/2 red onion, chopped fine
1/2 cup carrot, chopped fine
2 packets Diet Center Italian Dressing or 4 T
    low-calorie Italian dressing
1 1/2 tsp chopped fresh dill
1 T fresh chopped parsley
1/2 tsp lemon pepper
1/8 tsp garlic herb seasoning

Instructions:

Mix all ingredients together and chill well before serving, at least 2 hours.

Equivalent to:

2 Servings
Each =
1 oz protein
2 starch
1 1/4 cup raw
vegetable
1 oil

Woman Style:

2 Servings
Each =
1 legume
1 starch
1 1/4 cup raw
vegetable
1 oil

271 calories
5.6 g total fat
< 1 g saturated
0 cholesterol
600 mg sodium

POTATO SALAD WITH LEMON DRESSING

Ingredients:

2 potatoes, boiled, peeled and diced
1 stalk celery, chopped
2 T red onion, chopped
1 T light mayonnaise
2 T fat-free mayonnaise
3 T plain non-fat yogurt
1 tsp chopped parsley
1 tsp grated lemon rind
1 T lemon juice
1/4 tsp lemon pepper
1/4 tsp Parsley Patch Nice n Spicy or Season
  All
1/4 tsp salt

Instructions:

Mix mayonnaise, yogurt, parsley, lemon rind, and juice together; season to taste. Place potatoes, celery and onion in bowl; toss together. Pour on dressing, toss again and serve.

Equivalent to:

4 Servings
Each =
1 starch
1/2 oil
1/4 cup raw
vegetable
1 additional
food

82 calories
2.6 g total fat
< 1 g saturated
0 cholesterol
229 mg sodium

POTATO SALAD

Ingredients:

3 baking potatoes, not peeled
2 stalks celery, chopped fine
1 small red onion, chopped fine
1/2 each green & red pepper, chopped fine
1 tsp Teton Valley Nice n Spicy or Season All
Salt and pepper, to taste
Splash of seasoned rice vinegar

Dressing:
1 clove garlic, smashed and chopped very fine
1 1/2 tsp Dijon mustard
1/2 cup plain non-fat yogurt
2 T light mayonnaise
1 T fat-free mayonnaise

Instructions:

Wash potatoes, then boil gently until tender. Allow the potatoes to cool completely before cutting. Cut the potatoes into one-half inch cubes with the peel on. Place in a large bowl then add the rest of the ingredients. Add splash of rice vinegar and toss, this will add a touch of sweetness to the salad. In a separate bowl mix the dressing then add the potatoes and toss well.

Equivalent to:

6 Servings
Each=
1 starch
3/4 oil
1/2 cup raw
vegetable

111 calories
3.5 g total fat
<1 g saturated
1.6 mg
cholesterol
81 mg sodium

MONTEREY ROASTED POTATO SALAD

Ingredients:

4 small red potatoes
1 T olive oil
1 1/2 T fresh lemon juice
1 T raspberry or white wine vinegar
1 clove garlic
1 T fresh tarragon, or 1/2 tsp dried
1/4 tsp salt
1/4 tsp lemon pepper
1 T minced fresh flat parsley (Italian)
1/2 tsp grated lemon peel
1/8 tsp hot pepper sauce
3 oz fat-free jack cheese
Fresh parsley and tarragon sprigs, optional

Equivalent to:

4 Servings
Each =
1 starch
3/4 oil
3/4 dairy

157 calories
3.6 g total fat
< 1 g saturated
4 mg
cholesterol
477 mg sodium

Instructions:

Cook potatoes in boiling water until done still a bit firm, about 20 minutes. Combine oil, lemon juice, vinegar, garlic, tarragon, parsley, lemon peel and hot pepper sauce in a baking dish; toss with mixture. Let stand at room temperature 1 hour, stirring occasionally. Bake at 375 degrees for 20 minutes. Sprinkle with cheese, return to oven and bake 5 minutes.

LAYERED VEGETABLE SALAD

Ingredients:

2 1/2 cups torn lettuce greens
1/2 cup celery, chopped
1/4 cup green onion, chopped
4 T water chestnuts
1/2 cup green pepper, chopped
1/2 cup shredded carrots
1 cup frozen green peas
1 large tomato
1 large boiled egg
2 oz fat-free cheddar cheese, grated
1 T light mayonnaise
1 T fat-free mayonnaise
1/2 cup vanilla fat-free sugar-free yogurt
1/4 tsp lemon pepper
1/4 tsp Teton Valley Nice n Spicy or Season All

Instructions:

In a glass bowl, make an even layer of lettuce. Mix onion and celery and sprinkle over lettuce. Add water chestnuts and peas. Mix yogurt and mayonnaise together, add seasonings to taste. Spread mixture evenly over top of salad to sides of bowl. Layer tomato, egg, seasonings and cheese on top. Serve.

Equivalent to:

2 Servings
Each =
2 1/2 cup raw vegetable
1/2 oz protein
3/4 dairy
1 starch
3/4 oil
1 additional food

246 calories
8 g total fat
1.9 g saturated
114 mg cholesterol
601 mg sodium

ITALIAN TOMATO-BASIL SALAD

Ingredients:

2 package Diet Center Italian Dressing or 4 T low-calorie Italian dressing
3 cups tomato wedges
1 cup green bell pepper strips
1/2 cup red onion rings
2 T chopped fresh basil
1/4 tsp salt
1/8 tsp lemon pepper

Instructions:

Pour dressing over ingredients; mix lightly. Season to taste and refrigerate.

Equivalent to:

2 Servings
Each =
2 1/4 cup raw
vegetable
1 oil

104 calories
4 g total fat
< 1 g saturated
0 cholesterol
477 mg sodium

ITALIAN-STYLE CAULIFLOWER SALAD

Ingredients:

1/2 head cauliflower, cut into florets
3/4 cup sliced green or red bell pepper
1/4 cup sliced carrots
3/4 cup sliced celery
1 small jar pimentos, chopped
1 T chopped parsley
1/2 tsp dried basil, crumbled
1/4 tsp lemon pepper
1/4 tsp salt, or to taste
1/8 tsp garlic herb seasoning
2 packets Diet Center Italian Dressing or 4 T
  low-calorie Italian dressing

Instructions:

In a large saucepan, cook cauliflower in steamer basket over boiling water 8 minutes. Drain, transfer to large bowl. Pour dressing over warm cauliflower. Add remaining ingredients; toss to coat. Refrigerate covered overnight.

Equivalent to:

2 Servings
Each =
3 cups raw
vegetable
1 oil

128 calories
4.8 g total fat
< 1 g saturated
0 cholesterol
540 mg sodium

MARINATED BRUSSELS SPROUT SALAD

Ingredients:

1 package (10 oz) frozen Brussels sprouts, cooked and drained
1 cup yellow squash, sliced and blanched
1 cup fresh raw mushrooms, sliced
1/2 red onion, peeled and thinly sliced
2 packets Diet Center Dijon Dressing or 4 T low-calorie Dijon dressing
1/4 tsp lemon pepper
1/8 tsp Italian seasoning
1/8 tsp garlic herb seasoning
1/4 tsp salt

Instructions:

Arrange vegetables in a shallow dish. Mix dressing with seasonings and pour over vegetables. Cover and chill 2 hours or more. To serve, arrange vegetables in rows on platter; drizzle any remaining dressing over top of salad.

Equivalent to:

2 Servings
Each =
1 3/4 cup
cooked
vegetable
1 oil

141 calories
5 g total fat
< 1 g saturated
0 cholesterol
425 mg sodium

MINESTRONE PASTA SALAD

Ingredients:

3 cups cooked pasta
4 cups spinach, rinsed and stems removed
2 tomatoes, cut in eighths
1 (15 oz) cannellini or kidney beans
1 cup celery, sliced
1/2 cup carrots, thinly sliced
1/2 cup onion, chopped
2 T fresh chopped parsley
1 tsp lemon juice
1/4 tsp lemon pepper
1/2 tsp dried thyme leaves
1/2 tsp dried rosemary, crushed
6 packages Diet Center Italian Dressing or 3/4
    cup low-fat Italian dressing
2 oz fat-free swiss cheese

Instructions:

In a saucepan heat 1 cup water to boiling; add spinach. Cook, covered, 1 minute or until wilted; drain. Squeeze spinach dry or drain on paper towels. In a large bowl, gently toss pasta, vegetables, dressing and seasonings. Cover and refrigerate. Sprinkle with cheese before serving.

Equivalent to:

6 Servings
Each =
2 starch
1 cup raw
vegetable
1 oil

Woman Style:
6 Servings
Each =
2/3 legume
1 starch
1 oil
1 cup raw
vegetable

274 calories
5.3 g total fat
< 1 g saturated
13 mg
cholesterol
568 mg sodium

CABBAGE APPLE SLAW

Ingredients:

4 cups cabbage, chopped
1 Granny Smith apple, chopped
1/2 cucumber, chopped
1 green onion, chopped
1 T light mayonnaise
1 T fat-free mayonnaise
2 T lemon juice
1/4 cup plain non-fat yogurt
1/4 tsp salt
1/4 tsp garlic herb seasoning
1/2 tsp Teton Valley Nice n Spicy or Season All
1/4 tsp lemon pepper

Equivalent to:

2 Servings
Each =
3 cup raw
vegetable
3/4 oil
1/2 fruit
1 additional
food

157 calories
5.7 g total fat
1 g saturated
2.5 mg
cholesterol
413 mg sodium

Instructions:

Mix all ingredients together and chill to blend flavors.

COLESLAW

Ingredients:

3 T cider vinegar
2 tsp sweetener
1 T chicken stock, defatted and low-sodium
1 tsp oil
1 tsp Dijon mustard
1/4 tsp celery seeds
1/4 tsp mustard seeds
1 cup shredded green cabbage (1/4 small head)
1 cup shredded red cabbage (1/4 small head)
1 carrot, grated
1 stalk celery, finely chopped
1/4 tsp lemon pepper

Instructions:

In a medium bowl, whisk together vinegar, sweetener, chicken stock, oil, mustard seasonings and seeds. Add green and red cabbage, carrots, and celery; toss well. Season to taste.

Equivalent to:

1 Serving
Each =
3 cups raw
vegetable
1 oil

146 calories
5.8 g total fat
< 1 g saturated
< 1 mg
cholesterol
501 mg sodium

CHERRY WALDORF SALAD

Ingredients:

1 cup boiling water
1 (3 oz) size sugar-free cherry gelatin
1/2 cup cold water
1 T lemon juice
3/4 cup chopped celery
Lettuce leaves
Apple slices

Instructions:

Equivalent to:

4 Servings
Each =
1/4 fruit
1 additional
food

18 calories
< 1 g total fat
< 1 g saturated
0 cholesterol
72 mg sodium

In a medium bowl, pour boiling water over gelatin; stir until dissolved. Add cold water and lemon juice, chill until partially set. Fold in apples and celery. Chill and set, 4 hours.
Serve on lettuce leaves, garnish with apple slices.

MELON WEDGE SET SALAD

Ingredients:

1 cantaloupe or honeydew melon
1 package (4 oz) orange flavor sugar free
 gelatin
1 cup boiling water
3/4 cup cold Diet 7-Up
1/2 cup sliced strawberries

Instructions:

Cut melon in half lengthwise; scoop out seeds
and drain well. Dissolve gelatin in boiling
water. Add cold 7-Up. Chill until slightly
thickened; stir in fruit. Pour into melon halves.
Chill until firm, about 3 hours. Cut in wedges.
Serve with additional fresh fruit, cottage cheese
and crisp greens if desired.

Equivalent to:

4 Servings
Each =
1/2 fruit
1 additional
food

61 calories
< 1 g total fat
< 1 g saturated
0 cholesterol
62 mg sodium

FROZEN FRUIT SALAD

Ingredients:

1/2 cup frozen blueberries
1/2 cup frozen strawberries
1/2 cup frozen raspberries
1 apple, cubed
1 orange, sectioned and cubed
1 peach, sliced
1/2 cup cantaloupe, cubed
1 can Diet 7-Up

Instructions:

Toss fruit together in a large bowl.
Place fruit in dessert dish and top with Diet 7-up. Serve immediately.

Equivalent to:

5 Servings
Each =
1 fruit

71 calories
< 1 g total fat
< 1 g saturated
0 cholesterol
5 mg sodium

CRANBERRY SALAD

Ingredients:

1 package Crystal Light Berry Drink Mix
4 cups water
2 packages Knox Gelatin
1/2 cup cooked cranberries
2 apples, finely chopped
1/2 orange, with rind
1 1/2 cups strawberries, partially frozen and
    mashed
2 tsp sweetener

Instructions:

Dissolve drink mix in 4 cups water. Heat gelatin over low heat with 1/2 of drink mix. Stir until dissolved. Put orange in food processor and chop up, rind and all. Add sweetener. Mix all other ingredients together and chill.

Equivalent to:

4 Servings
Each =
1 fruit serving
1 diet drink

84 calories
< 1 g total fat
< 1 g saturated
0 cholesterol
1 mg sodium

NOTES

Seafood

BAKED STUFFED SHRIMP

Seafood

Ingredients:

8 oz jumbo shrimp, (about 6-8), peeled with
  tails
1/2 cup chopped mushrooms
2 T chopped onion
1/2 clove garlic, minced
4 Ryvita crackers, finely crushed
1 egg white, whipped
1 T chopped pimento
1/4 tsp lemon pepper
1/4 tsp salt
Lemon wedges, optional

Instructions:

Preheat oven to 400 degrees. In a skillet
sprayed with Pam, saute mushrooms, onion,
and garlic over medium heat until tender.
Remove from heat and stir in Ryvita crumbs,
pimento and whipped egg white. Cut a slit on
underside of each shrimp, don't cut all the way
through, remove vein. Spray each shrimp with
Pam to coat. Mound stuffing mixture in hollow
of each shrimp. Place in a baking dish sprayed
with Pam and bake 8 to 10 minutes or until hot.
Shrimp will turn pink.

Equivalent to:

2 Servings
Each serving =
2 oz protein
1 starch

219 calories
4.7 g total fat
1 g saturated
279 mg
cholesterol
512 mg sodium

SHANGHAI SHRIMP

Ingredients:

1 pound large shrimp*, shelled and deveined
4 scallions, cut in 1-inch pieces
1 tsp minced ginger
1/2 tsp Oriental seasoning
1/4 tsp salt
1 cup chicken broth
1/4 cup orange juice
1 (11 oz) can mandarin oranges, packed in
  water, drained
1 can water chestnuts, drained
Hot cooked rice
1 T cornstarch

Equivalent to:

4 Servings
Each =
2 oz protein
1/4 fruit
1 starch
Scant vegetable
1 additional
food

173 calories
2.6 g total fat
< 1 g saturated
174 mg
cholesterol
340 mg sodium

Instructions:

In a skillet sprayed with Pam, over medium-high heat, cook scallions and ginger 2-3 minutes, being careful not to let ginger burn. Add shrimp; cook 2-3 minutes.
Add cornstarch to chicken broth, stir into skillet with oranges and water chestnuts. Add seasonings and reduce heat; cover and simmer, until slightly thickened and heated through. Serve over rice.
* May also use chicken breast.

OVEN FRIED SHRIMP WITH CREOLE SAUCE

Ingredients:

12 oz jumbo shrimp, peeled and deveined
6 T bread crumbs
1/2 tsp Teton Valley Nice n Spicy or Season All
1 egg white, whipped
1/4 tsp lemon pepper
1/4 tsp onion powder

Instructions:

Add spices to bread crumbs. Cut shrimp along outside and remove vein, being careful not to cut all the way through shrimp. Spread cleaned shrimp apart to butterfly. Dip shrimp into egg wash then into bread crumbs.
On a baking sheet sprayed with Pam, cook shrimp 8 to 10 minutes at 400 degrees or until done. Serve with Creole Tarter Sauce.

Creole Tarter Sauce

Ingredients:

1/4 cup finely chopped green pepper
1/4 cup finely chopped celery

Equivalent to:

3 Servings
Each =
2 oz protein
1 oil

222 calories
7.7 g total fat
1 g saturated
174 mg
cholesterol
389 mg sodium

OVEN FRIED SHRIMP WITH CREOLE SAUCE

Ingredients Continued:

1/4 cup finely chopped parsley
3 T tomato paste
2 T Dijon-style mustard
1 T corn oil
1 T white wine vinegar
1/2 tsp Tabasco Pepper Sauce, (may use less)
1/2 tsp paprika

Instructions:

In a small bowl combine all ingredients until well blended. Serving = 1/3 cup

LEMON-BASIL SHRIMP KABOBS

Ingredients:

Marinade:
1/2 cup lemon juice
1 T oil
1 T finely chopped onion
1 T finely chopped fresh parsley
1 tsp basil leaves, crushed
1/2 tsp grated lemon peel
1/4 tsp salt
1/4 tsp lemon pepper

1 pound large fresh shrimp, peeled, deveined, tails left on
12 large mushrooms
6 thin lemon slices
1/2 large red bell pepper, cut into 1-inch pieces
1 small zucchini, cut into 1/2-inch pieces

Instructions:

In a bowl, combine marinade ingredients; mix well. Add shrimp; stir to coat. Cover; and chill in the refrigerate 1-3 hours.
Drain shrimp, reserving marinade.
Soak bamboo skewers 15 minutes in water.
On each of 6 skewers, arrange 3-4 shrimp, 2 mushrooms, 1 lemon slice, red pepper pieces

Equivalent to:

4 Servings
Each =
2 oz protein
1/2 cup cooked
vegetable
3/4 oil

165 calories
6 g total fat
< 1 g saturated
173 mg
cholesterol
324 mg sodium

LEMON-BASIL SHRIMP KABOBS

Instructions Continued:

and zucchini pieces. When ready to barbecue, place kabobs on grill 4-6 inches from medium-high coals. Cook 10 to 15 minutes or until shrimp are pink and vegetables are crisp-tender, turning once and brushing frequently with marinade.

SHRIMP PROVENCALE

Ingredients:

8 oz shrimp, peeled and deveined
1 garlic, smashed and chopped
1/2 red pepper, thinly sliced
1/2 zucchini, halved lengthwise and thinly
   sliced
1 tsp coarsely chopped fresh oregano
1 tsp chopped parsley
1/2 lemon, juiced
1/4 tsp lemon pepper
2 oz fat-free mozzarella cheese, grated

Instructions:

In a skillet sprayed with Pam, add shrimp and
garlic; season well. Cook 2 to 3 minutes on
each side over medium-high heat; stir
occasionally. Remove shrimp from pan and set
aside. Add vegetables, oregano, parsley, and
cook 2-3 minutes over medium-high heat.
Season well and sprinkle with lemon juice.
Replace shrimp in pan, stir and cook 1 minute.
Spoon into scallop shells, top with cheese, broil
until lightly browned.

Equivalent to:

2 Servings
Each =
2 oz protein
1 cup cooked
vegetable
1/2 dairy

165 calories
2 g total fat
< 1 g saturated
178 mg
cholesterol
659 mg sodium

HOT SHRIMP KABOBS

Ingredients:

8 oz fresh shrimp, peeled and deveined
2 tsp diet soft tub margarine
1 T lemon juice
1/4 tsp Tabasco sauce
1/2 orange, peeled and sectioned
1/2 apple, cut in wedges
1/4 tsp salt
1/2 tsp Teton Valley Nice n Spicy or Season All Pepper

Equivalent to:

2 Servings
Each =
2 oz protein
1 fruit
1 oil

172 calories
6 g total fat
1.2 g saturated
173 mg
cholesterol
534 mg sodium

Instructions:

Place shrimp, oil, lemon juice and Tabasco sauce in a bowl. Marinade 30 minutes.
Soak bamboo skewers in water for 15 minutes.
Alternate shrimp, orange and apple on skewers. Baste with marinade and season.
Broil 3 minutes on each side in oven or on barbecue over medium-hot coals. Shrimp are done when they turn pink.

BUTTERFLIED GARLIC SHRIMP

Ingredients:

1 pound medium shrimp, peeled, deveined and
*   butterflied*
1 clove garlic, smashed and chopped
1 green pepper, cut in thin strips
1/2 lemon, peeled and diced
1 tsp chopped fresh parsley
1/4 tsp lemon pepper
1/4 tsp salt
Dash garlic herb seasoning
1/8 tsp dill
1/8 tsp paprika

Instructions:

In a large skillet sprayed with Pam, cook shrimp 2 minutes each side over medium-high heat. Spray shrimp with Pam before you turn so they will brown. Add garlic and season well; continue cooking 1 minute. Stir in green pepper and diced lemon; cook 1 more minute.
Adjust seasonings, add parsley and paprika; mix and serve.

Equivalent to:

4 Servings
Each =
2 oz protein
Scant vegetable

111 calories
2 g total fat
< 1 g saturated
173 mg
cholesterol
314 mg sodium

SHRIMP SCAMPI ITALIANO

Ingredients:

*2 packages Diet Center Italian Dressing or 4 T
  low-fat Italian dressing
1 pound raw medium shrimp, cleaned
1/2 tsp lemon pepper
1/4 tsp salt*

Instructions:

In a large shallow non-aluminum broiler-proof
pan, pour Italian dressing over shrimp.
Cover and marinade in refrigerator, turning
occasionally, at least 2 hours.
Broil shrimp with dressing, turning and basting
frequently, until pink.
Garnish, if desired, with chopped parsley.

Serve with cooked rice.

Equivalent to:

4 Servings
Each =
2 oz protein
1/2 oil

123 calories
4 g total fat
< 1 g saturated
173 mg
cholesterol
397 mg sodium

ALASKA SNOW CRAB WITH SALSA VERDE

Ingredients:

1 large cucumber, peeled, seeded, and chopped
1/4 cup green bell pepper, chopped
1 T sliced green onions
1 T lemon juice
1 1/2 tsp olive oil
1 1/2 tsp chopped cilantro
1 clove garlic, chopped
1/2 jalapeno pepper, seeded and chopped
1/4 tsp salt
1/4 tsp lemon pepper
2 lbs. Alaska Snow crab clusters, thawed if
   necessary

Instructions:

Combine all ingredients except salt, lemon pepper, and snow crab in a food processor or blender and process briefly until finely chopped. Season to taste with salt and lemon pepper. Pour into serving bowl.
On a barbecue, 5-inches from coals, place crab. Grill 5 minutes or until thoroughly heated. Serve immediately, using Salsa Verde as dipping sauce.

Equivalent to:

2 Servings
Each =
3 oz protein
3/4 oil
1/2 cup raw
   vegetable

172 calories
5 g total fat
< 1 g saturated
101 mg
cholesterol
682 mg sodium

CRAB CAKES

Ingredients:

2 egg whites
1 cup crab (8 oz)
1/2 tsp Worcestershire sauce
1 tsp parsley
Dash tabasco
1/4 tsp dry mustard
1 T light mayonnaise
2 Ryvita Crackers, crushed
1/8 tsp lemon pepper

Instructions:

In a bowl, whip egg, add other ingredients and mix together well. Form into patties.
In a skillet sprayed with Pam, fry until browned, spray top of cakes with Pam, turn and brown on other side.

Diet Center Dressings can be used as dipping sauce for the cakes, 1000 Island or Dijon Herb are suggested choices.

Equivalent to:

2 Servings
Each=
21/2 oz protein
1 1/2 oil
1/2 starch

212 calories
6.5 g total fat
1 g saturated
103 mg cholesterol
481 mg sodium

SEA SCALLOPS CARTAGENA

Ingredients:

8 oz fresh sea scallops
2 T lime juice
1 1/2 tsp chopped fresh parsley
2 tsp chopped fresh shallot
1 tsp basil
1 tomato, peeled and diced
1/2 red pepper, diced
1/4 tsp lemon pepper
1/8 tsp salt
1 tsp diet soft tub margarine

Instructions:

Preheat barbecue to medium.
Place all ingredients on double sheet of foil, sprayed with Pam. Cover with single sheet and seal edges shut.
Place foil packet on hot grill. Cover and cook 8 minutes.
Serve over hot cooked rice.

Equivalent to:

2 Servings
Each =
2 oz protein
1/2 cup cooked
vegetable
1/4 oil

137 calories
2 g total fat
< 1 g saturated
38 mg
cholesterol
354 mg sodium

SEAFOOD FETTUCINI ALFREDO

Ingredients:

8 oz shrimp, shelled and deveined
8 oz crabmeat
1 small can mushrooms, sliced and drained
1 package Knorr Alfredo Pasta Sauce Mix
1 1/2 cups skim milk
1 T reduced calorie soft tub margarine
1/2 tsp parsley, chopped
1 T Parmesan cheese, grated
2 cups fettucini, cooked

Equivalent to:

4 Servings
Each =
2 oz protein
1/3 dairy
1 starch
3/4 oil

322 calories
6 g total fat
1.3 g saturated
143 mg
cholesterol
799 mg sodium

Instructions:

In a saucepan, whisk 1 1/2 cups skim milk and Alfredo sauce mix until blended. Add 1 T margarine. Stirring constantly, bring to a boil over medium-high heat. Reduce heat and simmer, stirring constantly, 2 minutes.
Add shrimp, crab, and mushrooms.
Toss seafood and sauce with pasta, sprinkle with Parmesan cheese and parsley and serve.

SEAFOOD MIX

Ingredients:

1/2 clove garlic, smashed and chopped
5 oz crabmeat, well drained
6 oz scallops
5 oz shrimp, peeled and deveined
2 cups canned tomatoes, drained and chopped
1 T tomato paste
1 tsp chopped parsley
1/4 tsp lemon pepper
1/4 tsp salt
2 oz fat-free mozzarella, grated

Instructions:

In a large skillet sprayed with Pam, saute garlic, scallops and shrimp; season well. Add crabmeat, cook 3-4 minutes over medium-low heat. Add tomatoes, simmer 2-3 minutes.
Stir in tomato paste and cook 1 minute over medium heat. Pour mixture into large oven proof dish. Top with parsley and cheese. Broil in oven until cheese melts.

Equivalent to:

4 Servings
Each=
2 1/2 oz protein
1/2 oil
1/2 cup cooked vegetable

118 calories
1.4 g total fat
< 1 g saturated
88 mg cholesterol
546 mg sodium

FISH FILLETS PRIMAVERA

Ingredients:

8 oz halibut or orange roughy fillets
1/4 tsp lemon pepper
1/8 tsp garlic herb seasoning
1/4 tsp Teton Valley Nice n Spicy or Season All
1/4 tsp basil leaves
Pam
Lemon juice
1/2 cup broccoli florets
1/2 cup cauliflower florets
1/2 cup cut carrots
1/2 cup mushrooms, sliced
1/2 cup celery, diced
2 oz fat-free jack cheese, grated

Equivalent to:

2 Servings
Each =
31/2 oz protein
1 cup cooked
vegetable
1/2 dairy

204 calories
2.9 g total fat
< 1 g saturated
41 mg
cholesterol
601 mg sodium

Instructions:

Heat oven to 450 degrees, place fish in a baking dish sprayed with Pam. Sprinkle with lemon juice and seasonings. Bake for 5 minutes.

Meanwhile, in a large skillet sprayed with Pam, add all ingredients except cheese.

Instructions Continued:

Cook vegetables until crisp-tender, about 5-7 minutes. Spoon vegetables over fish fillets, sprinkle with cheese and return to the oven and bake an additional 10-15 minutes or until fish flakes easily with a fork.

POACHED FISH WITH DILL SAUCE

Ingredients:

*7 oz white fish fillets (halibut, sole, orange
  roughy)
3/4 cup chicken broth
1 T lemon juice
1 T snipped fresh dill or 1 tsp dried dill
1/8 tsp salt
1/4 tsp lemon pepper
1/8 tsp garlic herb seaoning
1 T cornstarch*

Instructions:

Equivalent to:

2 Servings
Each =
3 oz protein
1 additional
food

157 calories
3.2 g total fat
< 1 g saturated
32 mg
cholesterol
239 mg sodium

In a skillet heat chicken broth to a boil; reduce
heat. Add fish, cover and simmer 6-8 minutes
or until fish flakes easily with fork. Carefully
remove fish with slotted spoon to heated
serving plate.

Mix cornstarch into small amount of cooled
chicken broth, add to skillet with chicken broth
and add other ingredients. Bring to a boil and
cook until slightly thickened. Spoon sauce over
fish.

Garnish with fresh dill.

PAN FRIED FISH

Ingredients:

2 tsp diet soft tub margarine
1 egg white, whipped
2 T skim milk
8 oz fish fillets
4 T fine seasoned bread crumbs
1/8 tsp garlic herb seasoning
1/4 tsp Oriental seasoning
1/4 tsp salt
1/8 tsp lemon pepper

Instructions:

In a small bowl, combine egg and milk. Dip fish in egg mixture; coat fish in cracker crumbs with seasonings added. In a skillet melt margarine over medium heat, cook fish about 5-7 minutes or until golden brown and fish flakes easily with a fork. Spray fish with Pam before turning so crumbs will brown. Serve with lemon slices.

Equivalent to:

2 Servings
Each=
31/2 oz protein
1 starch

201 calories
5 g total fat
<1 g saturated
37 mg cholesterol
511 mg sodium

POACHED FISH

Ingredients:

1 pound fish
1/2 tsp salt
2 pepper corns or 1/2 tsp lemon pepper
1 stalk celery, cut into pieces
1/2 carrot, cut into pieces
2 slices lemon
1 bay leaf
1/2 medium onion, sliced
2 cups water

Instructions:

Equivalent to:

4 Servings
Each =
31/2 oz protein

132 calories
2.6 g total fat
<1 g saturated
36 mg
cholesterol
362 mg sodium

Wrap fish in cheesecloth for ease in transferring after cooking (optional). In a large skillet, combine all ingredients except fish. Heat to boiling; simmer covered about 10 minutes. Carefully place fish in liquid, simmer covered about 10 to 12 minutes or until fish flakes easily. If liquid does not cover fish, turn fish over after 7 minutes for even cooking. Lift fish from liquid, carefully remove cheesecloth and place on platter. Serve with lemon slices.

DOUBLE FISH KABOBS

Ingredients:

4 oz shrimp, peeled and deveined
4 oz halibut, cubed
Marinade:
1/4 cup unsweetened apple juice
1 tsp lime juice
*1/2 tsp chopped ginger, or 1/4 tsp ground
  ginger*
1/4 tsp garlic herb seasoning
1/8 tsp crushed chilies
1 tsp low-sodium soy sauce
1/2 tsp oil

Instructions:

Preheat barbecue to high. Mix marinade ingredients together in bowl. Place shrimp and halibut in marinade for 30 minutes. Thread on skewers.
Grill on hot grill with cover for 8 minutes. Turn twice, basting occasionally.

Equivalent to:

2 Servings
Each =
2 oz protein
Scant oil

141 calories
3.4 g total fat
< 1 g saturated
104 mg cholesterol
128 mg sodium

FISH ROLLS WITH ASPARAGUS

Ingredients:

1 pound flounder fillets or orange roughy
1/2 pound fresh asparagus, cut into 4-inch
    spears, or 1 (10 oz) frozen asparagus spears
2 cups sliced fresh mushrooms
1 cup V-8 Juice
1 T fresh dill weed or 1/2 tsp dried
1-2 T cornstarch
1/4 tsp lemon pepper
1/2 tsp Teton Valley Nice n Spicy or Season All

Equivalent to:

4 Servings
Each =
31/2 oz protein
3/4 cup cooked
vegetable
1 additional
food

148 calories
1.8 g total fat
<1 g saturated
59 mg
cholesterol
316 mg sodium

Instructions:

Divide asparagus evenly among fish fillets. Roll up fillets jelly-roll fashion; secure with toothpicks, if necessary, set aside.

Spray 10-inch non-stick skillet with Pam, over medium heat cook mushrooms until lightly browned.

In a small bowl stir V-8 juice, seasonings and cornstarch until smooth. Gradually add to skillet. Cook over medium heat until mixture boils and thickens. Place fish rolls in sauce. Reduce heat to low, cover and simmer 15 minutes or until fish flakes easily when tested with a fork. Remove toothpicks before serving.

SKILLET FISH ITALIANO

Seafood

Ingredients:

1 small onion, sliced
1 pound fish fillets, fresh or frozen, thawed
1/4 cup fresh lemon juice
1/2 tsp Italian seasoning
1/2 tsp lemon pepper
1/4 tsp salt
2 cups sliced zucchini
1 cup fresh mushrooms, sliced
1/2 cup chopped tomatoes
4 oz fat-free swiss cheese

Instructions:

In a large skillet sprayed with Pam, cook onion until tender. Add fish fillets, lemon, seasonings, zucchini and mushrooms. Cover and simmer 10 minutes. Top with tomato and cheese; cover and simmer 2 minutes or until cheese melts. Serve immediately.

Equivalent to:

31/2 oz protein
1 oil
1 cup cooked vegetables
1/2 dairy

201 calories
2.9 g total fat
< 1 g saturated
41 mg cholesterol
645 mg sodium

SEAFOOD CURRY

Ingredients:

1 small onion, chopped
1 clove garlic, minced
1 tsp minced fresh ginger
1 T curry powder
1/2 tsp lemon pepper
1/4 tsp salt
1 1/2 cup low-fat buttermilk
6 ounces crabmeat or shelled shrimp
Fresh lemon juice, to taste
Lemon and lime wedges, (garnish)
1 cup cooked rice

Equivalent to:

3 Servings:
Each=
2 oz protein
1/2 dairy
1 starch

216 calories
2.3 g total fat
<1 g saturated
55 mg
cholesterol
480 mg sodium

Instructions:

In a skillet sprayed with Pam over low heat, add onion, garlic, ginger and cook 10 minutes. Add buttermilk and seasonings, simmer gently for 10 minutes. Add shrimp and crab, stir to blend, warm thoroughly. Add lemon juice to taste. Spoon curry over rice, surround with lemon wedges and serve.

FISH CREOLE

Seafood

Ingredients:

1 pound fish fillets
1/3 cup chopped onion
1/4 cup chopped celery
2 T finely chopped green pepper
1/2 tsp sweetener
1/4 tsp oregano leaves
1/8 tsp pepper
1 cup stewed tomatoes, cut in pieces
1/2 tsp Teton Valley Nice n Spicy or Season All

Instructions:

In a microwave safe dish sprayed with Pam, cook onion, celery, and green pepper for 3-4 minutes or until tender. Add sweetener, seasonings and tomatoes.
Arrange fish in a dish sprayed with Pam, placing thickest pieces on outside edge of dish. Spoon sauce over fish. Microwave on high for 5-7 minutes or until fish flakes easily with a fork, rearranging fish once halfway through cooking.

Equivalent to:

4 Servings
Each=
3 1/2 oz protein
1/4 cup cooked
vegetable

123 calories
1.5 g total fat
< 1 g saturated
59 mg
cholesterol
212 mg sodium

HADDOCK TOPPED WITH CHEESE

Ingredients:

8 oz haddock fillets
1 T lime or lemon juice
3 green onions, chopped
1/4 tsp fennel seed
1/4 tsp tarragon
1/4 tsp lemon pepper
1/4 tsp salt
Paprika, to taste
1 oz fat-free mozzarella cheese, grated

Instructions:

Equivalent to:

2 Servings
Each =
31/2 oz protein
1 dairy

138 calories
1 g total fat
< 1 g saturated
67 mg
cholesterol
523 mg sodium

Spray a microwave safe casserole with Pam, add fish, lime juice, and onions. Sprinkle with seasonings, cover and microwave about 3 minutes. Turn fillets over; cover and cook 1 minute more, or until fish is done.

Transfer fish to a serving platter, adjust seasonings, top with cheese; microwave 1 minute.

CAJUN CATFISH

Ingredients:

7 oz catfish fillets
1/4 cup bread crumbs
1/2 tsp cajun seasoning
1/4 tsp pepper
1/4 tsp salt
2 tsp diet soft tub margarine

Instructions:

Melt margarine in a skillet over medium-high heat. Dip fillets in bread crumbs and place in hot skillet. Brown on one side, about 4 minutes, turn and brown other side.
Serve with fresh lemon slices.

Equivalent to:

2 Servings
Each =
3 oz protein
1/2 starch
1/2 oil

184 calories
7.3 g total fat
1.7 g saturated
54 mg cholesterol
596 mg sodium

MARINATED TROUT FILLETS

Ingredients:

2 trout fillets, (8 oz)
1 package Diet Center Italian Dressing or 2 T
  low-fat Italian dressing
1/2 tsp Teton Valley Nice n Spicy or Season
  All
1/4 tsp salt
1/4 tsp lemon pepper

Instructions:

Equivalent to:

2 Servings
Each =
31/2 oz protein
1/2 oil

165 calories
5 g total fat
<1 g saturated
73 mg
cholesterol
713 mg sodium

Wash fish fillet and pat dry. Place in a dish and pour dressings over fish. Sprinkle with seasonings. Cover and refrigerate 1 hour. Place fish on barbecue and cook over med-hot coals just until fish turns white and flakes with a fork; basting with marinade. This only takes about 5 minutes on a gas barbecue, No need to turn the fish if you have a cover for your barbecue.

Oven method:
Cover and bake at 350 degrees for 15 minutes or until fish tests done.

BLACKENED RED SNAPPER

Ingredients:

8 oz red snapper fillets
1 tsp olive oil
Cajun Seasoning:
1 T paprika
1/4 tsp salt
1 tsp onion powder
1 tsp garlic powder
1/2 tsp cayenne pepper
3/4 tsp black pepper
1/2 tsp dried thyme leaves
1/2 tsp dried oregano leaves

Instructions:

Sprinkle cajun seasoning on both sides of fillets. Heat a heavy skillet until hot, add oil and swirl to coat pan. Place fillets in hot skillet; do not crowd. Cook 10 minutes for one-inch fillets (5 minutes on each side). Don't over cook. Adjust cooking time to thickness of fillet.

Equivalent to:

2 Servings
Each =
31/2 oz protein
1/2 oil

154 calories
4.5 g total fat
<1 g saturated
41 mg cholesterol
339 mg sodium

GRILLED TROUT WITH TARRAGON SAUCE

Ingredients:

8 oz trout fillets

Tarragon Cream Sauce:
4 tsp oil
1/4 cup plain non-fat yogurt
1 T skim milk
2 tsp red wine vinegar
2 tsp finely chopped parsley
1/2 clove garlic minced
1/4 tsp lemon pepper
1/4 tsp Oriental seasoning

Equivalent to:

2 Servings
Each=
31/2 oz protein
1 oil
(sauce)

205 calories
7 g total fat
1 g saturated
73 mg
cholesterol
369 mg sodium

Instructions:

Grill fish on a piece of aluminum foil sprayed with Pam. Cook over medium-high heat, turning once, about 3-4 minutes or until fish flakes easily when tested with a fork.
Sauce:
In a bowl, combine all ingredients; mix well with a wire whisk.
Serve cool. Makes about 1/3 cup.

GRILLED ORANGE ROUGHY

Seafood

Ingredients:

8 oz orange roughy fillet
1/4 small onion, cut in slices
Lemon slices
1/8 tsp lemon pepper
1/8 tsp garlic herb seasoning
1/8 tsp salt

Instructions:

On a piece of aluminum foil sprayed with Pam, layer fish, onions, lemon and seasonings. Wrap foil up and place on grill over medium-high heat for approximately 5-6 minutes per side.

Equivalent to:

2 Servings
Each=
31/2 oz protein

153 calories
7 g total fat
<1 g saturated
22 mg cholesterol
218 mg sodium

ORANGE ROUGHY WITH DILL

Ingredients:

8 oz orange roughy fillets
6 T flour or fine bread crumbs
1 egg white, whipped
1 tsp diet soft tub margarine
1/4 tsp dill weed
1/8 tsp lemon pepper
1/8 tsp garlic powder
1/8 tsp salt
Dash of Teton Valley Nice n Spicy or Season
   All

Instructions:

Equivalent to:

2 Servings
Each =
31/2 oz protein
1 starch
1/2 oil

197 calories
9 g total fat
< 1 g saturated
23 mg
cholesterol
475 mg sodium

Whip egg white, add seasonings to flour or crumbs. Dip fish fillet in egg wash then crumbs. Melt margarine in a skillet and swirl to coat pan. Cook fish on medium heat until browned on one side, turn continue to cook until fish tests done, about 4 minutes per side.

ORANGE ROUGHY WITH VEGETABLES

341

Seafood

Ingredients:

1 pound orange roughy fillets
1 small zucchini
1 small yellow crookneck squash
1/2 small onion
2 T lemon juice
1/4 tsp garlic herb seasoning
1/4 tsp dill
1/4 tsp salt
1/4 tsp lemon pepper

Instructions:

Julienne vegetables. Arrange in the center of a plate. Place the orange roughy around vegetables, turning thin ends under or rolling fillets, if necessary. Drizzle fish and vegetables with lemon juice. Cover with plastic wrap, vent. Microwave on high 4-5 minutes until thickest portion of fish is almost opaque when tested with a fork. Let stand 5 minutes to finish cooking. Drain and season to taste.

Equivalent to:

4 Servings
Each =
31/2 oz protein
1/2 cup cooked
vegetable

166 calories
7 g total fat
<1 g saturated
22 mg
cholesterol
221 mg sodium

MICROWAVE HALIBUT

Ingredients:

1 (4 oz) halibut fillet
lemon juice
1/8 tsp salt
Dash herb garlic seasoning
1/4 tsp dill
Lemon Pepper

Instructions:

Spray a microwave safe dish with Pam and place halibut on it. Squeeze lemon juice over fish and cover with plastic wrap. Microwave on high for 1 1/2 minutes. Let stand for a minute and check for doneness. Fish should no longer look translucent. Sprinkle with seasonings and serve with lemon wedges.
Other fish may be prepared in this same manner.

Equivalent to:

1 Serving
Each =
3 1/2 oz
protein

124 calories
2.6 g total fat
< 1 g saturated
36 mg
cholesterol
350 mg sodium

ORANGE-GINGER HALIBUT

Ingredients:

8 oz halibut steak
1/2 tsp grated ginger root or 1/4 tsp ground
    ginger
1/4 cup chicken broth
1/4 cup orange juice concentrate
1/2 tsp Crystal Lite Citrus Drink Mix
1 tsp low-sodium soy sauce
1 green onion, sliced

Instructions:

Place fish in a single layer on a broiler pan
sprayed with Pam. Spray fish with Pam also,
then sprinkle with seasonings. Broil fish 4
inches from heat for 6-8 minutes or until fish
flakes easily when tested with a fork. Turn fish
once.

In a small pan stir together ginger, chicken
broth, orange juice, citrus drink mix (dry) and
soy sauce. Stir in green onion. Heat until
warm. Place fish on a serving platter and top
with sauce.

Equivalent to:

2 Servings
Each =
31/2 oz protein

158 calories
3 g total fat
<1 g saturated
36 mg
cholesterol
91 mg sodium

TUNA-STUFFED SHELLS IN DILL SAUCE

Ingredients:

12 jumbo shell macaroni, cooked
1 stalk celery, finely chopped
1 small onion, finely chopped
2 slices bread
2 tsp olive oil
2 cups skim milk
2 T flour
4 oz fat-free cheddar cheese
1/4 tsp garlic herb seasoning
1/2 tsp dill weed
2 packets Diet Center Ranch Dressing or 4 T
   low-fat Ranch dressing
12 oz canned tuna, in water, drained

Instructions:

In a skillet, saute onion and celery in oil until tender. Remove to medium bowl. In same skillet over medium heat, heat milk, flour, and 1/4 tsp salt, to boiling, stirring until mixture thickens slightly. Stir cheese, dill and seasoning into sauce until blended. Pour sauce into a large baking dish. Into bowl with celery mixture, stir bread crumbs, dressing and tuna. Fill cooked shells with tuna mixture; arrange filled shells in sauce, in one layer. Spoon some of sauce over

Equivalent to:

6 Servings
Each =
1/3 oz protein
1 starch
2/3 oil
2/3 dairy
1 additional
food

305 calories
5.3 g total fat
< 1 g saturated
37 mg
cholesterol
665 mg sodium

LEMON PARSLEY FILLET OF SOLE

Ingredients:

1 pound sole fillets
2 T fresh lemon juice
1/2 tsp grated lemon rind
1 T light mayonnaise
1 T plain non-fat yogurt
1/2 tsp Teton Valley Nice n Spicy or Season All
3 T chopped fresh parsley
1/4 tsp garlic herb seasoning
1/4 tsp lemon pepper
1/4 tsp dill
1/4 tsp salt
Sliced lemon for garnish

Instructions:

Mix together the mayonnaise, seasonings and 1/2 of parsley.

In a baking dish sprayed with Pam, place fish in a single layer. Cover the fish with the mayonnaise mixture. Place dish on the lowest rack of a preheated 450 degree broiler and cook for 10 minutes.

Serve garnished with the lemon slices and the remaining parsley.

Equivalent to:

4 Servings
Each =
31/2 oz protein
1 oil

137 calories
3.9 g total fat
<1 g saturated
61 mg cholesterol
260 mg sodium

PAN FRIED SOLE WITH SHRIMP

Ingredients:

8 oz sole fillets
4 oz shrimp, peeled, deveined and cut in half
1/8 tsp paprika
6 T fine bread crumbs
1 cup fresh mushrooms, quartered
1 1/2 tsp chopped chives
1/2 tsp lemon pepper
1/4 tsp salt
Juice of one lemon

Instructions:

Preheat oven to 150 degrees.
Mix seasonings with flour or bread crumbs, dredge fish in crumbs and shake off excess.
In a skillet sprayed well with Pam, add fish and cook 2 minutes over medium-high heat. Spray top of fillet with Pam. Turn fillets over; season and continue cooking 2 minutes. Remove fish from pan and place in oven to keep warm.
Place remaining ingredients in pan and cook 3-4 minutes over medium-high heat. Serve with sole.

Equivalent to:

3 Servings
Each=
31/2 oz protein
1/2 starch
1/3 cup cooked
vegetable

173 calories
2.5 g total fat
< 1 g saturated
117 mg
cholesterol
420 mg sodium

SOLE AU GRATIN

Ingredients:

1 pound sole fillets
1/4 tsp fennel seed
3-4 fresh mint leaves
1/4 pound mushrooms, sliced thick
3/4 cup chicken broth
2 T lemon juice
1/2 tsp lemon pepper
Salt, to taste
1 T cornstarch
3 oz fat-free cheddar cheese

Instructions:

In a skillet sprayed with Pam, add fish, fennel seed, mint, mushrooms and lemon juice; season well. Add chicken broth; cover and bring to a boil. Turn fillets over, shut off heat and let stand 1 minute; remove fish. Mix a small amount of chicken broth with cornstarch to make a paste, add to broth and mushrooms, mix well and season. Cook 6 minutes over low heat. In a casserole dish, place fish. Pour sauce over fish and top with cheese. Broil in oven until cheese is melted.

Equivalent to:

4 Servings
Each =
31/4 oz protein
1/2 cup cooked
vegetable
3/4 dairy

146 calories
1.3 g total fat
< 1 g saturated
63 mg
cholesterol
414 mg sodium

FLOUNDER WITH TOMATOES

Ingredients:

1 (8 oz) flounder fillet
1 large tomato, cubed
1/3 onion, chopped
1/2 tsp low-sodium soy sauce
1 tsp lemon juice
1/4 tsp garlic herb seasoning

Instructions:

Preheat barbecue to high heat. Place ingredients on triple sheet of foil sprayed with Pam. Cover with single sheet and seal edges well. Place on hot grill and cover. Cook 15 minutes turning once.

Oven Method: Bake at 350 degrees for 15-20 minutes, depending on thickness of fillet.

Equivalent to:

2 Servings:
Each =
31/2 oz protein
1/2 cup cooked
vegetable

122 calories
1.5 g total fat
< 1 g saturated
59 mg
cholesterol
28 mg sodium

SHRIMP & MUSHROOM STUFFED SOLE

Ingredients:

1 package or 2 T low-fat Italian dressing
1 cup thinly sliced mushrooms
1/4 cup sliced green onions
4 oz uncooked medium shrimp, cleaned and
  coarsely chopped
1/4 tsp thyme leaves
1/4 tsp salt
1/8 tsp lemon pepper
1/8 tsp Oriental seasoning
2 Sesame Ryvita Cracker, crushed
8 oz sole or flounder fillets

Instructions:

Preheat oven to 400 degrees. In a skillet sprayed with Pam, heat Italian dressing and cook mushrooms and green onions over medium heat, stirring occasionally for 3 minutes. Add shrimp and cook, stirring, 2 minutes or until shrimp turn pink. Stir in seasonings and bread crumbs.

In a shallow baking dish, sprayed with Pam, evenly divide shrimp mixture into 2 mounds. Place 1 fillet over each mound; brush with more dressing.

Bake 10-15 minutes or until fish flakes.

Equivalent to:

2 Servings
Each=
5 oz protein
1/2 oil
1/2 starch
1/2 cup cooked
vegetable

217 calories
4.5 g total fat
<1 g saturated
146 mg
cholesterol
559 mg sodium

BARBECUED HALIBUT

Ingredients:

4 oz fish fillet
Seasonings, to taste
Lemon juice

Instructions:

Spray a sheet of tin foil large enough for the fish with Pam. Squeeze lemon juice over fish (any fish can way).

Cook with lid of the barbecue down if you have one, to smoke the fish. Cook over medium-high heat about 4-6 minutes, you may turn fish if you wish, however, with the lid down this isn't necessary.

Season to taste very last. Serve hot with lemon wedges.

Equivalent to:

1 Serving
Each =
31/2 oz protein

125 calories
2.6 g total fat
< 1 g saturated
36 mg
cholesterol
62 mg sodium

BAKED RED SNAPPER

Ingredients:

1 pound red snapper fillets
1 red bell pepper, cut julienne
1 green bell pepper, cut julienne
1 small yellow crookneck squash sliced
1 cup mushrooms, sliced
Lemon juice
1/4 tsp Oriental seasoning
1/2 tsp Teton Valley Nice N Spicy or Season All
1/8 tsp lemon pepper
1/4 tsp salt
1/4 tsp garlic herb seasoning

Instructions:

Place fish in a baking dish sprayed with Pam.
Squeeze lemon juice over fish and sprinkle with
seasonings.
Cut vegetables and saute in a skillet spayed
with Pam, until just crisp-tender, about 3-4
minutes. Sprinkle with seasonings.
Arrange vegetables on top of fish, cover with
foil and bake 20 minutes or until done, in a 350
degree oven.

Equivalent to:

4 Servings
Each =
31/2 oz protein
1 cup cooked
vegetable

132 calories
1.8 g total fat
< 1 g saturated
41 mg
cholesterol
196 mg sodium

BARBECUED SALMON

Ingredients:

8 oz salmon steaks or fillet
2 tsp oil
1 T fresh lemon juice
1/2 tsp Worcestershire sauce
1/4 tsp lemon pepper

Instructions:

Thaw salmon steaks if frozen.
In a bowl combine oil, lemon juice and Worcestershire sauce. Brush salmon steaks with sauce.
Place steaks on grill and cook over medium-hot coals 5-9 minutes or until lightly browned. Baste steaks with mixture and turn; grill 5-9 minutes longer, basting often until fish flakes easily when tested with fork.
(Cooking time is dependent on thickness of salmon).

Equivalent to:

2 Servings
Each =
31/2 oz protein
1 oil

184 calories
9 g total fat
1.5 g saturated
43 mg
cholesterol
65 mg sodium

LEMON POACHED SALMON

Ingredients:

2 cups water
2 T sliced green onions
1/2 lemon, sliced
1/4 tsp salt
1/8 tsp lemon pepper
8 oz salmon steak
Lemon wedges and fresh dill, if desired

Instructions:

In a large skillet, combine water, onion, lemon slices, seasonings. Bring to a boil; simmer 5 minutes to blend flavors. Add salmon. Cover; simmer 7-10 minutes or until salmon flakes easily with a fork. Lift salmon out of liquid onto a serving platter; garnish with lemon and dill.

Equivalent to:

2 Servings
Each =
31/2 oz protein

168 calories
6.6 g total fat
1 g saturated
43 mg cholesterol
340 mg sodium

CURRIED GRILLED MAHIMAHI

Ingredients:

1 pound mahimahi or swordfish fillets
Limey Red Onions:
1 1/2 cup red onion, thinly sliced
6 T fresh lime juice
1 tsp sweetener
1/4 cup cilantro

Curry Rub:
1 1/2 tsp cumin
1 1/2 tsp paprika
3/4 tsp ground coriander
3/4 tsp ginger
3/4 tsp cinnamon
1/2 tsp salt
1/4 tsp tumeric
1/4 tsp dry mustard
1/8 tsp ground red pepper

Equivalent to:

4 Serving
Each=
31/2 oz protein
Scant vegetable

124 calories
1 g total fat
<1 g saturated
89 mg
cholesterol
392 mg sodium

Instructions:

To make Limey Red Onions: mix all ingredients in a small bowl and let stand 30 minutes.
Combine ingredients in a small bowl for Curry Rub. Rub all over fish. Grill over med-hot coals for 5 minutes per side. Top with sauce.

DILL MARINATED SALMON STEAK

Ingredients:

2 T lemon juice
1/2 tsp oil
1 tsp dill weed
1/8 tsp garlic herb seasoning
1/4 tsp salt
1/8 tsp lemon pepper
8 oz salmon steak, cut 1-inch thick

Instructions:

In a small bowl, combine all ingredients except salmon steak; mix well. Pour over fish in a shallow non-metal container or plastic bag, turning to coat both sides. Cover, marinate 1 hour at room temperature, or several hours in refrigerator. Remove; *place on a sheet of heavy-duty foil and wrap securely.
Barbecue on grill 10-15 minutes or until fish flakes easily with a fork, turning once.

* May omit the foil and place directly on grill to get the flavor of the barbecue. Make sure grill is well seasoned so fish won't stick.

Equivalent to:

2 Servings
Each =
31/2 oz protein
1/4 oil

177 calories
7.8 g total fat
1.4 g saturated
43 mg cholesterol
199 mg sodium

BAKED SEA BASS

Ingredients:

8 oz sea bass fillets
1/4 tsp lemon pepper
1/4 tsp garlic herb seasoning
1/4 tsp salt

Instructions:

Spray a sheet of tin foil with Pam. Place fillet in middle, squeeze lemon over fish. Season to taste with seasonings. Place lemon slices on top of fillet, then seal foil around fish.

Bake in a 350 degree oven for about 30 minutes.

(This time is correct for a 1" thick fillet).

Equivalent to:

2 Servings
Each =
31/2 oz protein

124 calories
3.6 g total fat
< 1 g saturated
58 mg
cholesterol
676 mg sodium

LEMON SWORDFISH

Ingredients:

1 pound swordfish steaks
2 tsp grated lemon peel
1/2 cup fresh lemon juice
2 tsp oil
3 T chopped fresh parsley
1 T prepared horseradish
1 clove garlic, minced
3/4 tsp dried thyme, crushed
1/2 tsp salt
1/2 tsp lemon pepper
1 bay leaf

Instructions:

In a shallow dish, combine all ingredients except fish. Add swordfish; turn to coat with marinade. Cover and refrigerate at least 2 hours, turning fish occasionally.
Drain fish reserve marinade.
Grill swordfish on uncovered grill, over medium-hot coals about 7 minutes, basting lightly with marinade. Carefully turn swordfish and grill 5-6 minutes longer or until fish flakes easily when tested with fork, basting lightly with marinade.

Equivalent to:

4 Servings
Each=
31/2 oz protein
1/2 oil

168 calories
7 g total fat
1.5 g saturated
44 mg
cholesterol
399 mg sodium

SWORDFISH WITH DILL-MUSTARD SAUCE

Ingredients:

*1 package Diet Center Italian Dressing or 2 T
  low-fat Italian dressing*
8 oz swordfish steaks
1 T white cooking wine, optional
1/8 tsp lemon pepper
1 1/2 tsp snipped dill or 1/2 tsp dried
1 1/2 tsp Dijon-style mustard
1/4 cup non-fat plain yogurt

Instructions:

Equivalent to:

2 Servings
Each =
31/2 oz protein
1/2 oil

183 calories
6.7 g total fat
1.4 g saturated
44 mg
cholesterol
255 mg sodium

In a skillet sprayed with Pam, heat Italian dressing and cook fish over medium heat, turning once, 8 minutes or until fish flakes. Remove to serving platter and keep warm.
Into skillet, add wine (optional), pepper, dill and mustard. Bring to a boil; then simmer, stirring occasionally 8 minutes. Stir in yogurt and heat 1 minute.
Serve over fish.

ZESTY GRILLED SWORDFISH

Seafood

Ingredients:

8 oz swordfish fillets, boned
1 tsp low-sodium soy sauce
2 T orange juice concentrate
1 tsp oil
1 tsp tomato paste, thinned with water
1 tsp chopped fresh parsley
1/4 tsp herb garlic seasoning
1/4 tsp fresh lemon juice
1/8 tsp dried basil, crumbled
1/8 tsp lemon pepper
2/3 cup cooked rice

Instructions:

Arrange fish in a shallow baking dish sprayed with Pam.

Combine all remaining ingredients except rice in small bowl and mix well. Pour over fish, turning to coat well. Let stand at room temperature, turning once, 30 minutes.

Preheat broiler or prepare barbecue grill. Broil or grill fish 4 inches form heat source for 6-8 minutes. Baste with marinade, cook 6-8 minutes longer or until tests done. Serve over rice.

Equivalent to:

2 Servings
Each =
31/2 oz protein
1/2 oil
1 starch

247 calories
5.9 g total fat
1.4 g saturated
44 mg cholesterol
117 mg sodium

NOTES

Side Dishes

FRIED POTATOES & ONIONS

Side Dish

Ingredients:

2 medium potatoes
1/2 small onion, chopped
1/8 tsp lemon pepper
1/2 tsp Season All
1/4 tsp salt
2 tsp diet soft tub margarine

Instructions:

Scrub potatoes, pierce with a knife. Cook in a microwave on high about 8 minutes. Let cool, then peel (optional). In a heated skillet over medium-high heat, add margarine and swirl to coat pan. Slice potatoes thin, add chopped onion; continue cooking until crispy-fried, turning often. Season to taste.

Equivalent to:

4 Servings
Each =
1 starch
1/4 oil

71 calories
1 g total fat
< 1 g saturated
0 cholesterol
170 mg sodium

TWICE BAKED POTATOES

Ingredients:

2 medium baked potatoes
1/2 cup non-fat cottage cheese
2 oz fat-free cheddar cheese, shredded
1/8 tsp garlic herb seasoning
1/4 tsp Teton Valley Nice n Spicy or Season All
1/8 tsp lemon pepper
1/4 tsp salt
1-2 T skim milk
1 tsp diet soft tub margarine

Instructions:

Equivalent to:

2 Servings
Each =
1 starch
1/2 oil
1 dairy

204 calories
1 g total fat
< 1 g saturated
7 mg
cholesterol
611 mg sodium

Bake potatoes and cool slightly. Cut lengthwise and scoop out potato, leaving skin intact.
In a bowl, beat potato, seasonings, margarine, cottage cheese and skim milk together until smooth. Fill potato skins with potato mixture, top with cheese. Place in oven or microwave and heat until potatoes are warmed through and cheese melts.

POTATO CHIPS

Ingredients:

2 potatoes, thinly sliced
1/8 tsp salt
Teton Valley Nice n Spicy, Season All or Molly
*   McButter Sour Cream or Cheese Flavoring*

Instructions:

Slice unpeeled, raw potatoes very thin (use a cheese slicer, food processor or salad shooter). Place on a thick microwave safe plate sprayed with Pam. Sprinkle with selected flavor of seasoning. Microwave for 7-8 minutes, (check at 1-minute intervals after 4 minutes, because of the vast difference in microwave cooking temperatures).

Oven Method:
Sprinkle chips with seasonings. Bake on a cookie sheet sprayed with Pam, for 15-20 minutes at 350 degrees.

Equivalent to:

4 Servings
Each =
1 starch

44 calories
< 1 g total fat
< 1 g saturated
0 cholesterol
147 mg sodium

363

Side Dish

SKILLET POTATOES

Ingredients:

2 cups cubed potatoes
1/2 cup carrots, cut in julienne stirps
1/2 cup sliced celery
1/2 cup chopped onion
1 clove garlic
1 cup chicken broth
1/4 tsp lemon pepper
1/2 tsp salt
Chopped fresh parsley

Instructions:

Equivalent to:

4 Servings
Each =
1 starch
1/4 cup cooked
vegetable

79 calories
< 1 g total fat
< 1 g saturated
< 1 mg
cholesterol
49 mg sodium

In a skillet sprayed with Pam and over medium heat, cook celery, onion and garlic until vegetables are tender, stirring occasionally.
Add broth, potatoes, carrots and seasonings to skillet. Heat to boiling; reduce heat to low. Cover; simmer 15 minutes or until potatoes are tender. Uncover; over medium heat simmer 5 minutes or until broth is slightly thickened, stirring often.
Sprinkle with parsley before serving.

NOODLES ROMANOFF

Ingredients:

2 cups wide egg noodles, cooked
1/2 cup non-fat cottage cheese
1/2 cup plain non-fat yogurt
1 T chopped green onions
1/8 tsp garlic herb seasoning
1/2 tsp Teton Valley Nice n Spicy or Season All
1/4 tsp salt
2 oz fat-free mozzarella cheese

Topping:
1 Sesame Ryvita cracker, crushed
2 tsp diet soft tub margarine
1 tsp fresh parsley
1/2 tsp Worcestershire sauce

Instructions:

Heat oven to 350 degrees. Cook noodles to desired doneness as directed on package. Drain; rinse with hot water. In a casserole sprayed with Pam, combine noodles, cottage cheese, yogurt, green onions and seasonings; mix well. Top with cheese. In a small bowl, combine all topping ingredients; mix well. Spoon over noodles. Bake 350 for 25-35 minutes.

Equivalent to:

4 Servings
Each =
1 1/2 starch
1/4 oil
1/3 dairy

178 calories
2 g total fat
< 1 g saturated
3 mg cholesterol
412 mg sodium

POTATOES AU GRATIN

Ingredients:

2 T diet soft tub margarine
3 T flour
1/2 cup low-sodium chicken broth
1/2 cup skim milk
1/2 tsp salt
1/4 tsp garlic powder
1/4 tsp pepper
1/2 tsp Teton Valley Nice n Spicy or Season All
1/3 small onion, chopped
1/2 cup buttermilk
4 oz fat-free cheddar cheese
3/4 cup fat-free sour cream
6 medium potatoes, peeled, cooked and grated

Equivalent to:

6 Servings
Each=
1/2 dairy
2 starch
1 additional
food

190 calories
2.5 g total fat
< 1 g saturated
4 mg
cholesterol
576 mg sodium

Instructions:

Melt margarine in a saucepan over medium heat. Add flour and stir for 1 minute; don't brown. Add chicken stock and skim milk. Using a whisk, stir mixture until it comes to a boil. Add seasonings, set aside and cool. In a skillet sprayed with Pam, saute onion, add to sauce. Stir in buttermilk, cheese and sour cream. Place potatoes in a 9 by 13 baking dish sprayed with Pam. Pour sauce over potatoes. Bake in a 350 oven for 35-45 minutes.

PASTA PRIMAVERA

Ingredients:

2 cups cooked noodles
1/4 cup onion, chopped
1/8 tsp garlic powder
1/2 cup broccoli florets, cut into 1-inch pieces
1/2 cup thinly sliced carrots
1/2 cup sliced mushrooms
1/8 tsp basil leaves
1/2 tsp Teton Valley Nice n Spicy or Season All
1/2 small zucchini, cut in 1-inch slices
4 oz fat-free jack cheese, shredded

Instructions:

In a large skillet sprayed with Pam, over medium heat, saute onions and garlic for 2 minutes. Add broccoli, carrots, mushrooms and seasonings. Cover and cook 3-4 minutes. Add zucchini, stir-fry 4 minutes or until vegetables are crisp-tender. Toss with cooked noodles. Sprinkle with cheese.

Equivalent to:

4 Servings
Each =
1 starch
3/4 cup cooked vegetable
1/2 dairy

177 calories
< 1 g total fat
< 1 g saturated
5 mg cholesterol
443 mg sodium

MACARONI AND CHEESE

Side Dish

Ingredients:

2 tsp diet soft tub margarine
1 cup low-fat buttermilk
4 oz fat-free cheddar cheese, grated
Dash of hot pepper sauce
2 cups macaroni, cooked
1/4 tsp lemon pepper
1/4 tsp salt

Instructions:

Equivalent to:

4 Servings
Each=
3/4 dairy
1 starch
1/4 oil

181 calories
2 g total fat
< 1 g saturated
7 mg
cholesterol
668 mg sodium

In a skillet melt margarine. Add other ingredients and simmer until sauce is slightly thickened. Season to taste.

SPANISH RICE

Ingredients:

2 cups cooked rice
1/2 green pepper, chopped
1/2 red pepper, chopped
1 /2 onion, chopped
1 hot chili pepper, seeded and chopped,
   (optional)
1 small can tomato paste
Water to thin tomato paste
1/2 tsp Teton Valley Nice n Spicy or Season All
1/2 tsp Mexican seasoning
1/4 tsp garlic powder

Instructions:

In a skillet sprayed with Pam, saute vegetables until done. Mix water into tomato paste to get consistency of tomato sauce. Add seasonings to sauce and vegetables. Add cooked rice and adjust seasonings.

Equivalent to:

6 Servings
Each =
1 starch
1/3 cup cooked
vegetable

112 calories
< 1 g total fat
< 1 g saturated
0 cholesterol
6 mg sodium

MEXICAN FRIED RICE

Ingredients:

1/2 cup long grain rice
1 cup water
1/2 cup Pace Picante Sauce
1/4 cup chopped green pepper
1/2 small onion, chopped
1/8 tsp garlic herb seasoning
1/8 tsp Mexican seasoning
Salt, to taste

Instructions:

Equivalent to:

6 Servings
Each =
1 starch
1/3 cup cooked
vegetable

70 calories
< 1 g total fat
< 1 g saturated
0 cholesterol
126 mg sodium

In a skillet sprayed with Pam, cook rice until lightly browned, stirring often. Stir in remaining ingredients. Bring mixture to a boil; reduce heat. Cover; simmer 15-20 minutes or until rice is tender.

WILD-RICE PILAF

Ingredients:

2 tsp diet soft tub margarine
1/4 cup finely chopped onion
1 cup low-sodium chicken broth
1/4 cup water
1/4 cup wild rice
1/4 cup rice
2 T chopped fresh parsley leaves
1/8 tsp salt
1/4 tsp lemon pepper
1/2 tsp Teton Valley Nice n Spicy or Season All

Instructions:

In a 2-quart saucepan melt margarine, saute onion until transparent, stir in broth, water, wild rice. Heat to boiling over high heat. Cover pan and reduce heat to low; simmer mixture 20-25 minutes. Add regular rice and simmer another 25 minutes or until liquid is absorbed and rice is tender.
With a fork; stir parsley and seasonings into rice mixture and serve.

Equivalent to:

4 Servings
Each=
1 starch
1/4 oil

108 calories
1.8 g total fat
<1 g saturated
< 1   m g
cholesterol
117 mg sodium

Side Dish

GARDEN MEDLEY RICE

Ingredients:

3/4 cup Minute Rice
3/4 cup chicken broth
1 cup assorted vegetables, (broccoli, sliced
  yellow or green squash, grated carrots,
  mushrooms)
1 tsp onion flakes
2 tsp snipped fresh rosemary or 1 tsp dried
1/4 tsp lemon pepper
1/2 tsp garlic herb seasoning

Instructions:

Equivalent to:

4 Servings
Each =
1 starch
1/4 cup cooked
vegetable

73 calories
< 1 g total fat
< 1 g saturated
< 1 mg
cholesterol
26 mg sodium

Stir together broth, vegetables, onion flakes, rosemary and other seasonings in a saucepan and bring to a boil.
Stir in rice, cover and remove form heat. Let stand 5 minutes. Fluff with a fork and adjust seasonings.

Microwave Directions:
Stir together all ingredients, cover with plastic wrap and cook at high for 3 minutes. Stir and continue to cook another 2-3 minutes. Fluff with a fork, adjust seasonings.

RICE & VEGETABLE STIR-FRY

372

Side Dish

Ingredients:

1/2 cup egg substitute
1/2 cup frozen broccoli cuts
4 T chopped onion
1/4 cup coarsely chopped green pepper
1 stalk celery, cut diagonally into 1/4-inch
  slices
1 T chopped pimento
1 1/3 cup rice, cooked
1/4 tsp garlic powder and dill
1/4 tsp oregano leaves
1/2 tsp low-sodium soy sauce

Instructions:

In a small skillet sprayed with Pam, add beaten egg. Cook eggs until hard without stirring, gently lifting edges to allow uncooked egg to flow to bottom of skillet. Cut into chunks, set aside. In a skillet sprayed with Pam over medium-high heat, add broccoli, onion, green pepper, celery; stir-fry 2 minutes. Add 1 T water and cover and cook 3 more minutes, until vegetables are crisp-tender. Add seasonings, rice, and egg, stir-fry another 3 minutes. Adjust seasonings and serve.

Equivalent to:

4 Servings
Each =
1/2 cup cooked vegetable
1/2 oz protein
1 starch

126 calories
1.3 g total fat
< 1 g saturated
0 cholesterol
82 mg sodium

BAKED BARLEY CASSEROLE

Ingredients:

4 tsp diet soft tub margarine
1/2 cup pearl barley
1 large onion, chopped
1/2 tsp salt
1/4 tsp lemon pepper
1/2 tsp Teton Valley Nice n Spicy or Season All
3 cups chicken or beef broth
1/2 cup mushrooms, sliced

Instructions:

Equivalent to:

6 Servings
Each =
1 starch
1/4 cup cooked
vegetable
1/4 oil

81 calories
2 g total fat
< 1 g saturated
0 cholesterol
247 mg sodium

In a skillet melt 2 T margarine, brown barley slightly. Place in a casserole. Add the other 2 tsp of margarine to skillet, saute onion and mushrooms. Mix with barley and add seasonings. Add 1 1/2 cup chicken or beef broth, cover and place in a 350 degree oven for 1 hour, or until moisture is almost absorbed. Add the other 1 1/2 cup broth, cover and cook until absorbed.

Soups & Stews

BEEF STEW

Ingredients:

1 pound top round steak, cubed (may also use
  elk or deer).
1/2 cup asparagus, optional
1/2 cup green pepper, chopped
1/2 cup red pepper, chopped
2 medium potatoes, cut in chunks
1/2 cup zucchini, sliced
1/2 cup yellow squash, sliced
3/4 cup fresh mushrooms, sliced
1 large onion, chopped
1/2 cup carrots, sliced
2 T tomato paste
1 tsp Teton Valley Nice n Spicy or Season All
1/2 tsp salt
1 bay leaf
1/2 tsp pepper, or to taste
1/4 tsp garlic powder
1/2 tsp onion powder
2 T cornstarch

Instructions:

In a crock pot, place meat and 1/2 of the onion,
1 cup water, and seasonings and cook on high
for 3 hours, stir occasionally.
Add cut up vegetables; except the squash and

Equivalent to:

4 Servings
Each=
31/2 oz protein
1 cup cooked
vegetable
1 starch
1 additional
food

263 calories
5.8 g total fat
1.9 g saturated
70 mg
cholesterol
352 mg sodium

BEEF STEW

Instructions Continued:

asparagus tips, cook 1 1/2 hour. Add remaining
ingredients and cook until at desired doneness,
about 1 hour longer. (May need to add more
water if needed while cooking).
Add cornstarch to 1/2 cup water to make a
thickening for the juices in crock pot.
Adjust seasonings and stir until stew starts to
thicken.

VEGETABLE BEEF SOUP

Ingredients:

2 tsp diet margarine
1 pound beef round stead, cubed
1 can low-sodium beef broth
3 cups water
1 cup carrots, sliced
1 cup onions, chopped
1/2 green pepper, chopped
1 cup celery, chopped
3/4 cup mushrooms, sliced
1/3 cup barley, uncooked
1/2 tsp salt
1 tsp Teton Valley Nice n Spicy or Season All
1/4 tsp pepper
2 bay leaves
1/2 tsp garlic powder
1 cup stewed tomatoes

Instructions:

In a large dutch oven heat margarine and brown beef. Add water, broth and seasonings and bring to a boil. Reduce heat; cover and simmer 20 minutes. Add all other ingredients and continue cooking about 30-45 minutes longer or until vegetables and barley are tender. Remove bay leaves, adjust seasonings and serve.

Equivalent to:

4 Servings
Each =
1 cup cooked
vegetable
31/2 oz protein
1 starch

274 calories
7 g total fat
2 g saturated
70 mg
cholesterol
407 mg sodium

CLEAR VEGETABLE SOUP

Ingredients:

1 can chicken broth
1 can water
1/2 cup sliced carrots
1/2 cup sliced celery
1/2 cup chopped onion
1/2 cup uncooked rotelle or other pasta
1 tsp chopped fresh parsley
*1 tsp Teton Valley Good Stuff Seasoning or
  chicken seasoning*

Instructions:

Equivalent to

2 Servings
Each =
1/2 cup cooked
vegetable
1 starch

128 calories
2 g total fat
< 1 g saturated
1 mg
cholesterol
107 mg sodium

In a 2 quart saucepan over high heat, heat chicken broth, water, seasonings and vegetables to boiling. Add rotelle or pasta and reduce heat to low, cover and simmer until pasta is done, about 20 minutes.
Ladle soup into bowls; top with fresh parsley.

RED-HOT CHILI SOUP

Ingredients:

9 oz extra lean ground round beef
1 cup chopped onion
1/2 cup chopped red pepper
1 clove garlic, minced
2 tsp cumin
1 tsp Mexican seasoning
1/8 tsp ground red pepper
1 can (13 3/4 oz) chicken broth
1 can (14 1/2 oz) stewed tomatoes
1/2 cup uncooked elbow macaroni
2 cups kidney beans, drained and rinsed
2 T chopped fresh cilantro
1/4 tsp salt

Instructions:

In a saucepan sprayed with Pam, cook beef, onion, garlic, seasonings and pepper until browned. Stir in chicken broth and tomatoes. Cover and bring to a boil. Add macaroni, cover, cook 5 minutes. Add kidney beans cook 3 minutes longer. Stir in cilantro and serve.

Equivalent to:

4 Servings
Each =
1 1/2 starch
3 oz protein
1 cup cooked
vegetable

Woman Style:
4 Servings
Each =
1 legume
1/2 starch
2 oz protein
1 cup cooked
vegetable

279 calories
5 g total fat
1.4 g saturated
40 mg
cholesterol
609 mg sodium

SEAFOOD STEW

Ingredients:

8 oz scallops, cut in 1-inch pieces
8 oz raw shrimp, shelled and deveined
4 oz cod or other white fish, cut in 1-inch
   cubes
1/2 tsp garlic seasoning or powder
1 medium onion, chopped
1/2 cup celery, diced
2 1/2 cups canned tomatoes, chopped, including
   liquid
1 bay leaf
Pinch of cayenne pepper
1/2 tsp each of thyme, basil and oregano
1 tsp Teton Valley Nice n Spicy or Season All
1/2 tsp salt
1/4 tsp lemon pepper

Equivalent to:

3 Servings
Each =
31/2 oz protein
1 cup cooked
vegetable

191 calories
2.3 g total fat
< 1 g saturated
157 mg
cholesterol
663 mg sodium

Instructions:

Combine garlic, onions, celery, water, tomatoes
and seasonings in a saucepan. Simmer for ten
minutes. Add cod and simmer gently 2 minutes.
Add scallops and simmer 2 minutes. Add
shrimp and simmer 3-4 minutes, just until
shrimp turn pink.
Ladle into bowls and serve.

SHRIMP & CHEESE CHOWDER

Ingredients:

1 pound shrimp, cooked and shelled
2 tsp diet soft tub margarine
1 cup cooked rice
1 onion, chopped
2 stalks celery, sliced
2 cups cut green beans
4 cups low-fat buttermilk
4 oz fat-free cheddar cheese, shredded
1/2 tsp salt
1/2 tsp lemon pepper
1/2 tsp Teton Valley Nice n Spicy or Season All
1/2 tsp thyme

Instructions:

In a skillet melt margarine, cook onion and celery until tender. Add green beans, cover and simmer 3 minutes. Add buttermilk, cheese and shrimp to vegetable mixture. Stir until heated and cheese melts. Adjust seasonings.
To serve: Place 1/3 cup rice in bottom of bowl; spoon chowder over rice, serve.

Equivalent to:

3 Servings
Each =
21/2 oz protein
2 dairy
1 starch
1/3 oil
2/3 cup cooked vegetable

459 calories
6 g total fat
1.9 g saturated
246 mg cholesterol
996 mg sodium

LITE MARKET STREET CLAM CHOWDER

Ingredients:

1 T diet soft tub margarine
4 cans chopped clams with juice
2 cups diced potatoes
2 cups diced celery
2 cups chopped onions
2 cups chopped green leeks
2 cups chopped green pepper
1-2 tsp ground fresh pepper, or to taste
1/2 tsp salt
2 tsp whole thyme
6 bay leaves
1 tsp tabasco
3/4 cup sherry
1 cup water
1 qt low-fat buttermilk
1 qt skim milk
4 T cornstarch
2 T flour

Equivalent to:

10 Servings
Each =
1 oz protein
1/2 cup cooked
vegetable
1 starch
1/3 oil

203 calories
2.5 g total fat
< 1 g saturated
23 mg
cholesterol
720 mg sodium

Instructions:

In a large pan, melt diet margarine, add onions, leeks, celelry, and green pepper; saute for 3-4 minutes. Add potatoes, seasonings, clam juice and water; simmer until vegetables are tender.

Instructions Continued:

To vegetables add buttermilk and skim milk, turn heat down to medium-low. Stirring constantly to keep milk from scorching on bottom of pan.

Mix cornstarch and flour together, whisk in sherry until smooth. Add to chowder, continue to heat and stir until just below boiling point and chowder is thickened. <u>Don't boil.</u>

CHICKEN NOODLE SOUP

Ingredients:

1 can chicken broth
1 can water
*8 oz chicken breasts, skinned and boned,
    cut in bite-size pieces*
1/2 cup egg noodles, uncooked
1/2 cup sliced carrots
1/2 cup celery, sliced
1/2 cup onion, chopped
1/2 cup sliced mushrooms, optional
1 tsp fresh dill weed (or dry dill)
1/4 tsp lemon pepper
1 tsp Teton Valley Nice and Spicy or Season All
1/4 tsp salt

Instructions:

In a large saucepan, over medium-high heat, heat chicken broth, chicken, carrots, onion, celery and seasonings to boil. Add noodles and return to boil, reduce heat and simmer 20 minutes.

Equivalent to

2 Servings
Each =
31/2 oz protein
1 starch
3/4 cup cooked
vegetable

252 calories
3.4 g total fat
< 1 g saturated
67 mg
cholesterol
455 mg sodium

ORIENTAL SOUP

Ingredients:

1 1/2 cups chicken broth, home made preferred
3 ounces Lite Mori-Nu Tofu, pressed
1/4 cup green pepper, chopped
1/4 cup red pepper, chopped
1/2 cup fresh mushrooms, sliced
1/2 cup fresh zucchini, chopped
1/4 cup celery, chopped
1/2 onion, chopped
4 oz shrimp, shelled (may use 2 oz chicken if
   preferred)
2 spinach leaves, sliced
Seasonings: all to taste...
Teton Valley Nice n Spicy or Season All
Garlic herb seasoning
Oriental seasoning

Instructions:

Bring broth to a boil, add vegetables and reduce heat and simmer 5 minutes. Add shrimp or chicken and cubed tofu, cook 3-5 minutes. Turn off heat. Place spinach leaves in last to steam. Adjust seasonings and serve.

Equivalent to:

1 Serving
Equals=
3 oz protein
1 cup cooked
   vegetable

Woman Style:
1 Serving=
1 legume
2 oz protein
1 cup cooked
vegetable

317 calories
7 g total fat
1.6 g saturated
177 mg
cholesterol
446 mg sodium

CHICKEN CHILI

Ingredients:

1 medium onion, chopped
1 stalk celery, chopped
1 hot pepper, chopped or to taste
Equivalent to: *8 oz chicken breast, cubed*
2 cups canned white beans
4 Servings   *Dash crushed chilies, optional*
Each=   *1 tsp chopped cilantro*
1/2 cup cooked   *1/8 tsp oregano*
vegetable   *1/8 tsp cumin*
1 starch   *1/4 tsp Mexican seasoning*
3 oz protein   *2 oz fat-free mozzarella cheese*
1/4 dairy   *1 1/2 cup chicken broth*

Woman Style
1 legume
2 oz protein
1/2 cup cooked
vegetable
1/4 dairy

201 calories
2.2 g total fat
< 1 g saturated
36 mg
cholesterol
400 mg sodium

Instructions:

In a skillet sprayed with Pam, saute onion, celery, chicken and seasonings until chicken is white and tender.

Add remaining ingredients, except cheese, and simmer 15-20 minutes.

Adjust seasonings, top with cheese. Serve.

CHEESY VEGETABLE CHILI

Soups & Stews

Ingredients:

1/2 cup green pepper, chopped
1/2 cup red pepper, chopped
1 cup mushrooms, sliced
1 cup onion, chopped
1 1/2 cup canned tomatoes
1 small can tomato paste
1/2 to 1 tsp Mexican seasoning
1/2 tsp herb garlic seasoning
1/4 tsp Teton Valley Nice n Spicy or Season All
1/4 tsp cumin
1 1/2 cup kidney beans
3/4 cup corn
3/4 cup diced zucchini
3 oz fat-free cheddar cheese, shredded

Instructions:

In a skillet sprayed with Pam, cook peppers, mushrooms and onions 5 minutes or until tender. Add tomatoes, seasonings, tomato paste and enough water to make paste into sauce consistency. Bring to a boil. Reduce heat and add corn, zucchini, beans. Simmer 5-8 minutes. Top with grated cheese and serve.

Equivalent to:

3 Servings
Each =
1 oz protein
1 1/4 starch
1/2 dairy
1 1/2 c cooked vegetable

Woman Style
3 Servings
Each =
1 legume
1/4 starch
1/2 dairy
1 1/2 cup cooked vegetable

271 calories
1.9 g total fat
< 1 g saturated
5 mg cholesterol
835 mg sodium

MACARONI AND SQUASH SOUP

Ingredients:

1 leek, washed and thinly sliced
1 yellow crookneck squash, diced
1/2 cup carrot, thinly sliced
1 medium zucchini, sliced
4 cups chicken broth, preferably low sodium
1 bay leaf
1 tsp Italian blend or 1/4 tsp thyme, 1/2 tsp
    basil
1/4 tsp lemon pepper
1/2 tsp Teton Valley Nice n Spicy or Season All
Salt to taste
1/2 cup elbow macaroni

Instructions:

In a microwave safe casserole sprayed with Pam, cook leek and squash 6 minutes, covered on high.
Add remaining ingredients; cover and microwave 12-15 minutes.
Serve hot.

Equivalent to:

4 Servings
Each =
1 starch
1 1/2 cup
cooked
vegetable
1/4 oil

142 calories
3.9 g total fat
< 1 g saturated
3 mg
cholesterol
275 mg sodium

CHICKEN STEW

Ingredients:

12 oz chicken breast, skinned and boned
1 onion, chopped
1 cup celery, chopped
1 cup mushrooms, sliced
1 cup green pepper, chopped
2 medium potatoes, diced
1 cup carrots, sliced
2 T chopped parsley
1 clove garlic, minced
1/2 tsp Teton Valley Nice n Spicy or Season All
1/2 tsp Teton Valley Good Stuff Seasoning
1/4 tsp basil and thyme
3 T cornstarch

Instructions:

Place chicken in a pan with 2 quarts water.
Add seasonings and small amount of onion and
celery leaves. Simmer until chicken breasts are
done. Remove chicken and cut into cubes. Add
vegetables to stock and simmer until vegetables
are done, about 30 minutes. Return chicken to
stew. Mix cornstarch with 1/2 cup cold water
to make a thin paste, add to the stew and
simmer until it comes to a boil and thickens,
stirring often.

Equivalent to:

4 Servings
Each =
21/2 oz protein
1 cup cooked
vegetable
1 starch

201 calories
1.4 g total fat
< 1 g saturated
49 mg
cholesterol
99 mg sodium

CREAM OF MUSHROOM SOUP

Ingredients:

1 leek or 1 large onion, chopped
2 tsp diet soft tub margarine
1 pound mushrooms, sliced
2 medium russet potatoes, peeled and thinly sliced
1 can (14 1/2 oz) chicken broth
1 1/2 cup skim milk or buttermilk
1/2 tsp basil
1/2 tsp Italian blend
1/2 tsp salt
1/4 tsp lemon pepper
1 T chopped parsley
Dash low-sodium soy sauce

Equivalent to:

4 Servings
Each =
1 starch
3/4 dairy
1 cup cooked
vegetable

153 calories
3.2 g total fat
1 g saturated
4 mg
cholesterol
461 mg sodium

Instructions:

In a skillet heat margarine, add leek or onion and 1/2 of mushrooms; cook 5 minutes. Remove leek mixture, set aside. Add potatoes and broth to skillet. Cover and cook over medium-high heat just until potatoes are tender, about 10 minutes. Pour into blender container, add 1/2 cup milk, blend until smooth, then return to skillet. Stir in mushrooms, cooked leek and mushrooms, rest of milk and seasonings. Bring just to boil. Serve.

CREAM OF VEGETABLE SOUP

Ingredients:

2 cups asparagus or chopped broccoli
1/2 cup carrot, sliced
1/2 cup chicken stock
1/2 cup zucchini, sliced
1/4 cup sliced green onion
1/2 tsp salt
1/4 tsp garlic powder
1/4 tsp lemon pepper
1/2 tsp all purpose seasoning
1/2 tsp Season All
1 can (12 oz) evaporated skim milk
1 cup skim milk
2 T cornstarch

Instructions:

In a large saucepan stir together asparagus, carrot, chicken stock, green onion, seasonings. Bring to a boil, reduce heat and simmer covered for 5 minutes. Stir in zucchini, cook covered, about 2 more minutes until just tender. Add the milks. Stir together a small amount of milk & cornstarch to make a thin paste. Stir into soup, cook and stir until thick, about 2 more minutes, but don't boil. Serve.

Equivalent to:

2 Servings
Each =
1 1/2 cup
cooked
vegetable
1 1/4 dairy
1 additional
food

212 calories
3 g total fat
1.5 g saturated
9 mg
cholesterol
578 mg sodium

BOUILLABAISSE

Ingredients:

1 medium onion, chopped
2 cloves garlic, minced
1 T olive oil
1/4 tsp chopped parsley
1 tsp salt
1/4 tsp curry powder
1/4 tsp pepper
1 bay leaf
4 cups water
1 tsp lemon juice
1 lb fish fillets, cut in 2-inch pieces
12 oz fresh or frozen shrimp,
12 oz frozen crab or lobster meat
1 pint fresh oysters or clams, undrained
8 oz can tomato sauce

Equivalent to:

10 Servings
Each =
3 oz protein
Scant cooked
vegetable

137 calories
3.7 g total fat
< 1 g saturated
91 mg
cholesterol
396 mg sodium

Instructions:

In a dutch oven or large saucepan, saute onion and garlic in oil until tender. Add remaining ingredients; mix well. Heat just to boiling. Simmer covered over low heat, 20-30 minutes or until seafood is done, stirring occasionally. Remove bay leaf. Serve in large soup bowls.

SPLIT PEA SOUP

Ingredients:

1 can low-sodium chicken broth
1 quart water
3/4 cup dried split peas
1/2 cup carrot, finely diced
1 cup onion, chopped
1/2 tsp salt
1/8 tsp lemon pepper
1/2 tsp dill weed, crushed
1/4 tsp herb garlic seasoning

Instructions:

Bring water and broth to a boil in large saucepan; add split peas, carrot, onion, and seasonings, except dill weed. Simmer, covered, until thick, about 2 1/2 hours. Add dill weed and simmer 5 minutes longer.

Equivalent to:

4 Servings
Each =
1 starch
1 oz protein
1/2 cup cooked
vegetable

Woman Style:
4 Servings
Each =
1 legume
1/2 cup cooked
vegetable

64 calories
< 1 g total fat
< 1 g saturated
0 cholesterol
298 mg sodium

ZUCCHINI, RICE AND BEAN SOUP

Equivalent to:

3 Servings
Each =
1 cup cooked
vegetable
2 starch
1/3 oil
1/3 dairy

Woman Style:
3 Servings
Each =
1/3 legume
1 starch
1 cup cooked
vegetable
1/3 oil
1/3 dairy

64 calories
< 1 g total fat
< 1 g saturated
0 cholesterol
298 mg sodium

Ingredients:

1 cup chopped onion
2 tsp diet soft tub margarine
1 clove garlic, minced
1 quart low-sodium chicken broth
2 cups zucchini
1/4 tsp salt
1 tsp Teton Valley Nice n Spicy or Season All
1/2 tsp lemon pepper
1/2 tsp ground thyme
1/2 cup uncooked rice
1 cup kidney beans
2 oz fat-free cheddar cheese, grated

Instructions:

In a skillet heat margarine and cook onion and garlic until tender but not brown. Add remaining ingredients, except cheese. Bring to a boil, stirring once or twice. Lower heat and simmer 15-20 minutes, or until rice is tender, adjust seasonings.
To serve, ladle into bowls and top with cheese.

TOMATO SOUP

Ingredients:

3 cups tomatoes, peeled and seeded
1 cup plain non-fat yogurt
1/2 tsp Worcestershire sauce
1 clove garlic, quartered
1 cup tomato or V-8 juice
1/4 tsp lemon pepper
1/4 tsp salt

Instructions:

Pour tomato juice, yogurt, Worcestershire sauce and garlic in the blender. Whirl until smooth. Add tomatoes and blend for one minute. Season to taste, serve chilled.

Equivalent to:

4 Servings
Each =
1 cup raw
vegetable
1/4 dairy

65 calories
< 1 g total fat
< 1 saturated
0 cholesterol
322 mg sodium

Soups &
Stews

MINESTRONE SOUP

Ingredients:

1/2 large onion, chopped
1 medium zucchini, sliced
2 tsp diet soft tub margarine
2 (10 oz) cans low-sodium beef broth
1 cup kidney or lima beans
1/2 cup macaroni or pasta, uncooked
2 cups stewed tomatoes
1/2 tsp Teton Valley Nice n Spicy or Season All
1/4 tsp pepper
1/8 tsp cayenne pepper
1/4 tsp garlic powder
1/4 tsp basil

Equivalent to:

4 Servings
Each =
1 cup cooked
vegetable
1 1/2 starch
1/4 oil

Instructions:

In a large saucepan over medium heat, saute onion and zucchini in margarine until vegetables are crisp-tender. Add beans to vegetables. Stir in remaining ingredients. Simmer, stirring occasionally, about 15 minutes or until pasta is tender but still firm.

Woman Style:
4 Serving
Each =
1/2 legume
3/4 starch
1/4 oil

188 calories
2.4 g total fat
< 1 g saturated
0 cholesterol
293 mg sodium

Vegetables

VEGETABLE MEDLEY CASSEROLE

Ingredients:

1 cup broccoli florets
1 cup cauliflower florets
1/2 onion chopped
2 carrot, sliced
1 cup sliced mushrooms
2 tsp diet soft tub margarine
1/2 tsp Teton Valley Nice n Spicy or Season All
1/4 tsp salt
1/4 tsp lemon pepper
Dash garlic herb seasoning
2 oz fat-free cheddar cheese, shredded

Instructions:

In a steamer basket, place broccoli, cauliflower and carrots, steam until tender, don't overcook. In a microwave safe casserole, cook onion and mushrooms over high heat 1-2 minutes or until tender. In the same casserole, add steamed vegetables. Sprinkle with seasonings, adjust to taste. Top with cheese. Microwave until cheese is melted and warmed through.

Equivalent to:

4 Servings
Each =
1 cup cooked
vegetable
1/4 oil
1/2 dairy

95 calories
1.3 g total fat
< 1 g total fat
< 1 g saturated
0 cholesterol
527 mg sodium

TANGY MUSTARD CAULIFLOWER

Ingredients:

4 cups cauliflower
1 T light mayonnaise
1 T fat-free mayonnaise
1 to 1 1/2 tsp prepared mustard
1 green onion, sliced
2 oz fat-free cheddar cheese
1/4 tsp lemon pepper
1/2 tsp Teton Valley Nice n Spicy or Season All

Instructions:

Equivalent to:

2 Servings
Each =
2 cups cooked
vegetable
2 oil
1/2 dairy

169 calories
5.9 g total fat
1.9 g saturated
7.5 mg
cholesterol
580 mg sodium

In a large saucepan, steam cauliflower until crisp-tender, about 10 minutes; drain well.
Place hot cauliflower in serving dish. In a small bowl, combine mayonnaise, mustard, onion and seasonings. Spread over cauliflower. Sprinkle with cheese. Cover; let stand a few minutes until cheese is melted. Sprinkle with Nice n Spicy.

DILLY SUMMER SQUASH

Vegetables

Ingredients:

2 tsp diet soft tub margarine
2 T sliced green onions
2 medium crookneck or zucchini squash, thinly
  sliced (3 cups)
1/2 tsp salt
1/2 tsp dill weed or 1 1/2 tsp chopped fresh dill
1/4 tsp lemon pepper
3/4 cup plain non-fat yogurt

Instructions:

In a large skillet, saute green onions 1 minute
or until crisp-tender in margarine. Add squash
and seasonings. Cover; cook over medium-low
heat until crisp-tender, stirring occasionally.
Stir in yogurt. Garnish with additional fresh
dill, if desired.

Equivalent to:

2 Servings
Each =
1 1/2 cup
cooked
vegetable
1/3 dairy
1/2 oil

83 calories
2.4 g total fat
< 1 g saturated
0 cholesterol
323 mg sodium

BROCCOLI WITH ORANGE SAUCE

Ingredients:

4 cups broccoli florets
1/2 cup plain non-fat yogurt
1/4 tsp salt
1/4 tsp lemon pepper
1/8 tsp thyme leaves
1/2 tsp grated orange peel
1/4 cup orange juice concentrate
Orange slices, for garnish
1 tsp cornstarch

Instructions:

Equivalent to:

2 Servings
Each =
2 cups cooked
vegetable
Scant dairy

112 calories
< 1 g total fat
< 1 g saturated
0 cholesterol
376 mg sodium

In a 2-quart microwave-safe casserole, place broccoli and 1/4 cup water; cover. Microwave on high for 6-8 minutes or until crisp-tender; drain well. Place broccoli in serving dish; keep warm.
Mix remaining ingredients together and microwave on medium power for one minute or until warmed. Stir until smooth. Pour orange sauce over broccoli. Garnish with orange slices.

SPECIAL SPAGHETTI SQUASH

Ingredients:

1 spaghetti squash
2 T fresh lemon juice
2 tomatoes, chopped
1/4 tsp lemon pepper
1/2 tsp Teton Valley Nice n Spicy or Season All
1/4 tsp salt
2 oz fat-free cheese, any flavor

Instructions:

Cut squash in half, remove seeds. Sprinkle with seasonings. Cover with plastic wrap and microwave on high for about 10 minutes. Run a fork around squash, it will look like strands of spaghetti.

Remove from shell and place in a microwave safe serving bowl. Add chopped tomatoes. Sprinkle with lemon juice, and seasonings, top with grated cheese.

Place back in microwave for 1-2 minutes to melt cheese.

Equivalent to:

4 Servings
Each =
2 cups cooked vegetable
1/4 dairy

72 calories
< 1 g total fat
< 1 g saturated
2.5 mg cholesterol
367 mg sodium

MIXED VEGETABLE KABOBS

Ingredients:

1 red pepper, cut in bite size pieces
1/2 zucchini, cut in thick slices
1 red onion, cut in large pieces
2 tsp low-sodium soy sauce
1/2 tsp Worcestershire sauce
1 tsp olive oil
1 clove garlic, smashed and chopped
1/4 tsp tarragon
1 tsp sweetener
1 tsp Teton Valley Nice n Spicy or Season All
1/2 tsp lemon pepper
1/4 tsp salt

Equivalent to:

2 Servings
Each =
1 cup cooked
vegetable
1/2 oil

65 calories
2.6 g total fat
< 1 g saturated
0 cholesterol
333 mg sodium

Instructions:

Prepare barbecue or grill, (may also broil in oven).

In a bowl mix soy sauce, Worcestershire sauce, oil, garlic and seasonings. Marinate vegetables for 30 minutes at room temperature.

Drain and reserve marinade. Alternate vegetables on skewers and baste. Cook 8 minutes, turning and basting with marinade. Adjust seasonings and serve.

QUICK VEGETABLE MIX

Ingredients:

1 medium onion, chopped
1 clove garlic, smashed and minced
1 pound fresh okra, end snipped
4 tomatoes, peeled and chopped
1 green pepper, diced
1/2 tsp chopped jalapeno pepper, optional
1 T curry powder
1 T cumin powder
1 tsp olive oil
1/2 tsp lemon pepper
1/2 tsp salt
2 oz fat-free jack cheese

Instructions:

In a microwave safe casserole sprayed with Pam, cook onion and garlic 1 minute. Add okra and mix, microwave 2-3 minutes. Stir in tomatoes, green pepper, jalapeno, seasonings and oil; cover and microwave 7 minutes. Mix well, finish microwaving 8 minutes, covered. Sprinkle with cheese.

Equivalent to:

4 Servings
Each =
1 1/2 cup
cooked
vegetable
1/4 dairy

133 calories
2.8 g total fat
< 1 g saturated
2 mg
cholesterol
384 mg sodium

CAULIFLOWER WITH CHEESE

Ingredients:

4 cups cauliflower, cut in florets
2 oz fat-free cheddar cheese, shredded
1/2 tsp Teton Valley Nice n Spicy or Season All
1/4 tsp lemon pepper

Instructions:

steam cauliflower until just tender don't overcook. Transfer to serving bowl. Sprinkle with seasonings.
Shred cheese; sprinkle on top and microwave for 1-2 minutes until cheese melts.

Equivalent to:

2 Servings
Each =
1 cups cooked
vegetable
1 oz protein
1/2 oil

106 calories
< 1 g total fat
< 1 g saturated
5 mg
cholesterol
502 mg sodium

BAKED ZUCCHINI & TOMATO FLATS

Ingredients:

1/2 large zucchini, cut in 1/4-inch slices
1 large tomato cut in 1/4-inch slices
1/2 cup seasoned bread crumbs
2 egg whites
Lemon pepper, to taste
1/4 tsp salt
fresh lemon juice

Instructions:

Preheat oven to 375 degrees. Pour oil on cookie sheet and distribute evenly. In a small bowl, whip egg whites and 1 T water. Dip zucchini and tomato flats in egg wash then bread crumbs. Place on cookie sheet in a single layer. Spray top of zucchini and tomatoes with Pam. Sprinkle with seasonings and bake in a 375 degree oven, about 10 minutes on each side, or until golden brown and tender.
Top with fresh lemon juice.

Equivalent to:

2 Servings
Each =
1 starch
1/2 oz protein
2 cup cooked vegetable

176 calories
3.8 g total fat
< 1 g saturated
2 mg cholesterol
637 mg sodium

SESAME BROCCOLI

Ingredients:

3 cups broccoli florets
1 package Diet Center Italian Dressing or 2 T
  low-fat Italian dressing
2 tsp sesame seeds, toasted
1/2 tsp low-sodium soy sauce
Pinch lemon pepper
Pinch garlic herb seasoning

Instructions:

In a large saucepan, steam broccoli over boiling water 5 minutes; drain. In a small bowl combine other ingredients. In a serving bowl, toss broccoli with sesame dressing mixture. Serve.

Equivalent to:

3 Servings
Each =
1 cup cooked
vegetable
2/3 oil

66 calories
3.9 g total fat
< 1 g saturated
0 cholesterol
143 mg sodium

ZUCCHINI AND GREEN CHILI CASSEROLE

Vegetables

Ingredients:

2 tsp diet soft tub margarine
3 medium zucchini
1 small onion, chopped
1/2 can green chilies, chopped
2 tomatoes, sliced
1/2 tsp Teton Valley Nice n Spicy or Season All
1/4 tsp lemon pepper
1/8 tsp garlic herb seasoning
1/4 tsp salt
2 oz fat-free cheddar cheese

Instructions:

Wash and slice zucchini, cut diagonally 1/2 inch thick. Melt margarine in a skillet, saute onion and zucchini with seasonings until just crisp-tender. Transfer to a casserole. Sprinkle with seasonings and green chilies; layer tomatoes slices over chilies. Top with cheese. Heat in microwave 2-3 minutes until cheese is melted.

Equivalent to:

4 Servings
Each =
2 cups cooked
vegetable
1/4 oil
1/2 dairy

94 calories
1.3 g total fat
< 1 g saturated
5 mg
cholesterol
608 mg sodium

GREAT GREEN BEANS

Ingredients:

1 can green beans, drained
1 tsp diet soft tub margarine
5 mushrooms, sliced
1/2 cup onion, chopped
Dash lemon pepper
Salt, to taste

Instructions:

In a microwave safe dish add margarine, cook mushrooms and onion on high for 40 seconds. Add green beans and toss with vegetables. Heat until warmed, about 2 minutes. Sprinkle with seasonings.

Equivalent to:

2 Serving
Each=
1 cup cooked
vegetable
1/4 oil

75 calories
1.5 g total fat
< 1 g saturated
0 cholesterol
315 mg sodium

ASPARAGUS WITH YOGURT SAUCE

Vegetables

Ingredients:

2 cups asparagus spears, tough ends removed
Sauce ingredients:
1 cup plain low-fat yogurt
1/2 tsp garlic, minced
1 tsp lemon zest
1 T lemon juice
1/4 tsp dill weed

Instructions:

Cook asparagus until crisp-tender, about 4 to 5 minutes.
Mix all ingredients together for yogurt sauce and pour over asparagus.
Amount depends on personal taste.

Equivalent to:

2 Servings
Each =
1 cup cooked
vegetable
1 dairy

91 calories
< 1 g total fat
< 1 g saturated
0 cholesterol
86 mg sodium

ASPARAGUS WITH LEMON DRESSING

Ingredients:

24 thin asparagus spears
1 T grated lemon rind
2 T fresh lemon juice
2 tsp olive oil
1/2 tsp fresh tarragon, or 1/4 tsp dried
1/4 tsp garlic herb seasoning
1/4 tsp salt

Instructions:

Cook asparagus until crisp-tender. Drain and chill.
In a small bowl prepare dressing and make sure to whisk well, chill.
To serve, arrange asparagus on plate and top with dressing.

Equivalent to:

2 Servings
Each =
1 1/4 cup
cook vegetable
1 oil

111 calories
5.7 g total fat
< 1 g saturated
0 cholesterol
299 mg sodium

BAKED POTATO TOPPERS

Vegetables

Ingredients:

Broccoli Buttermilk:
1/2 cup raw broccoli florets
1/2 cup non-fat yogurt
1/3 cup buttermilk
3 T chopped red pepper
2 T green onion
1/8 tsp pepper
1 tsp Season All
salt, to taste

Mexican Cheese Topping:
1/2 cup non-fat yogurt
1/2 cup salsa
2 oz fat-free cheddar cheese
1/8 tsp garlic powder

Instructions:

Combine all ingredients; spoon onto hot baked potato, store covered in refrigerator up to 5 days.

Equivalent to:

2 Servings
Each =
3/4 dairy
Scant vegetable

52 or 79 calories
< 1 g total fat
< 1 g saturated
0 cholesterol
377 or 692 mg sodium

CURRIED MUSHROOMS

Ingredients:

2 cups mushrooms, sliced
2 green onions, sliced
1/4 tsp curry powder
1/4 tsp garlic powder
1/4 tsp onion powder
1/4 tsp oregano
1/4 tsp basil
1/4 tsp lemon pepper

Instructions:

In a skillet sprayed with Pam, saute mushrooms, stirring occasionally. Sprinkle with seasonings and continue to cook 4-5 minutes. If mushrooms seem too dry add a bit of water.

Equivalent to:

1 Serving
Each =
1 1/2 cup
cook vegetable

59 calories
< 1 g total fat
< 1 g saturated
0 cholesterol
7 mg sodium

SWISS ASPARAGUS AU GRATIN

Ingredients:

4 cups asparagus spears, trimmed
2 oz fat-free swiss cheese, shredded
1/2 cup seasoned bread crumbs
4 tsp diet soft tub margarine
1/2 tsp dry mustard
1/8 tsp lemon pepper
1/4 tsp salt

Instructions:

Heat oven to 400 degrees.
Bring 1/2 cup water to a boil in a 10 inch skillet; add asparagus and cook 2 minutes, drain. (Asparagus will still be crisp). Place in a 10x6-inch baking dish. Mix remaining ingredients; sprinkle over asparagus. Bake 8-10 minutes or until cheese mixture is lightly browned.

Equivalent to:

4 Servings
Each =
1 cup cooked
vegetable
1/4 dairy
1/4 oil
1/4 starch

113 calories
2 g total fat
< 1 g saturated
2.5 mg
cholesterol
390 mg sodium

CREAMED CUCUMBERS

Ingredients:

4 large cucumbers, sliced
1 small red onion, sliced
8 oz plain non-fat yogurt
2 green onions
1 T tarragon vinegar
1 T lemon juice
1 package sweetener
1 tsp celery seed
1/4 tsp garlic herb seasoning
1/4 tsp salt

Instructions:

Arrange cucumber slices and red onion slices in a shallow bowl.
In a food processor or blender blend remaining ingredients; pour over cucumbers and onion, chill and serve.

Equivalent to:

4 Servings
Each =
1 cup raw
vegetable
1/4 dairy

87 calories
< 1 g total fat
< 1 g saturated
0 cholesterol
194 mg sodium

ITALIAN-STYLE ROASTED PEPPERS

Ingredients:

6 large red, green or yellow peppers
2 packages Diet Center Italian Dressing or 4 T
  low-fat Italian dressing
1/3 cup fresh basil leaves or 3/4 tsp dried basil
1/8 tsp lemon pepper
1/4 tsp salt
2 tomatoes, sliced
2 oz fat-free mozzarella cheese, sliced julienne

Instructions:

Over a gas flame, under broiler or on a barbecue grill, char peppers until completely black. Immediately place in a paper bag; close tightly and let cool about 30 minutes. Under cold running water, peel off skin, then remove stems and seeds; slice into long thick slices.

In a large bowl, combine peppers with remaining ingredients. Cover and marinate in refrigerator, stirring occasionally, at least 4 hours. For best flavor, serve peppers at room temperature with mozzarella cheese and sliced tomatoes.

Equivalent to:

4 Servings
Each =
1 cup cooked
vegetable
1/2 oil
1/4 dairy

95 calories
3 g total fat
< 1 g saturated
3 mg
cholesterol
454 mg sodium

VEGETARIAN STUFFED PEPPERS

Ingredients:

3 yellow or green bell peppers
1 cup kidney beans, rinsed and drained
3/4 cup chopped plum tomatoes
1 cup cooked rice
1/2 can chopped green chilies, undrained
1/4 cup chopped onion
1/2 tsp Mexican seasoning
1/2 tsp cumin
2 oz fat-free cheddar cheese, sliced

Equivalent to:

3 Servings
Each =
1 cup cooked
vegetable
2 starch
1/3 dairy

Woman Style:
3 Servings
Each =
3/4 legume
3/4 starch
1 cup cooked
vegetables
1/3 dairy

235 calories
1 g total fat
< 1 g saturated
4 mg
cholesterol
543 mg sodium

Instructions:

Cut off tops of peppers; remove seeds. In a microwave safe dish, cover and microwave on high 4 minutes.
Mix remaining ingredients together, except cheese. Cover and microwave on high 10 minutes or until thoroughly heated. Top with cheese and microwave 2 more minutes or until cheese melts.

STUFFED TOMATOES

Side Dish

Ingredients:

2 medium tomatoes
2 T chopped celery
1 T chopped onion
2/3 cup cooked brown rice
1 tsp fresh snipped parsley
1/2 tsp dried basil leaves
1/8 tsp lemon pepper
Dash garlic herb seasoning
2 oz fat-free mozzarella cheese, sliced

Instructions:

Cut a thin slice from each tomato top. Set top aside. Scoop out center of tomatoes; chop pulp and set aside. Place shells upside down on paper towels to drain.

Preheat oven to 350. In a medium saucepan sprayed with Pam, saute onion and celery until tender. Remove from heat. Add reserved tomato pulp, rice, and seasonings; mix well. Fill tomato shells with rice mixture. Top with cheese; replace tomato tops, if desired.

In a baking dish sprayed with Pam, place tomatoes and cover with aluminum foil. Bake at 350 degrees for 30-45 minutes, or until tender.

Equivalent to:

2 Servings
Each =
1 starch
1/2 dairy
1 cup cooked
vegetables

152 calories
< 1 g total fat
< 1 g saturated
5 mg
cholesterol
511 mg sodium

SNAP PEAS AND PEPPERS

Instructions:

2 large yellow peppers
2 large celery stalks
2 cups snap peas or Chinese pea pods
2 tsp olive oil
1/4 tsp salt
1/2 tsp coarsely ground black pepper
Basil sprigs for garnish

Instructions:

Equivalent to:

4 Servings
Each =
1 cups cooked
vegetable
1/2 oil

66 calories
2.7 g total fat
< 1 g saturated
0 cholesterol
309 mg sodium

Cut peppers into 2" by 3/4" pieces. Cut celery diagonally into 1/4-inch thick slices. Remove stem and strings along both edges of each pea pod.
In a non-stick skillet over medium-high heat, heat 1 tsp olive oil, cook peppers, celery, 1/4 tsp salt and 1/4 tsp black pepper, stirring frequently, until tender and lightly browned, about 10 minutes. Remove vegetables to bowl. In the same skillet in 1 tsp olive oil, cook snap peas, and 1/4 tsp black pepper, stirring frequently, until peas are crisp-tender, about 4 minutes. Stir pepper mixture into snap peas in skillet. Spoon vegetables onto platter. Garnish with basil sprigs.

SWEET SAUTEED CABBAGE

Ingredients:

2 tsp diet margarine
2 cans (11 oz) mandarin orange segments
6 cups shredded cabbage
1 medium onion, chopped
1 clove garlic, pressed
1/4 cup white wine vinegar
1 tsp caraway seeds
1/4 tsp salt

Instructions:

Drain oranges, reserve 1/3 cup liquid. In a large skillet melt margarine, saute cabbage, onion and garlic until onion is soft. Stir in reserved juice, vinegar, caraway seeds and salt. Cover and simmer 5 minutes. Stir in oranges. Cover and cook 2-3 minutes longer.

Equivalent to:

4 Servings
Each =
1 1/4 cup
cooked
vegetable
1/2 fruit
1/4 oil

93 calories
1.4 g total fat
< 1 g saturated
0 cholesterol
177 mg sodium

SCALLOPED SPINACH

Ingredients:

1 package (10 oz) frozen chopped spinach,
  cooked and drained well
1/3 cup skim milk
2 oz fat-free cheddar cheese
2 eggs, beaten
1/4 tsp lemon pepper
1/2 tsp Teton Valley Nice n Spicy or Season All

Instructions:

Combine spinach with other ingredients and half of cheese. Turn mixture into a baking dish sprayed with Pam; top with remaining cheese. Bake at 350 degrees for about 35 minutes, or until knife inserted in center comes out clean. Let stand 5 minutes before serving.

Equivalent to:

2 Servings
Each =
1/2 cup cooked
vegetable
1 oz protein
1 additional
food

169 calories
5 g total fat
1.6 g saturated
219 mg
cholesterol
647 mg sodium

CHINESE SPINACH

Ingredients:

12 oz fresh spinach, washed, trimmed, torn in
  bite size pieces
1 tsp low-sodium soy sauce
1 tsp lime juice
1 packet sweetener
1/8 tsp lemon pepper
1 clove garlic, minced
1/2 cup diagonally cut green onion, 1-inch
  pieces
1/4 cup sliced water chestnuts
1 jar (2 oz) sliced pimento, drained

Instructions:

Heat soy sauce, lime juice, sweetener and
lemon pepper in a large skillet sprayed with
Pam. Add garlic, stir-fry over medium-high
heat 1 minute. Add spinach, water chestnuts,
and pimento. Stir-fry 2-3 minutes longer, or
until spinach is tender.

Equivalent to:

1 Serving
Each =
1 1/2 cup
cooked
vegetable

198 calories
1.8 g total fat
<1 g saturated
0 cholesterol
226 mg sodium

SWEET POTATO WITH BLACK BEAN CHILI

Ingredients:

4 small sweet potatoes
2 tsp olive oil
2 cups diced red bell pepper
1 1/2 cups chopped onions
1 T minced garlic
1 T chili powder
2 tsp ground cumin
1 16-oz can peeled tomatoes with juice
1 15-oz can black beans, rinsed and drained
2 cups diced yellow crookneck squash
1 T minced seeded jalapeno chili
4 lime wedges
Plain nonfat yogurt, optional
Chopped fresh cilantro, optional

Instructions:

Bake sweet potatoes at 400 degrees about 1 hour. Heat oil in a skillet over medium-low heat. Add bell pepper and onions and saute about 7 minutes. Add garlic, cook 2 minutes. Add seasonings, tomatoes and beans, bring to simmer. Reduce heat to low, cover and cook 20 minutes. Add squash and jalapeno, cover and cook 6 minutes. Split potato; spoon some chili into center, squeeze lime juice, top with yogurt.

Equivalent to

4 Servings
Each =
3 1/2 starch
1/2 oil
1 3/4 cup
cooked
vegetable

Woman Style:
4 Servings
Each =
2 starch
1 legume
1/2 oil
1 3/4 cup
cooked
vegetable

297 calories
4.2 g total fat
< 1 g saturated
0 cholesterol
462 mg sodium

Index

INDEX

To Order
"Eating Lite And Loving It"
Write To:
Rebecca Young
777 East 200 North
Payson, Utah 84651

801-465-9013

You may order as many copies of *"Eating Lite And Loving It"* as you wish for the regular price plus postage and packing per book ordered. Mail to:

    Rebecca Young
    777 East 200 North
    Payson, Utah 84651

Please mail _____copies of *"Eating Lite And Loving It"* @ _____each, plus postage and packing per book ordered.
Mail Books To:

Name _____

Address _____

City, State, Zip _____

You may order as many copies of *"Eating Lite And Loving It"* as you wish for the regular price plus postage and packing per book ordered. Mail to:

    Rebecca Young
    777 East 200 North
    Payson, Utah 84651

Please mail _____copies of *"Eating Lite And Loving It"* @ _____each, plus postage and packing per book ordered.
Mail Books To:

Name _____

Address _____

City, State, Zip _____